The DAM Book Guide to

Organizing Your Photos with Lightroom 5

A Multimedia Book

By Peter Krogh

DAM Useful
PUBLISHING

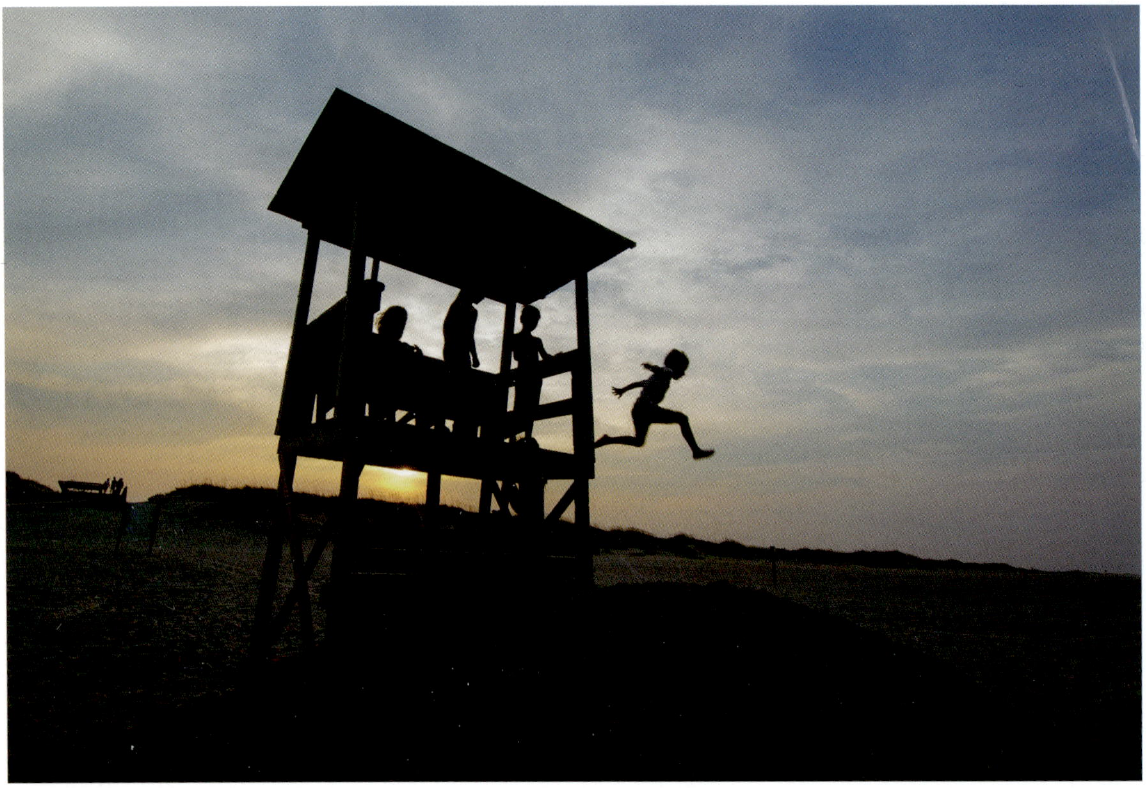

The DAM Book Guide to
Organizing Your Photos
with Lightroom 5

All photos by Peter Krogh, except where otherwise credited.
Photograph of Peter Krogh by Alyson Krogh.

Editing by Dominique le Roux, Moonshine Media.
Proofreading by Alyson Krogh.
Design by Elinore Wrigley de Lisle, Me Jayne Design.

Video/Audio Production and
Design Production by Benjamin Mowrey.

Published by DAM Useful Publishing
3301 Oberon St. Kensington, MD 20895
USA

DAM Useful Publishing provides information tools for photographers and other creative professionals. For more information or to request a review copy, contact us at info@DAMuseful.com or 301-529-5506.

ISBN 978-0-9898514-7-3

Acknowledgements

This book continues the work that I have done in digital photographic education for more than a decade, and grows out of my thirty-year career in professional photography. There have been a number of important people and organizations along the way.

I need to thank my family first, for being supportive, and giving me something fun and valuable to photograph. My wife, Alyson, has also been invaluable as a partner in the business, running marketing and operations. Dominique le Roux has been a valuable collaborator in a number of projects, and her work on this book and for this publishing venture have been essential. Ben Mowrey has done great work in video and design production, showing real dedication and an ability to work like hell until everything is done. Thanks to Elinore de Lisle for her design work on the cover and book content, as well as on promotional material.

I could not accomplish the work I do without the help of a number of people in the industry. Tom Hogarty at Adobe has provided insight, advice and support that is crucial to my work, and I'd also like to thank him for the great work he does providing the vision for Lightroom. Mikkel Aaland remains one of my closest collaborators and best friends in the industry. And my long collaboration with Richard Anderson continues to inspire much of my writing. I also need to thank O'Reilly Media for giving me a start in the publishing industry, and being so gracious in letting me continue this venture on my own. The Library of Congress's NDIIPP program has been one of the best supporters of my work, and a great place to learn. Finally, Gene Mopsik and ASMP have provided ongoing support for my work, as well as a platform for outreach.

Other individuals and organizations that have helped me in this work include Victoria Bampton, George Jardine, Eric Chan, Sharad Mangalick, Winston Hendrickson, Kathy Waite, Russell Brown, Katrin Eismann, John Beardsworth, Robert Edwards, Jeff Dunas, Steve Uzzell and Sam Kittner.

The thesis of this book was first presented at the Society for Photographic Education in 2012. These ideas were further refined in presentations at the Look3 Festival, The Palm Springs Photographic Festival, Brooks Institute, and South by Southwest Interactive festival.

Dominique le Roux is a publisher and editor passionate about helping creatives tell their stories. Her work and travel itch have taken her all over the world, but home and office right now are an Internet-connected wooden cabin on the banks of the Mekong River in Asia. www.moonshinemedia.co.za

Elinore de Lisle is a graphic designer based in Cape Town, South Africa. Specializing in magazine design and layout, she believes that consistency and legibility are key factors in creating an easy-on-the-eye design. www.mejaynedesign.com

Benjamin J. Mowrey is a student, currently attending Landmark College, VT for 3D Animation and Game Development. He is building a startup game company, Project x studios. www.ProjectXStudios.net

Alyson Krogh brings a decade of marketing experience in the publishing industry to her position as head of Database Marketing and Operations at DAM Useful Publishing.

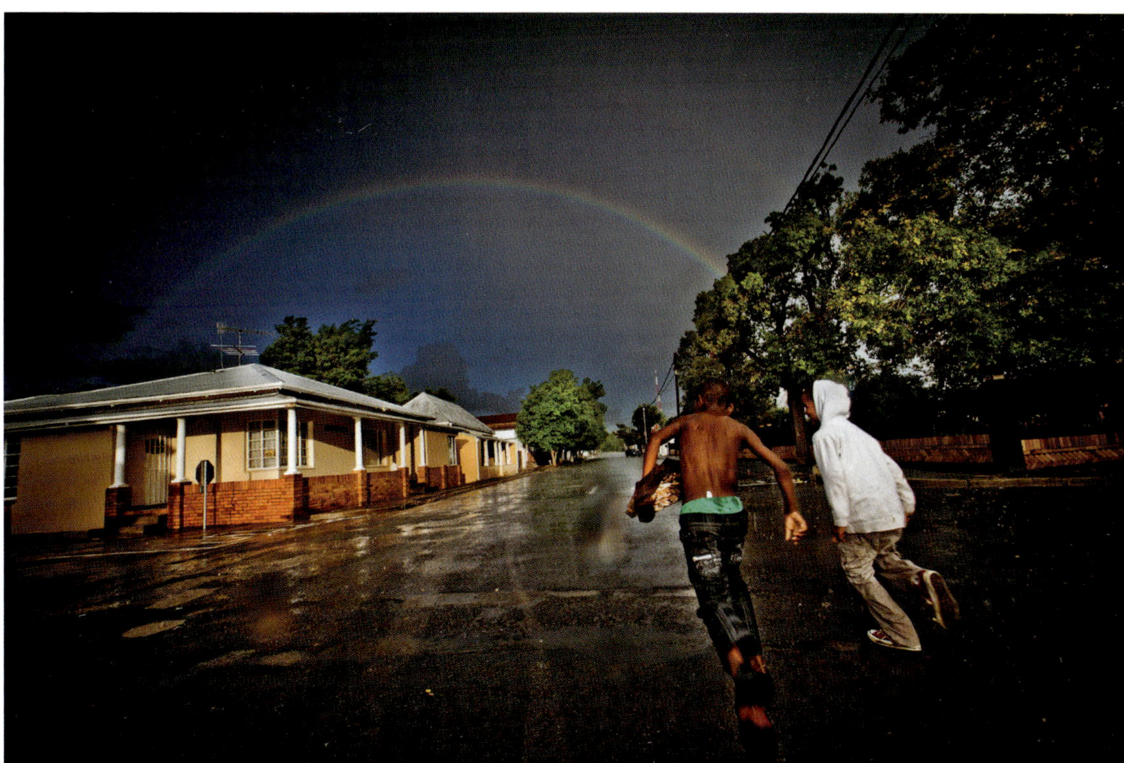

CONTENTS

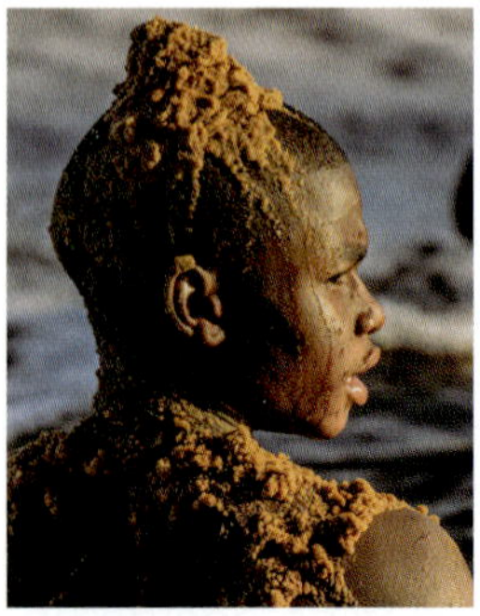

The foundation of an organized Photo Library is a layered approach to storing the images, tagging them for content, and making creations from them. This chapter lays out the basic principles of organization.

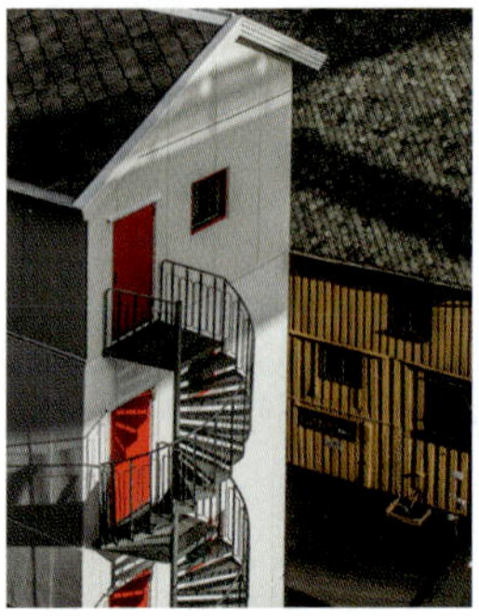

The Lightroom catalog is the hub of your organized Photo Library. This chapter outlines the basics of catalog storage, naming and backup. We'll also look at the process for combining your existing catalogs into a single Master Catalog.

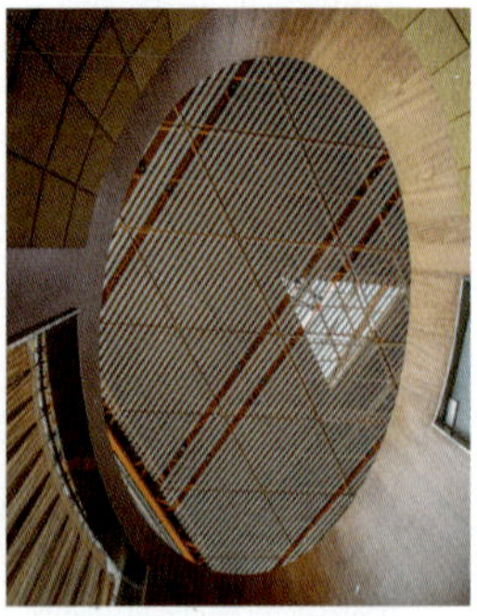

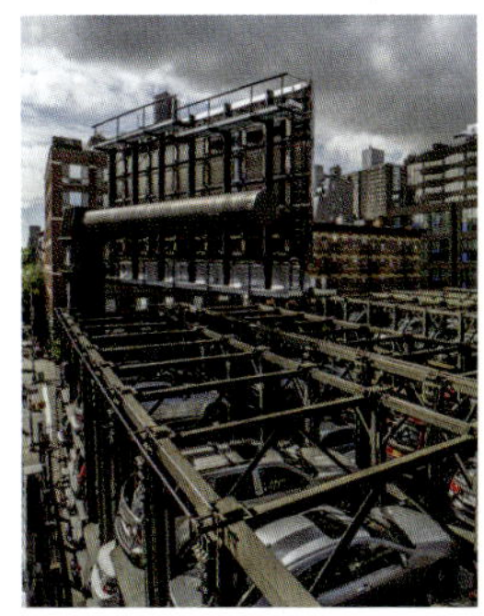

CHAPTER 4 - FINDING & FILTERING WITH TAGS 87

This chapter describes tagging strategy for organizing your Photo Library. You'll see how to tag the images to describe the content and the quality of the photos. You'll also see how to use the the Library Filter and Smart Collections to find and filter by tags.

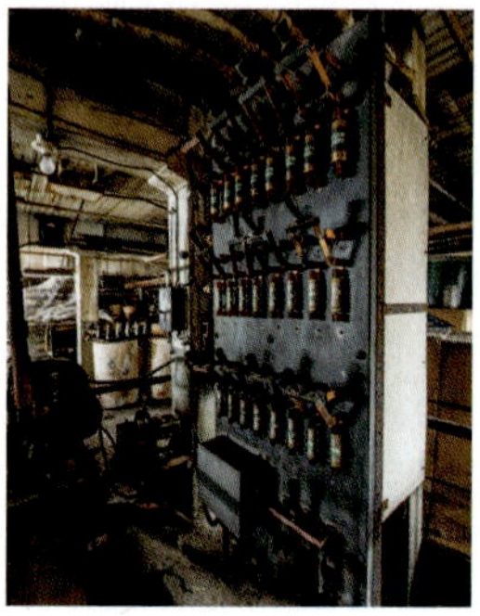

CHAPTER 5- KEYWORDS 111

Keywords are the most versatile tagging tool in Lightroom. We'll examine how to create keywords, organize them, and filter with them. You'll see how to get started with Keywords, and tag your Library methodically.

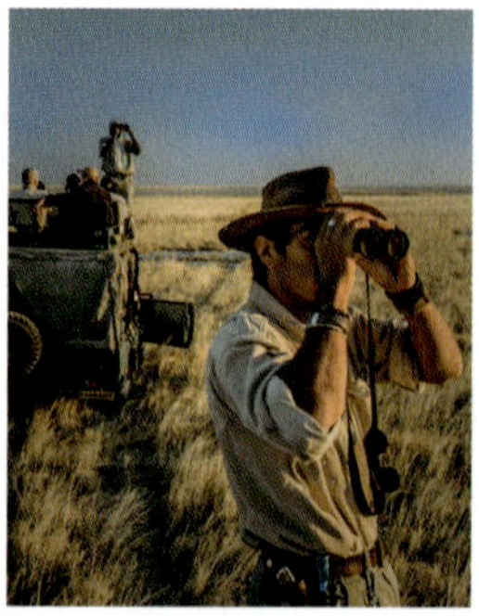

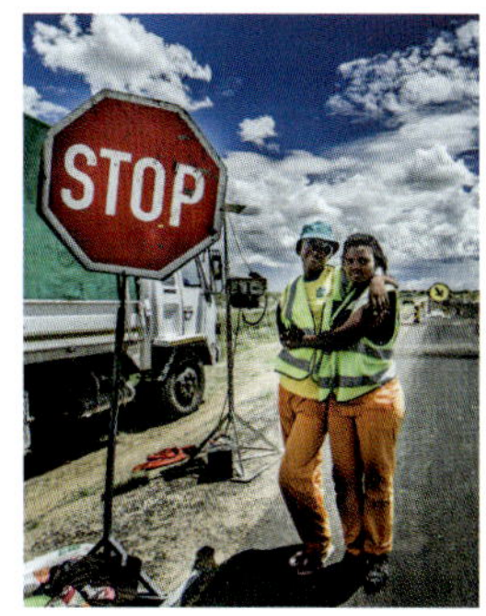
STOP

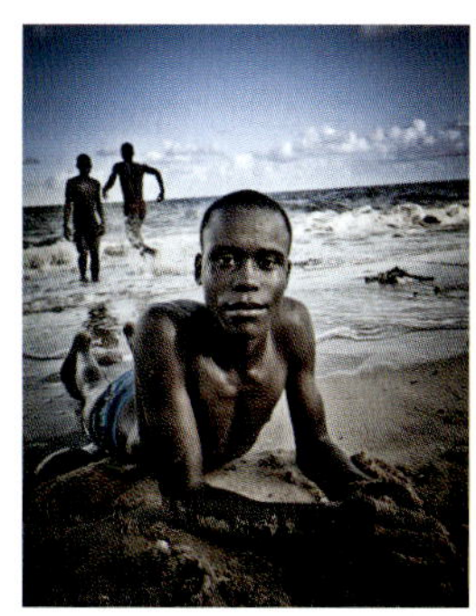

CHAPTER 8 - COLLECTIONS AND PROJECTS 155

The Collections panel in Lightroom is the place where you can bring your photos together in useful ways. This chapter outlines how Collections work, and how they can be employed to creative purposes and to streamline workflow.

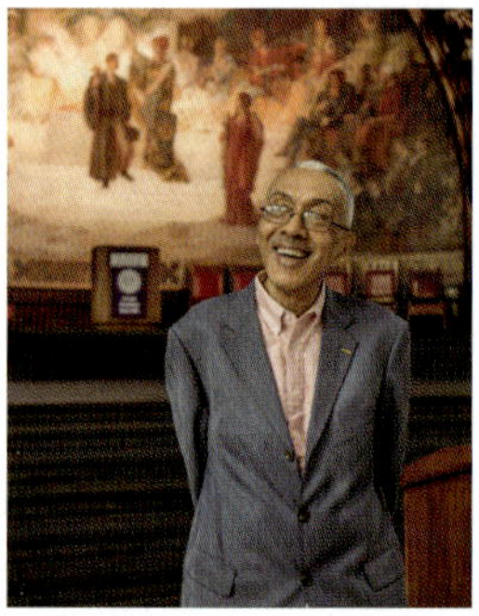

CHAPTER 9 - USING PUBLISH SERVICES 173

Publish Services allow you to share your photos to your own devices, to sharing services, to social media and to other web services. This chapter explains how to make and use Publish Services.

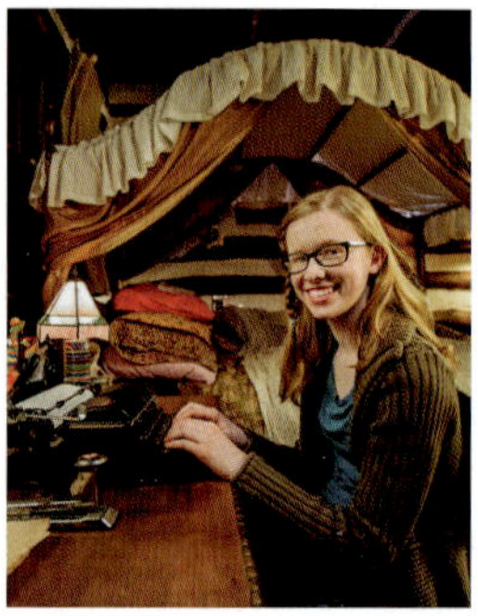

CHAPTER 10 - MANAGING DERIVATIVE FILES 189

Sometimes you'll need to create a new version of the file to send to another person or program. This chapter explains the workflow and storage options for the creation and management of Derivative Files.

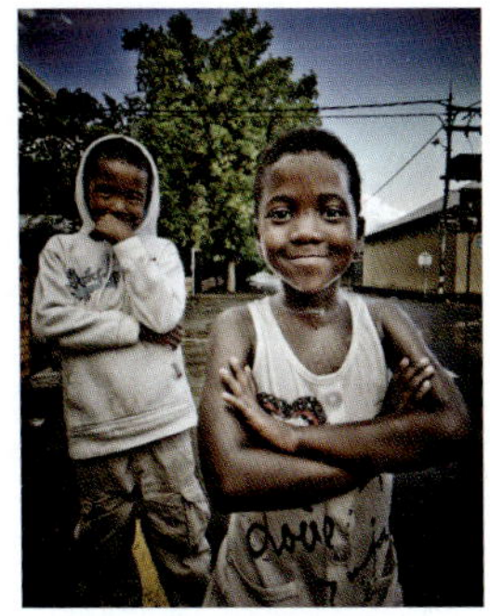

AFTERWORD 206

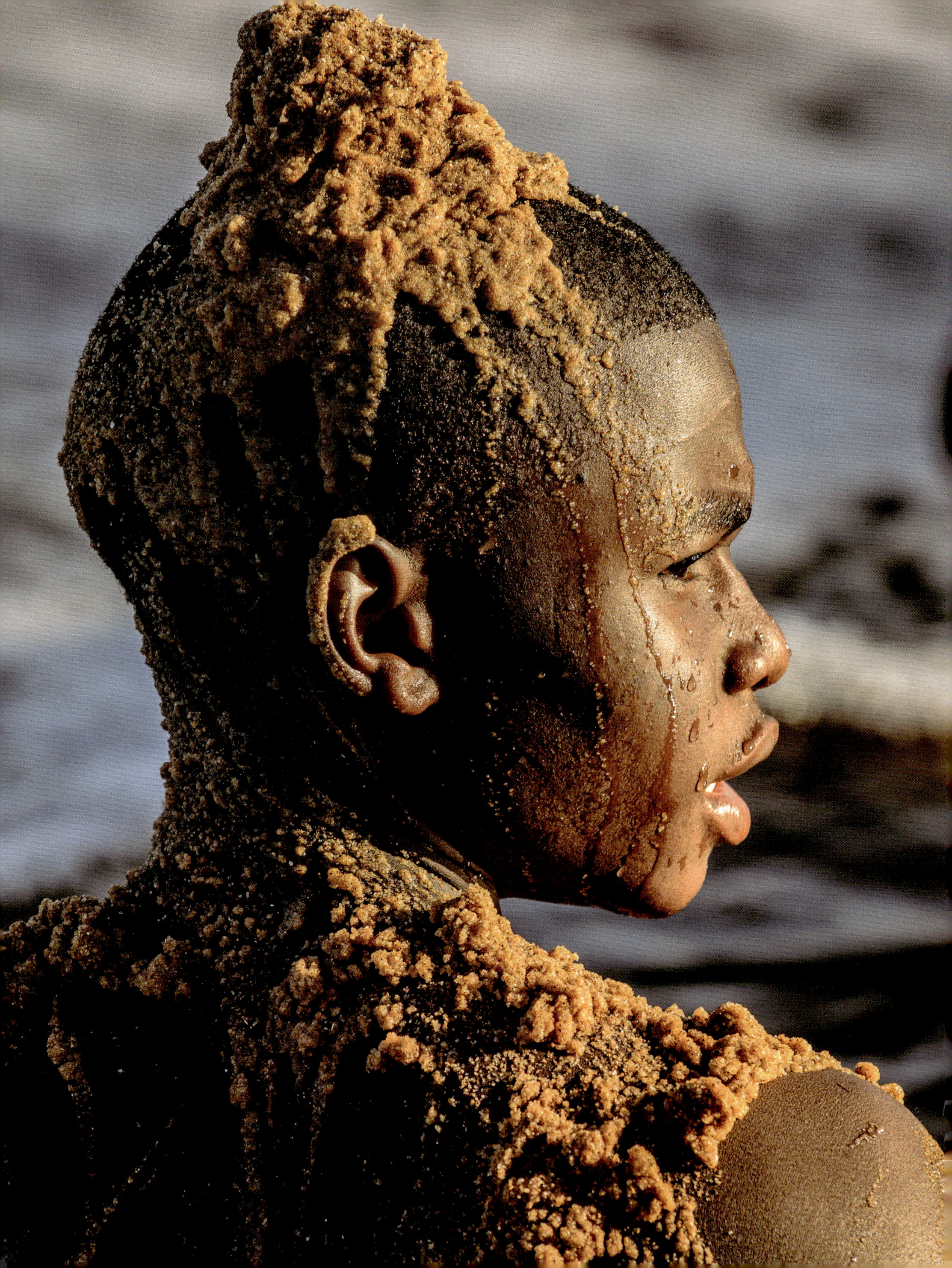

INTRODUCTION

I want you to have your photographs forever. I want you to be able to find them forever, and to be able to put them together to tell stories. This could be the story of your life, of your family, of the places you've been and the people you've met. If you are a professional, you will be telling the stories of your clients. It may be a small chapter: what someone looked like at this point in time. Or it may be a book's worth of information about a company or other institution.

The photographic record of our time is rich and extensive. With cameras everywhere, the experience of an event is, more than ever, directly tied to the photographs of that event. If there's no photo, it's like it didn't happen. That's important for the present, and it's going to be even more important in the future as we come to rely ever-more on this visual legacy.

Because we're taking so many photos, and because those photos have so much significance, it's essential that we understand how to preserve them, and how to find them when we want them, how to put them together in compelling ways and how to share them.

Photography is important as memory-keeping, and photography is becoming ever more important as its own visual language. Sharing photographs has become central to interpersonal communication. Don't just tell me what happened, you need to show me. We now have a generation of adults who have always known a world where taking and sharing photos is as easy as making a phone call.

This photographic capability has created an explosion of people who use the medium as their art form of choice. For them, photography goes beyond memory keeping and sharing. Photography is their central means of artistic self-expression, a way to comment on the world and their place in it.

Whether for memory keeping or self-expression, Adobe Lightroom is becoming the application of choice. Lightroom allows you to seamlessly blend storytelling with your personal photographic vision. When used to its full capacity, Lightroom allows you to share that craft and vision with the world. This could be the whole world, or a few selected individuals, or you may hold it privately for your own enjoyment.

All of this rich new capability must be built on a solid foundation. At the base of the foundation is the need to store and preserve the image itself. Building on top of that storage, you need to be able to find the photo when you want it. And on top of this foundation you create the highest value - the point of view you express, the stories you tell, the images you share.

This book helps you understand the process of organization according to those three layers: storing, tagging and creating. This universal framework is clear and easy to put into practice. In fact, this philosophy is at the core of Lightroom's design.

In this book, I'll help you understand how these layers can be built, and how you can use Lightroom to help you get the most out of your photographs. You'll see how to safely build and store a Photo Library, and you'll see how to make sense of it easily: how to tag the images in useful and meaningful ways for your own needs.

And most important, we'll see how you can make compelling creations from your photos in a seamless and fluid way. We'll do this in a way that allows you to find and revisit the creations, and to refine them in the future. Once those creations are made, we'll also see how they can be shared with clients, family and friends.

MY ASSUMPTIONS ABOUT THE READER

I have written this book for every Lightroom user, from the novice to the advanced professional. That's a pretty broad claim, considering the vast gulf between those two groups, but I think it's appropriate.

It's valuable for the novice user to understand the fundamentals of Photo Library design, and the purpose of the tagging and creation tools. Getting started on the right foot will make Lightroom an even more enjoyable experience.

Intermediate users will surely gain insight on Lightroom's capabilities. Not only will they get a better understanding of the tools, they will benefit from the tips on sorting out the messes they've made over the years.

And even most advanced users will have some aha! moments. I have met comparatively few who really use Collections to its full potential or understand the capabilities of Published Services and file verification.

I do assume that any reader has a working knowledge of Lightroom, and has been able to get started. I strongly recommend Victoria Bampton's free Getting Started Guide if you're a new Lightroom user. And her The Missing FAQ Book is a resource that I consider essential for all Lightroom users.

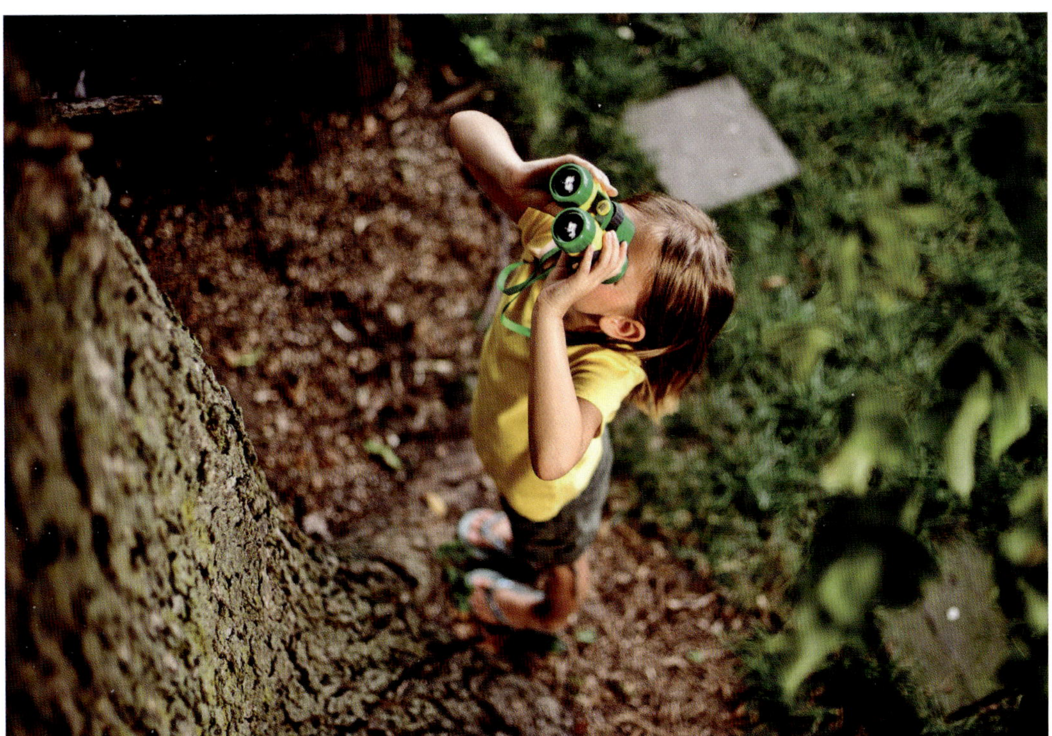

ABOUT THE DEMONSTRATION MOVIES

The techniques that I outline in this book are the ones I use for my own personal and professional Photo Library. You'll see a lot of my work here, and you'll be able to see how I integrate the storage, tagging and creation tools. I think it's essential that a book like this use a large photo collection for demonstration purposes.

The Photo Library we'll be working with has about 75,000 photos that have been pulled from my collection of nearly a half-million images. It shows a selection of shoot types, both personal and professional. In some cases, we'll see only a handful of images from a larger shoot, and in some cases we'll see entire shoots. Each of these is valuable in a demonstration like this.

What about the other 400,000 photos?

While I have included a large number of photos in the demonstration catalog, it's not my entire collection. I've found that Lightroom gets too sluggish for daily use with catalogs this large. I have my own collection split between several catalogs, and the one we'll be looking at is based on my own works-in-progress catalog that contains current shoots as well as the "greatest hits" from my archive.

If you have a Photo Library that is too large for a single catalog, then you should consider reading The DAM Book Guide to Multi-Catalog Workflow with Lightroom 5 in addition to this book, as it scales the techniques here for a larger library or a multi-user environment.

WHAT ABOUT ORGANIZING MY VIDEOS?

Lightroom has the ability to import and catalog your videos in addition to your still photos. As currently designed, this functionality is geared to people who shoot some videos along with their photos. Almost everywhere in this book where you read the word "photos" you could substitute the words "photos and videos."

Lightroom's tools to import, tag and make collections of your videos work pretty well, with some important limitations. The embedded metadata tags in videos are typically not as complete as the ones you find in still images. And the exported files won't carry most of the tags you create in Lightroom.

Once you have imported the videos into your Lightroom catalog, you can tag the files with any of the metadata you use to tag stills: keywords, creator information, locations and ratings. You can add them to web galleries and slideshows, and even make prints from videos.

But Lightroom does not offer a timeline editor, which is part of nearly every video workflow. Basically, Lightroom allows you to store, tag and create with your video as though it is a "moving snapshot" and not a whole lot more.

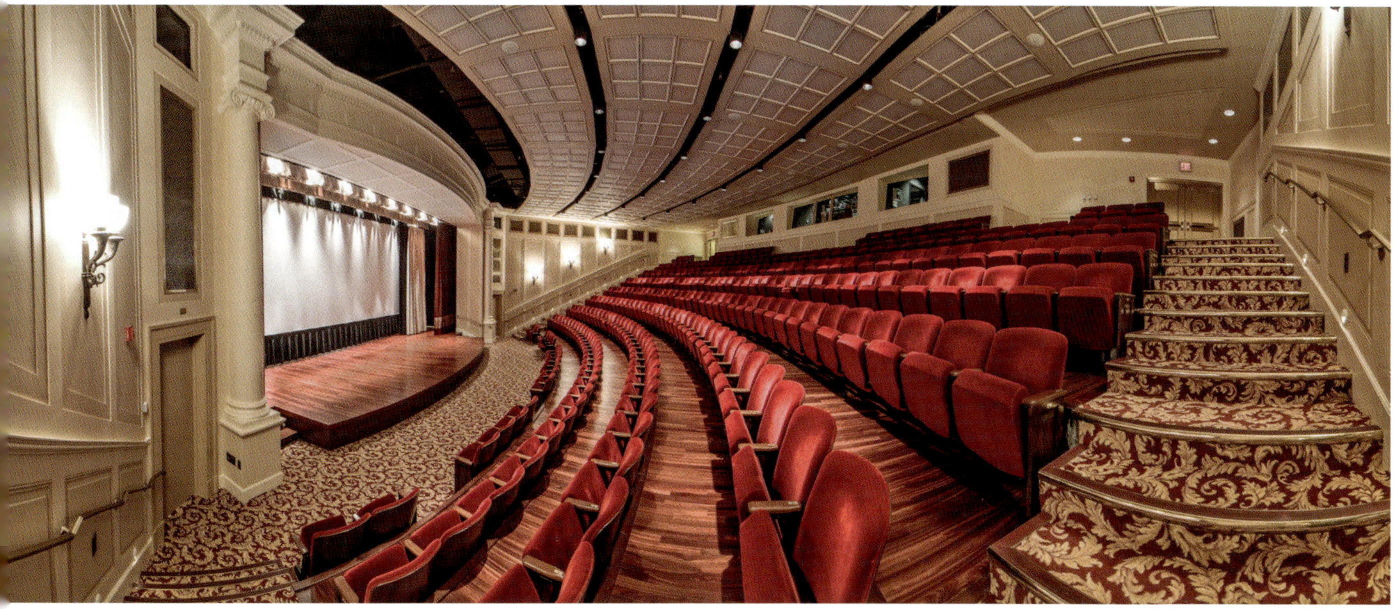

SUSTAINABILITY

Ever since I started as a photographer, the long-term preservation of photos has been a priority for me. *The DAM Book* was written specifically to address the issues of photo preservation and access. I have a deep commitment to my readers to help them preserve their images, even as the technology of digital photography changes.

I've had the good fortune to be involved in the development of some important standards and technology in the world of imaging. I know that my books have helped to inform the decision-makers in standards bodies, government and technology companies.

If you have been following my recommendations, I promise not to leave you hanging. I'm happy to report that eight years into this publishing effort, the structure and practices I outlined have proven to be solid and reliable, and have enabled my readers to move gracefully into the future of imaging technology.

When new technology does trigger a change, I'll be sure to point it out to you. In this book, you'll see two examples of important changes in my practices - one with ratings definitions and one with storage "buckets". Each of these is called out clearly. And in each case, I explain why I suggest the change, and how I suggest you make the change in your own collection.

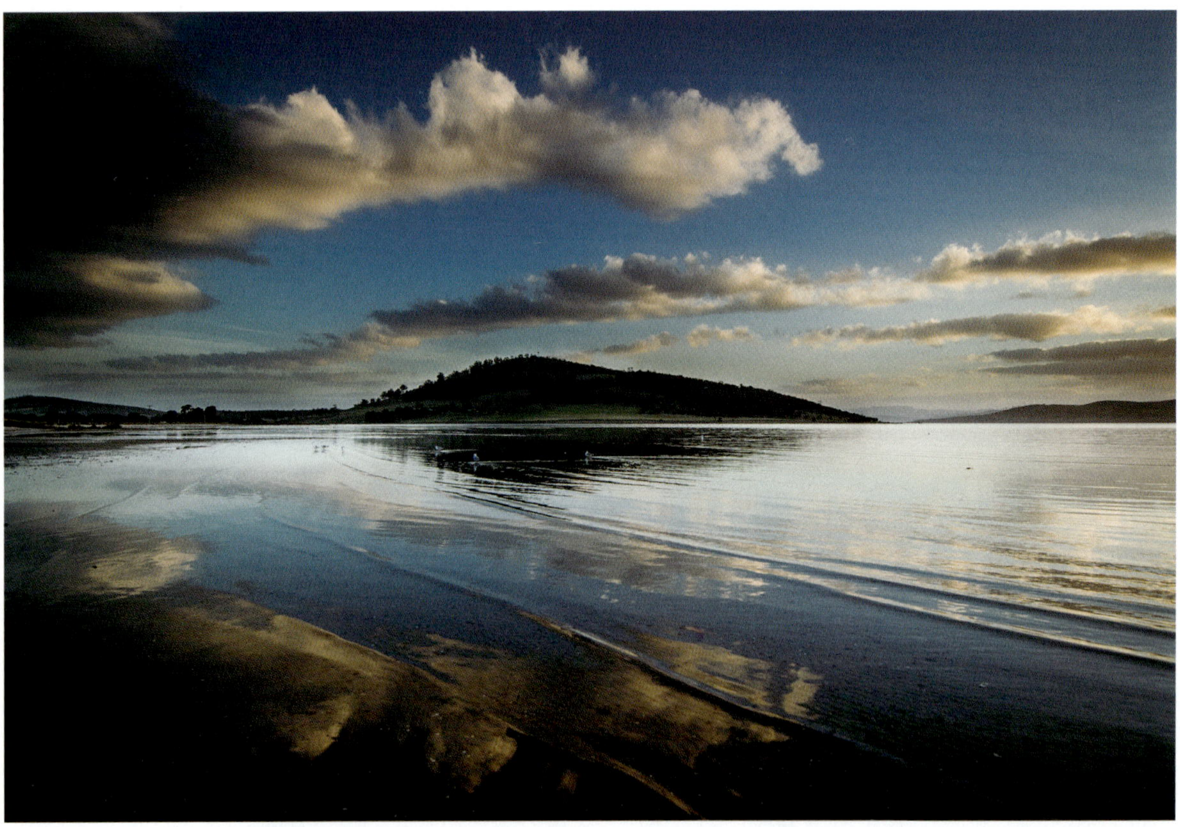

HOW THIS BOOK IS ORGANIZED

This book is divided into ten chapters that describe the structure of an organized Photo Library.

- Chapter 1 describes the basic structure of an organized Photo Library, including the relationship between the storage, tagging and creation layers.
- In Chapter 2, I outline some important basics of Lightroom structure and workflow. We'll be doing the most important work to the collection inside this application, so we'll need to make sure to know how it works. We'll also want to know how to preserve the catalogs.
- Chapter 3 outlines the methods to store your images, including storage hardware, file and folder naming, backup and file integrity-checking.
- Chapters 4 to 7 discuss the methods of tagging and filtering your photos.
- Chapters 8 and 9 show how you can use Collections and Published Collections to create projects out of your images and manage workflow.
- Chapter 10 discusses the approaches to Derivative Files.

Book notes

I've used a number of callout tags in this book for specific types of information.

You Might Be Wondering addresses common questions about a subject we've just covered.

I've used the **Digging Deeper** headline when I'm introducing some technique that is more advanced and won't be needed by all readers.

Whenever you see the **Warning** section, I'm pointing out the possibility of some kind of data loss. This could be loss of the photo files themselves or the tags that you have made.

DAM Book Changes point out the sections where I outline changes to my recommendations from previous books.

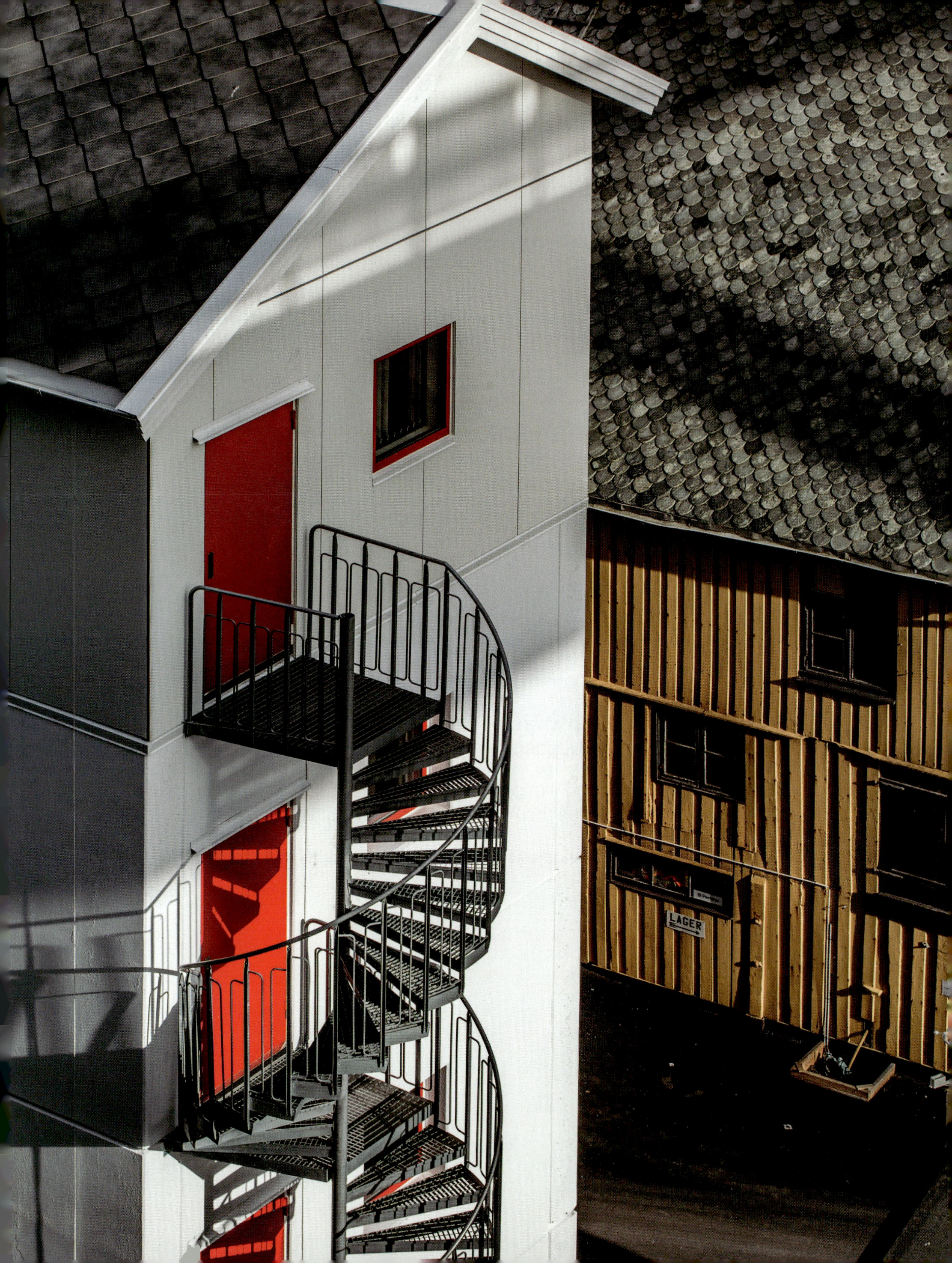
LAGER

CHAPTER 1

STORE, TAG, CREATE

In this chapter, we're going to outline the elements of an organized Photo Library, and how those elements relate to each other. We'll break the process into three pieces: storing the photos, organizing the photos, and creating projects. Seeing each of these processes as a separate operation can add simplicity and clarity to your work in Lightroom.

In the last part of this chapter, we'll look at some strategies to bring order out of chaos, and to do so without going crazy. You can use some simple techniques to make your life easier now, while at the same time you make your Photo Library much easier to manage in the long term. And at the end of this chapter, we'll see a sample workflow that puts these principles into action.

Let's start by looking at the three layers of an organized library and see how each one works.

CREATING AN ORGANIZED LIBRARY

The three pieces of an organized collection can be seen as layers.

The foundation of the Photo Library is the storage layer. You need an orderly place to keep your image files, and we will accomplish this by creating a folder structure and a file naming structure.

On top of the storage layer is the classification and organization of the files. This is accomplished by a set of tags that can be used to tell you some facts about the images, such as when they were created, where they were created and what they are pictures of.

Layered on top of these two is the work we do to put the photos into useful groups or creations. This could be a collection of images to send to someone, a portfolio, a slideshow, or perhaps a book that tells a story.

The layers move from something that should be very simple, stable and objective up through to something that is complex and ever-changing and quite subjective. When you structure things this way, you allow your creative process to work freely. You can spend less time worrying about storing your images, and spend more time making something cool out of them. The following video helps to explain the layers and how they relate to each other.

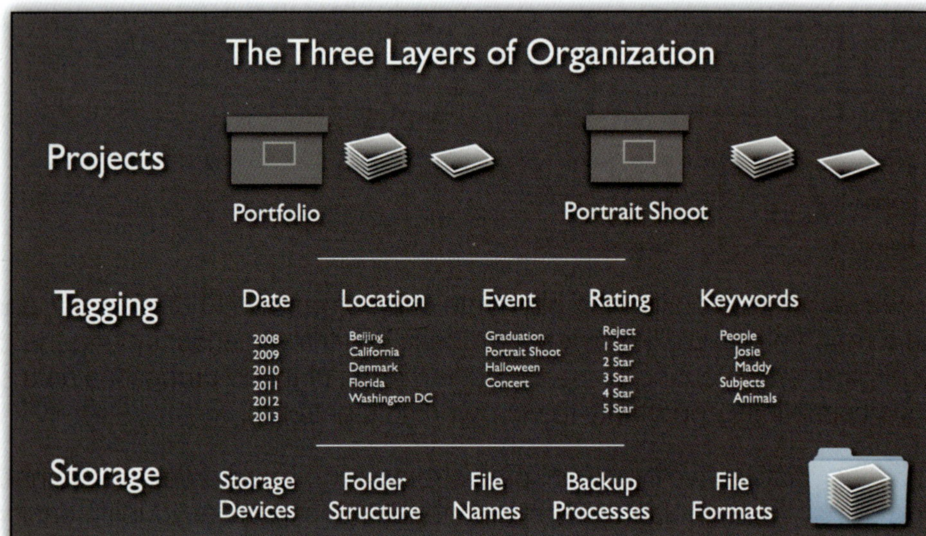

VIDEO 1-1 THE THREE LAYERS OF ORGANIZATION (7:43)
This video outlines the three layers of an organized Photo Library: the Storage, Tagging and Creative Layers.

YOU MIGHT BE WONDERING....

What do you mean by Layers?
In the IT world, the term *Layer* refers to all the elements that make up a particular task. So the Storage Layer is not just the storage hardware you need, like disk drives. It also includes the folder structure, file naming, backups, etc. I think it's very helpful to group all of these together under the umbrella of Storage Layer, so that we can better understand that they are all related and that each is dependent on the other.

STORING THE PHOTOS

The most fundamental part of a Photo Library is the Storage Layer. The goals of the Storage Layer are pretty straightforward: we need to store the image files, make them available for use, and protect them from loss. Short and simple.

The tools of the Storage Layer are listed below.

Storage devices: You'll need somewhere to put your files. Your main Photo Library should be on a hard drive (or two, if necessary). You'll also need a backup drive (or two), and maybe even some DVDs or Blu-ray discs.

Folder names: We need to create a simple and orderly folder structure for storing the files. It needs to expand easily as we shoot new photos.

File names: Each file needs to have a unique name. This will help to avoid confusion for you, for Lightroom, and for anyone you send the photos to.

Backup procedures: Data backup is an essential part of Photo Library management. We will need to backup the files themselves as well as the catalog.

File format: If you shoot raw files with your camera, you'll need to make some choices about the storage format. There are some real advantages to storing the files as DNG, a format designed by Adobe specifically for photo archiving.

Catalog: Your Lightroom catalog is an essential part of your storage layer because it can tell you all the files are present. If the files are DNGs, the catalog can also tell you that they are in good health.

The video below shows my basic recommendation for how these should be set up for most Lightroom users. In Chapter 3, we'll look more deeply into this subject, and show you how to accomplish this in a workflow.

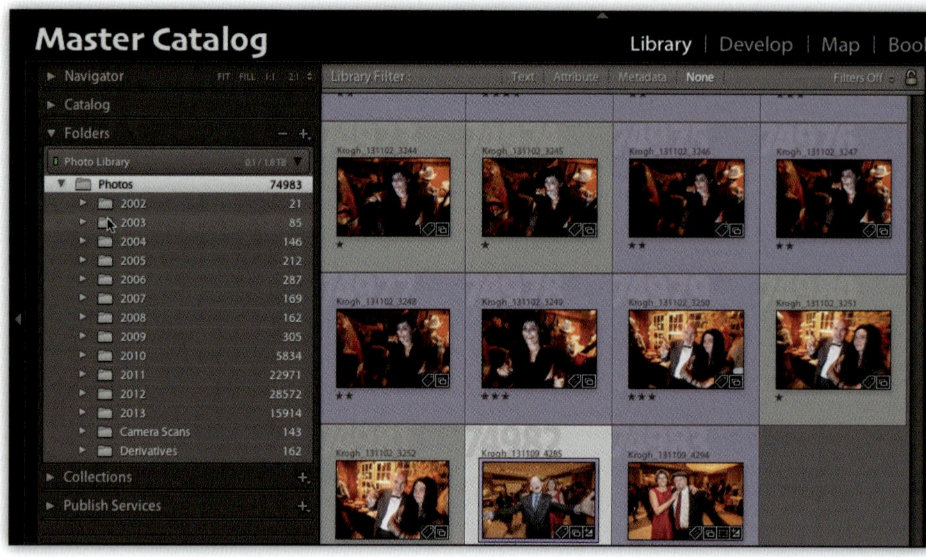

VIDEO 1-2 THE STORAGE LAYER (4:54)

This video shows the basics of a good Storage Layer in Lightroom.

Here are the elements:

- Make a parent folder for your Photo Library called *Photo Library* or *Photos*.
- Choose a photo folder structure that is simple and expandable, like *Year/Month/Project*.
- Choose a file name that can be applied automatically, like *MyName_Date_####*.
- Keep at least one copy of the Photo Library backed up to another hard drive.
- Consider converting raw files to DNG for added safekeeping.
- Use Lightroom to organize your photos without moving them around on the hard drive.
- Lightroom can help you confirm that all your files are present and have good integrity.

ORGANIZING WITH TAGS

Now that the files are put away safely, we can use some tags to organize them. Let's think of these tags as a bunch of facts about the photos. Some of these facts are recorded by the camera, such as the date and time the photo was taken. Some of these facts will be added in Lightroom as keywords or other metadata.

Automatic tags are added by your camera or computer, well, automatically. This includes the camera model, exposure information, date and time of capture and more. Some cameras will add GPS tags at the time of capture as well.

Bulk tags can be added to a whole shoot with a single action. This includes the name and contact information of the photographer, as well as location information and keywords that may describe the entire shoot.

Custom tags are added on a more individual basis. This can include ratings to describe how good a photo is, or specific keywords identifying people or subjects that may appear in individual photos. (The work described in Creative Collections in the next section is also Custom Metadata.)

Filtering and Finding

Taken together, the organizational tags can help you filter and find specific photos pretty easily. Let's think of Filtering as "show me all photos with this classification." For instance, you might want to see "all photos that were shot in my house" by filtering on a location tag. Or you may want to see "photos from Halloween" by filtering on a date tag.

Filtering can be really powerful when you use multiple filters at once. You can filter the rating stars against a person's name, for instance, to show "best pictures of Maddy."

Let's think of Find slightly differently. When we want to find something, we start by filtering, and then we pick a specific photo. I might want to find dog photos to send to Maddy. First, I'll filter down to photos with the keyword *dog*, and then I will pick ones to send. So Finding is adding a selection to the Filter process. (Of course, you could find a photo without filtering first. But, as you will see, using a filter makes the finding part much easier.)

YOU MIGHT BE WONDERING

What's the difference between tags and metadata?

In general, you can use the terms *tags* and *metadata* interchangeably. A keyword is a *metadata tag*. The word *tag* may seem less sophisticated, but it has a few advantages. It's shorter, and it sounds less intimidating. And unlike *metadata*, you can use the word *tag* as a verb, which is a whole lot easier to say than "applying metadata."

The most useful tags

There are lots of different kinds of tags you can apply to your photos. In fact, there are hundreds of tag types that Lightroom supports. But most people don't want to spend a lot of time tagging images. I know I certainly don't.

Let me outline the tags that I find most useful. With a modest amount of work, you can make your Photo Library easy to filter and navigate. With just a handful of tags, it's easy to identify photos from a specific shoot or location, or to identify all your best photos. Listed below are the ones I use the most when Finding and Filtering.

Date tags: Just remember to set your camera's clock correctly, and you're done. Each photo will be tagged with the date and time it was taken. Lightroom shows you this information in the filter bar.

Location tags: After the Date tags, I find Location tags the most useful. I can find all images from a trip I've taken, or all photos that were taken at my house. (We have a whole chapter on how to make and use these.)

Ratings and Flags: I use Ratings to remember which photos I like best. I also use the Reject Flag to tag images for deletion. The Ratings tag will be useful in many different filtering situations. I keep this process simple and standardized throughout my Photo Library.

Keywords/Collections – Shoot or Event Name: I like to put a keyword tag on any images that are part of a shoot so I can find the shoot later. This might be the name of an assignment, or the name of a performance I photographed. Not every photo is part of a real shoot. Sometimes I may take a few photos around the house, which are not part of any shoot.

Keyword – Person Photographed: I use keywords to tag images with the names of people who appear in them. In many cases, I'll just tag them as a group, without tagging individual people. I can tag all photos from my in-laws' house, for instance, without having to tag each person individually. When the need arises, I may go through these groups to tag specific people for some project I'm doing. I'll show you some techniques to do this very quickly.

Keyword - Ongoing Projects: If you have a project you are working on, or a subject matter you return to, you can use keywords to help organize those images. In my case, this might be *Lensbaby* photos, *Architecture*, or *Halloween*. These keywords will be determined by what you like to shoot.

Smart Collections for saved searches: You can use Smart Collections to save searches you find useful. I use these to find by ratings, or to find all photos with the *Panorama* label, or to find all TIFF files in the Catalog.

I deliberately left subject matter keywords out of the list above. I don't think that most people need to make use of keywords like *tree* or *strength* unless it's part of an important ongoing project or when preparing images for stock photo submissions.

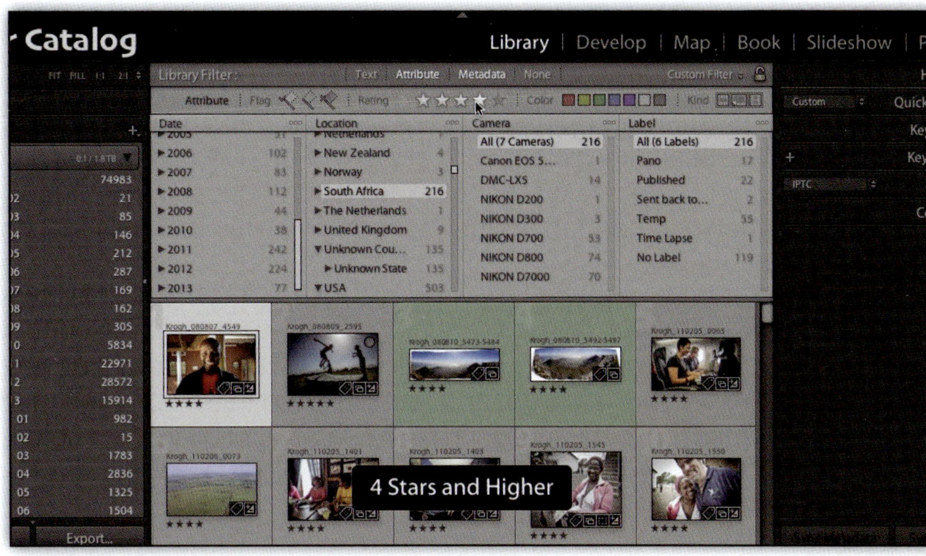

VIDEO 1-3 TAGGING YOUR PHOTOS (5:09)
This video shows how tags can be used for organization. We also see how you can filter on this metadata, and how we can find particular images.

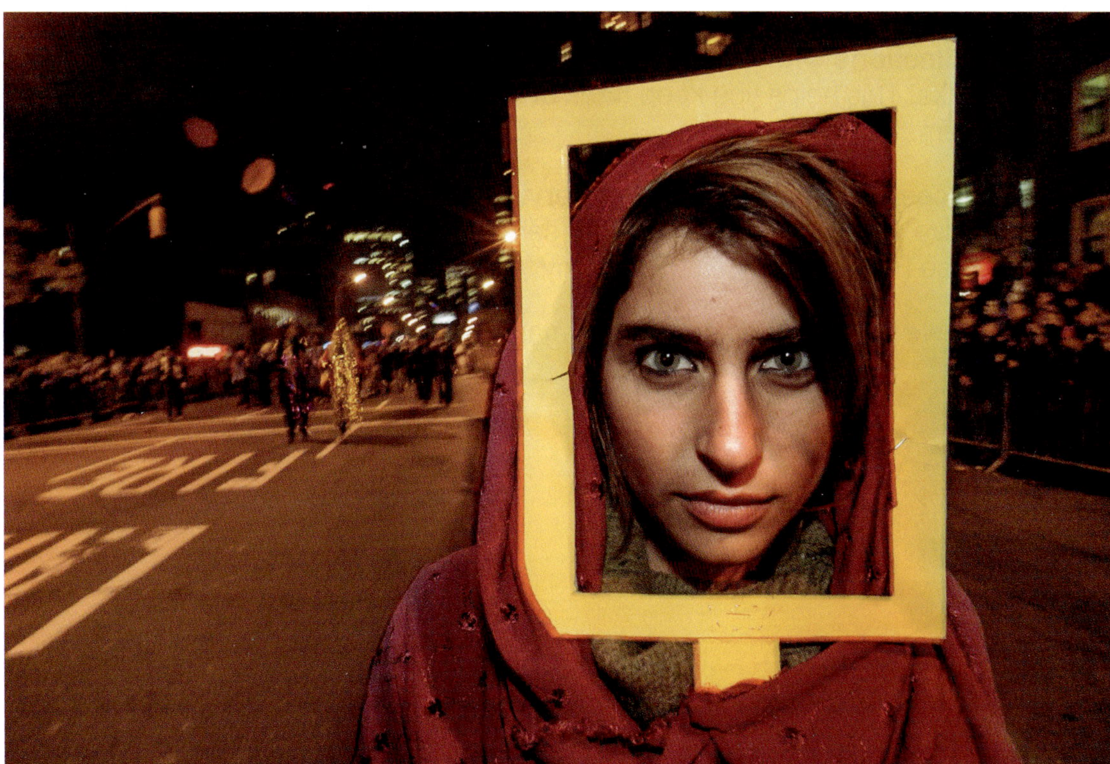

CREATING PROJECTS

Lightroom allows you to layer your own creative work on top of both the storage and organizational layers. This is where we put the images together in some kind of valuable way. Perhaps you want to create a set of images to tell the story of an event, or to show a person growing up. At its core, this is a subjective process. You need to choose the images from the possible candidates, and then you need to sequence them in a way that tells the story.

Lightroom provides a wonderful environment for making these creations. It provides many ways to turn your photos into finished works, including books, slideshows, web galleries, videos, PDFs, exported files and uploaded collections. And along the way Lightroom allows you to add to these creations, refine the Develop settings, and to repurpose them from one medium to another. All of this can be done while the image files are safely stored in the Photo Library Drive.

Here are the basic techniques I suggest.

Use Collections for your creations: The Collections tool in Lightroom is built for exactly this purpose. You can gather photos into collections, and then put the photos in a sequence. This is where I bring images together to tell a story, or prepare for client delivery.

Use module-specific Collections: There are specialized Collections for Web, Print, Slideshow and Books that will remember all the settings. You can have as many of these Collections as you would like.

Organize your Collections with Collection Sets: You can use Collection Sets to organize the Collections you make. This helps you keep track of the Collections, which can be important if you have lots of them.

Use Publish Services to connect with other services and devices: I use Publish Services to upload my creative collections directly to web services like Facebook, PhotoShelter or SmugMug. I also use Publish Services to push my favorite photos out to my iPhone and iPad.

In the video below, we'll see how it's possible to make and use these creations in Lightroom.

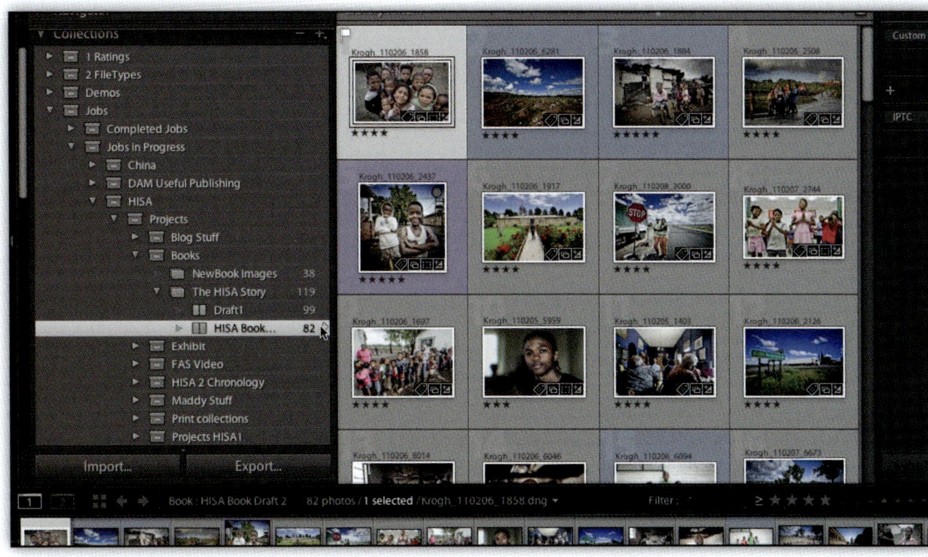

VIDEO 1-4 MAKING PROJECTS (4:35)

This video shows how we can use Lightroom's Collections tool to manage shoots and create projects. These creative collections allow us the flexibility to experiment with groupings of images and with different sequencing. And all of this can be done without disturbing the storage foundation of the collection.

THE LIGHTROOM CATALOG

Lightroom is the key reason that the "layers" described above can work so well. By bringing the tools for managing storage, organization and creations together, Lightroom enables us to seamlessly merge these three functions.

Comprehensive catalogs, unified Library

All of the work outlined above — storing, tagging, and creating projects — is easier when you are working with comprehensive catalogs and a unified library. Remember that Lightroom does not allow you to search multiple catalogs, or even open more than one catalog at a time. So it's harder to manage your files across multiple catalogs, and it's even harder to tag consistently.

Because of this, you'll want to gather all your image files into one place, if possible. And you'll want to use as few Lightroom catalogs as possible. If you can fit everything in one single catalog, that **is** the best way to go. Creating the single Master Catalog in Lightroom really does allow you to have maximum creative freedom with your images.

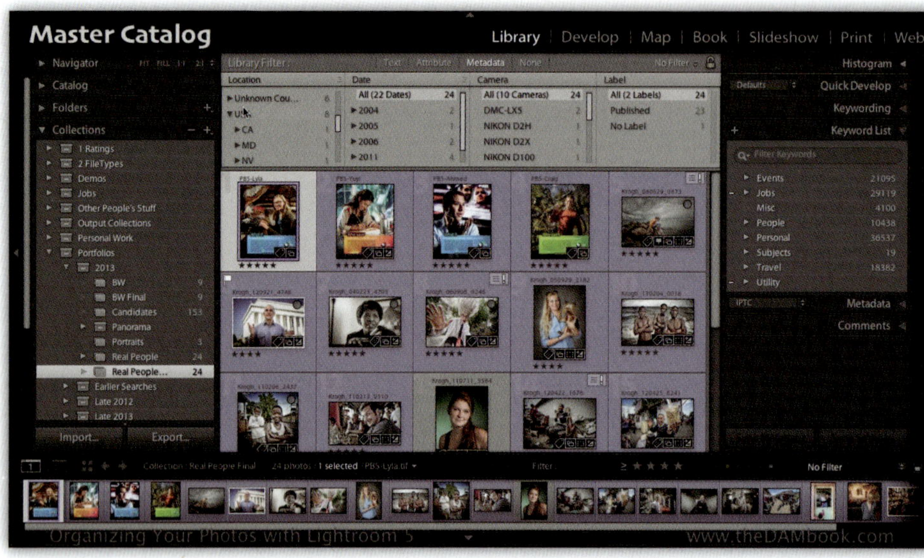

VIDEO 1-5 THE LIGHTROOM CATALOG (3:24)
This video shows some of the advantages you get by using a unified Master Catalog, compared to using multiple smaller catalogs.

In Chapter 2, I'll provide some tips on merging catalogs together into a single Master Catalog. And in Chapter 3, I'll add some tips on bringing your image files together into a unified Photo Library.

ADDING INTELLIGENCE TO YOUR IMAGE COLLECTION

Being faced with a large collection of images to tag can be daunting. You might have hundreds (or thousands) of different shoots, people, locations, and subjects. How do you approach this without driving yourself crazy?

Listed below are a few simple guidelines that can make the process a manageable one.

Bring everything together (as best you can)

You'll want to work as comprehensively as possible. This means that you'll want to bring all your photos together into a single catalog, if possible. I realize that this may be tough for people who have made a big mess of things. I'll give you some tips later in the book to help smooth the way on this.

Regardless of the state of the existing photos, it's important to have a vision of what an organized future can look like. So the video below will help you understand how being comprehensive can help you.

Leverage what you already have

If you are only starting to use metadata tags, you might have a bit of work in front of you. Let's begin by making use of the tags that we already have. You probably have a lot of folder names, and hopefully you have some date information. (You did set your camera's clock, right?) You can use this existing information to help you build a tag structure.

You can use Lightroom's Find command to show all images in folders with a particular name. It may be very easy to find images with a shoot name in the folder, and build out a keyword hierarchy from these terms.

You may also be able to filter your collection by the camera model and add some other keyword to all these photos (for instance, you may primarily use a point-and-shoot camera while on vacation). And the date tags make the photos line up in order taken, so that you can select entire shoots quickly for adding bulk tags.

Do your searching and grouping in the catalog

Whenever you need to search for some images, you should do the searching in the catalog. And when you find what you are looking for, add a tag or two to help you find the files next time you search. This can be a tag that says what the photos are about (keyword: *People > Family > Krogh > Josie* or *Location > Oberon St.*) or it could be a creative collection (*Photos for My Portfolio*).

Over time, you will add lots of internal intelligence to your Photo Library without doing any additional work. The video below shows this in action.

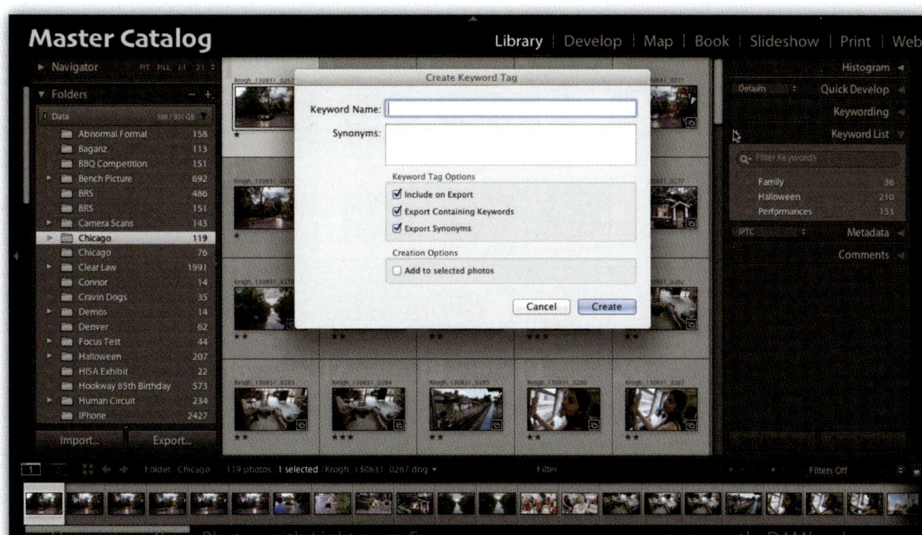

VIDEO 1-6 GETTING STARTED (6:38)

This video outlines some approaches for getting started with your newly organized Photo Library.

START BIG AND SUBDIVIDE

We're going to use the technique *Start big and subdivide* a lot in this book. It's an extremely helpful technique for building a tag structure efficiently, especially if you are starting from scratch on a large collection of images.

We'll start by creating large groups, and then subdividing the images as necessary. I touched on this earlier when talking about how to tag people in groups. We can use the same technique for many types of keyword tags. As you start tagging, I suggest you put your photos in large groups that you can divide up as time allows.

This is generally going to be a lot more efficient than starting at the bottom level of the hierarchy. Instead of starting your tagging by assigning hundreds or thousands of place, people and shoot names, you can start by making a few dozen big groups that let you filter your Photo Library in valuable ways immediately. You can make more specific tags as time goes on.

Use the tools that tell you where tags are missing

We can use Smart Collections, as well as the Library Filter to help find images that don't have a type of tag. The Smart Collections that come with Lightroom include one that is called Without Keywords and it can be useful on your first pass of keywording. We'll look at this technique more in the Keywording chapter, as well as the Location Tagging chapter.

The video below shows this process in action.

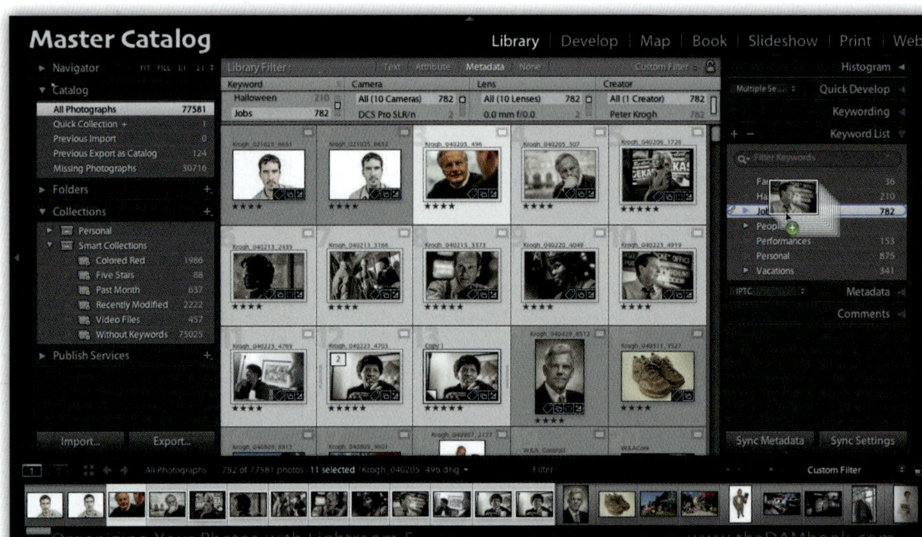

VIDEO 1-7 START BIG AND SUBDIVIDE (4:00)
This video shows how you can use a few large groups to start filtering your Photo Library immediately and then subdivide easily later.

MULTIPLE FILES AND MULTIPLE VERSIONS

One of the biggest challenges of any Photo Library is the management of lots of copies of the same files. Lightroom's Develop and creative capabilities can really reduce the number of additional files you need to make and save. Many people can do all of their image optimization work entirely inside of Lightroom and need never go over to Photoshop.

I will present some methods that Lightroom offers for you to create multiple interpretations of an image file without having to make additional copies. We'll use Virtual Copies and Snapshots to help us out here.

When we need to simply export files to send out, we can often "export and forget" them. The originals stay in the Lightroom catalog, and can be easily recreated. We can also use *Publish Services* to export the photos and keep a connection directly to the master copy in Lightroom.

And when we do need to use Photoshop for some image compositing or for heavy retouching, we'll see how to organize those files as well. As a matter of fact, we have a whole chapter on the options for managing multiple versions and copies.

The video below presents an overview of the options for multiple copies.

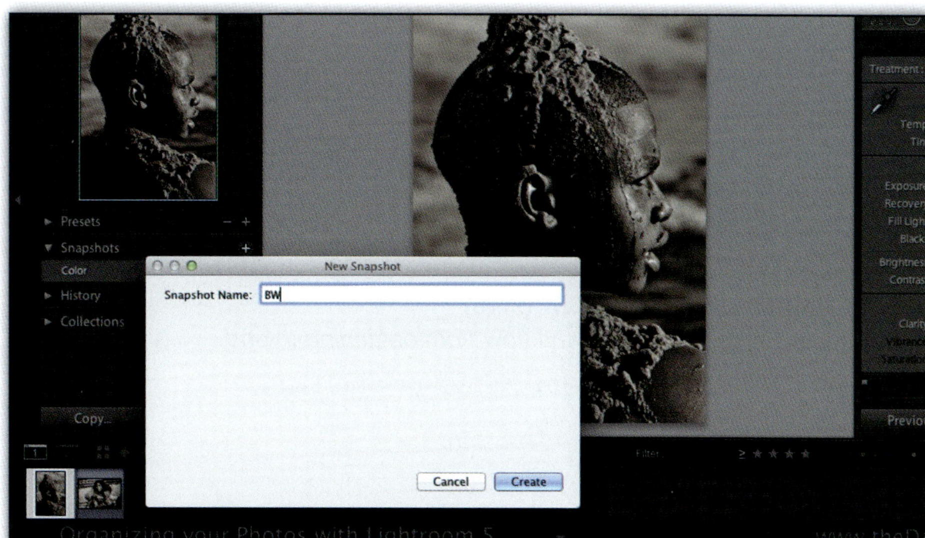

VIDEO 1-8 MULTIPLE VERSIONS (5:12)
This video outlines the several different ways that Lightroom allows you to make versions of your photos. This includes Snapshots, Virtual Copies, Published copies and Exported files.

SAMPLE IMPORT WORKFLOW

So far in this chapter, we've discussed the elements of storage, the idea behind tagging, and the use of projects to organize a shoot. Before we move on to the rest of the book's detailed discussion of these tools, I'd like to show you how a shoot can be downloaded, tagged, put into a project and shared. We'll make use of all these tools in an integrated workflow.

The video below outlines the workflow for the importing, naming, storage, tagging, sorting, project creation and sharing of a shoot. We'll be looking at the details of all of these tasks later in the book.

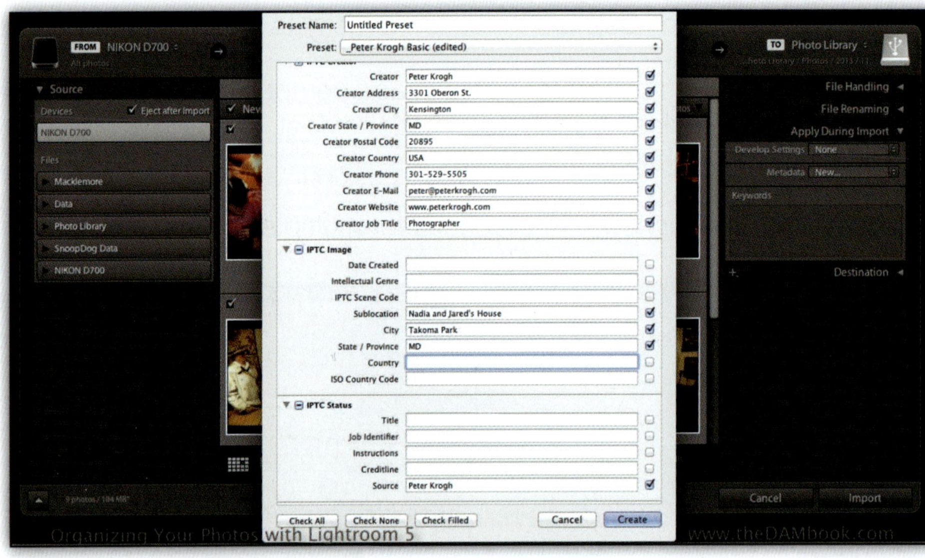

VIDEO 1-9 SAMPLE WORKFLOW (9:48)

In this video, we see a sample workflow from beginning to end.

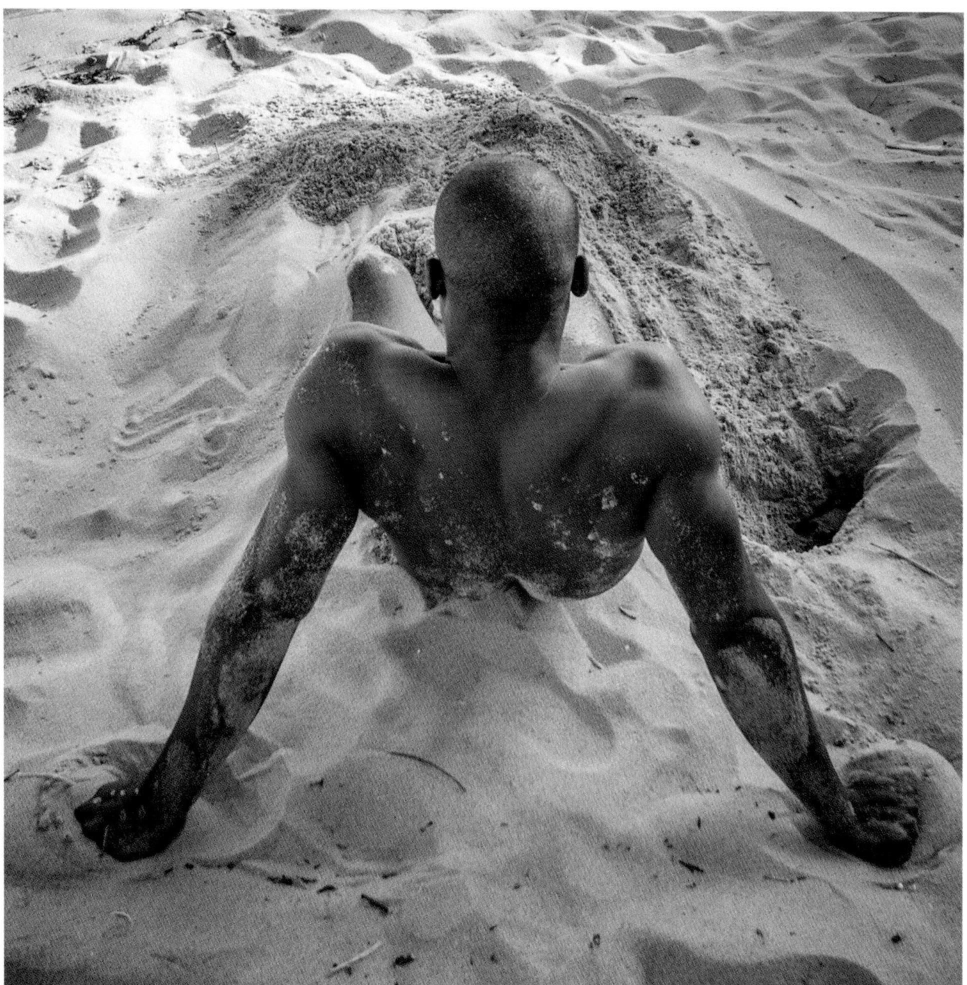

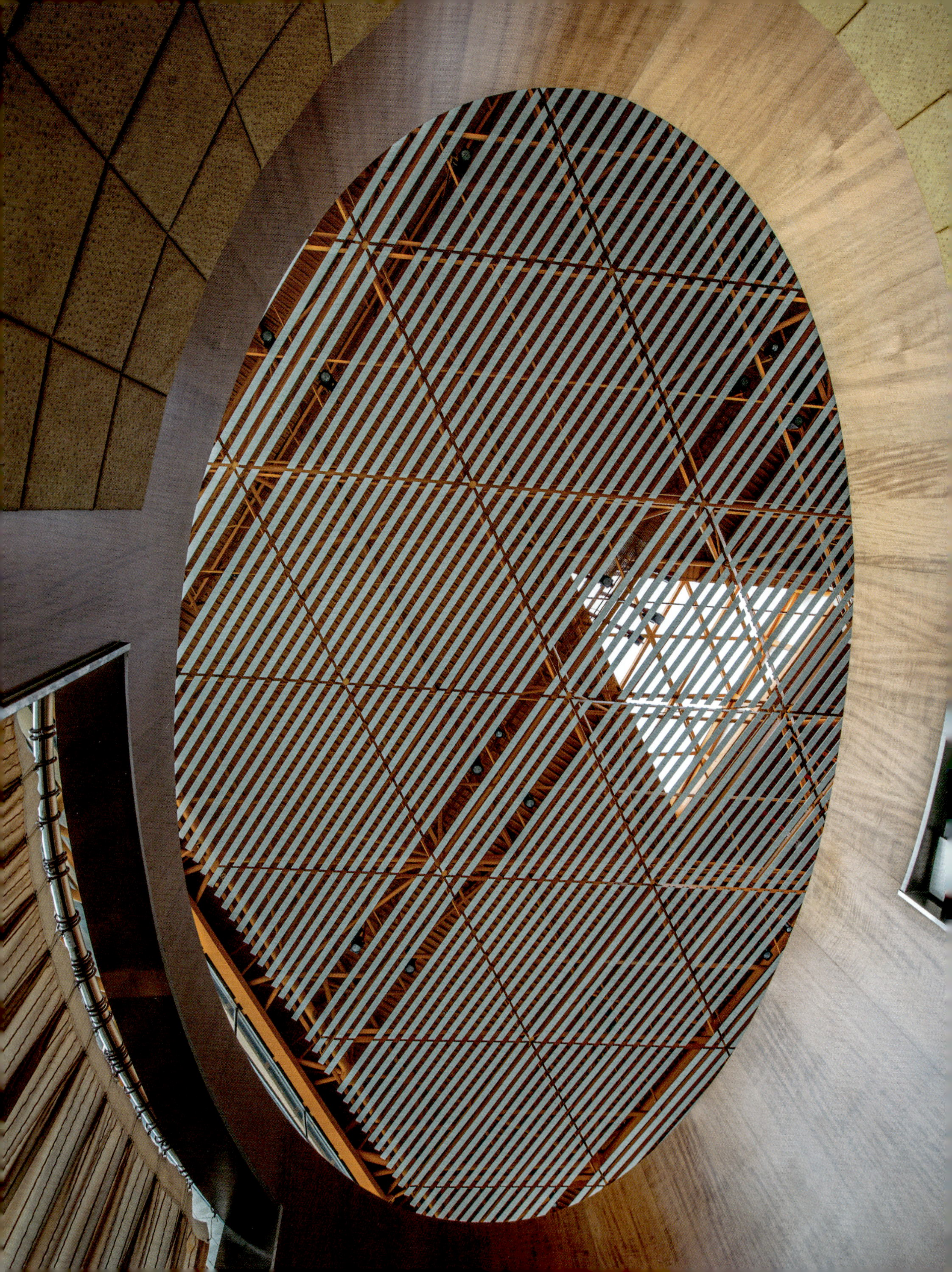

CHAPTER 2

THE LIGHTROOM CATALOG

Lightroom is the lynchpin of your organized Photo Library. Before we dive into the workings of the storage, tagging and project-creation tools, I want to spend a little time reviewing the way Lightroom works.

This chapter focuses on the functions of the catalog. I want to make sure that you understand the basic structure of the catalog, and some of the most important functions from an organization point-of-view.

WHAT WE'LL COVER IN THIS CHAPTER

This chapter does not provide a guide for your initial setup of Lightroom, nor does it cover all catalog-handling functions. Victoria Bampton provides a free Quick Start Guide that can help new users get up and running. And Victoria's *The Missing FAQ* book will answer your questions about what each individual option or control does.

I'm limiting my discussion here to the stuff you need to know in order to organize your photos. These topics have been chosen because they are central to the comprehensive, long-term use of your Lightroom Catalogs in the management of your Photo Library. We can split that into several parts.

Understanding and working with catalogs

We're investing a lot of work in the catalog, so it's important to understand how a catalog is structured. You'll need to know the relationship between a catalog and the photo files. And you'll need to know some basics about the catalog document itself, such as what the parts of the catalog are, and where to store the catalog.

Creating a unified Master Catalog

In order to make maximum use of the organizational tools in Lightroom, you'll want to bring all your photos into a single Master Catalog. We'll see how we can merge any of your existing catalogs into a single Master. We'll also look at some tips for managing the size of your catalog.

Preserving the catalog

The catalog holds lots of important tags and other settings, so it's essential to make sure it's backed up properly. We'll look at the ways you can protect the catalog through good backup procedures.

CATALOG BASICS

Let's start at the very beginning (a very good place to start).

The Lightroom Catalog stores all your settings

All the work you do to organize and tag your photos is stored in the Lightroom catalog.

Each tag you make in Lightroom, each Develop setting you make, and all your creations are stored in the catalog. This is very different from working with your photos in Photoshop, or using a word processor program. In those cases, the changes you make are stored inside the file itself.

The photo files themselves are not stored in the catalog. The photos should be stored in a set of folders that are organized in an easy-to-understand manner such as date taken. Put the files into their folders and leave them there.

Catalogs provide a lot of advantages, particularly when you want to organize a large number of photos. You can tag and filter the photos in multiple ways, such as by date, location, subject matter or rating.

Catalogs can allow you to view your photos, even when the Photo Library drive is not currently connected. This allows you to view, tag and organize your photos when you are away from home, as long as you have the catalog with you.

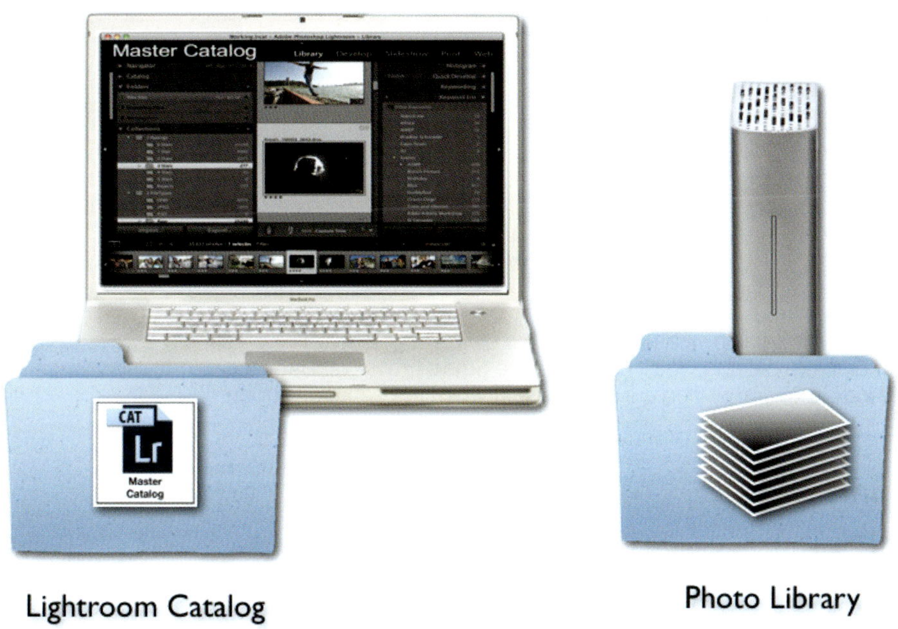

Figure 2-1 Your catalog and your photos should probably be stored in different places. The catalog can live in your Pictures or My Photos folder, but your Photo Library will often need to be stored on its own dedicated hard drive.

THE ELEMENTS OF A CATALOG

Lightroom stores your catalog in a folder, and inside that folder are several pieces. Let's review these.

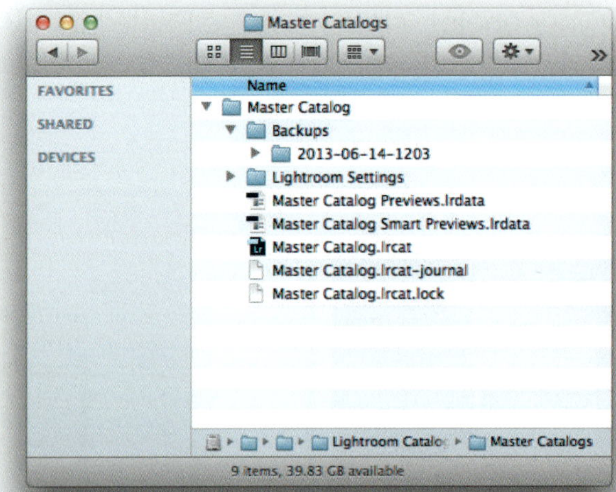

Figure 2-2 Here is a Lightroom catalog with all the possible stuff it might include. You should always have the .lrcat and Previews.lrdata in any complete catalog. You'll only have the Smart Previews, Backups and Presets when you've chosen those options. And the lock and journal files are only present when the catalog is open.

Here are the parts:

- The .lrcat file: This is the catalog database that contains all the settings you make: Develop settings, keywords, collections, history, saved books, etc. This is the most important part of the catalog.
- The Previews.lrdata file (which shows as a folder on Windows): This contains the previews for the catalog. This is what you see when you are looking at the Lightroom Library module. Previews can be recreated, as long as you have the .lrcat file and the original images. You'll notice that the previews are the biggest part of the catalog.
- The Smart Previews.lrdata file (which shows as a folder on Windows): This contains any Smart Previews you may have made. It will only exist if you have made Smart Previews. It was introduced in Lightroom 5. This can also get large if you have a lot of Smart Previews.
- The Backups folder: This is an optional duplicate copy of the .lrcat file. It is created when you choose to backup the catalog upon exit. Lightroom creates a folder named for the date and time the backup is created, and copies the .lrcat file to the folder. Note that, while it's an option, I definitely think it's an option you should use.
- The Settings folder: This is an optional folder that is created when you tell Lightroom to "Store presets with this catalog" in the Preferences menu. I don't suggest using this option, so I'll ignore it in this book.

- The .lrcat-lock file and the .lrcat-journal files: These only exist when that catalog is actively open in Lightroom.

Upgrading Lightroom

When you upgrade your Lightroom application by a whole number (4 to 5, as opposed to 5.0 to 5.3), Lightroom will make a new copy of the .lrcat file with a number appended to the file name, leaving the old one in place. Once you are satisfied that the new version works fine, it's okay to delete the older version of the catalog.

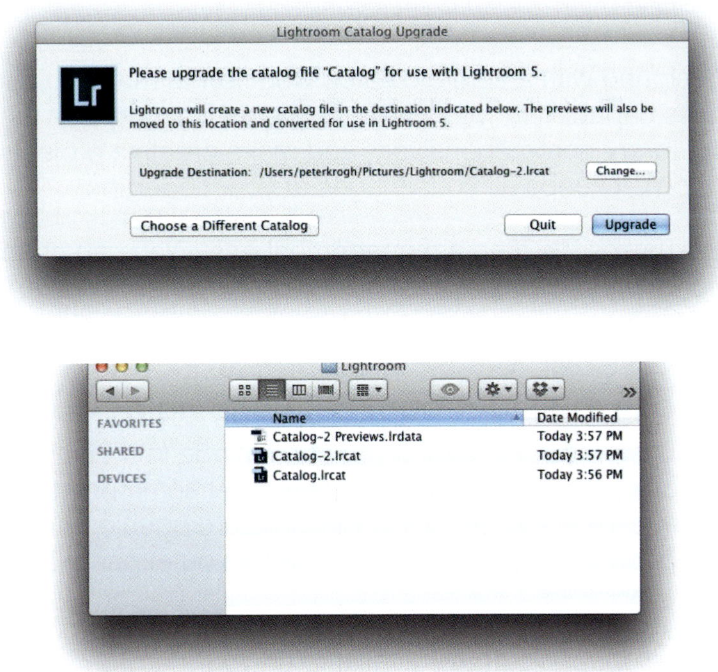

Figure 2-3 When you upgrade to a new "full number" version, Lightroom requires you to upgrade the catalog. It creates a new version of the catalog with a number after the name, and adds the number to Previews.lrdata. It leaves the old .lrcat file in place.

Don’t move files around behind Lightroom’s back

Lightroom will lose track of the photos if you move or rename them outside of Lightroom. So don’t do that.

It’s possible to reconnect the catalog and the photos after they have been moved. If you’ve only moved a folder, it’s very easy to tell Lightroom to reconnect. If you have renamed files, or moved them into many different folders, it can be really difficult. We’ll see how to reconnect files and folders that have been moved in the next chapter.

THE IDEAL NUMBER OF CATALOGS IS 1

Lightroom has been designed with a single-catalog workflow in mind. To take greatest advantage of Lightroom’s capabilities, you’ll want to use as few catalogs as possible. This lets you search your Photo Library comprehensively, and make creative projects all within a single place (the Master Catalog). It keeps all your images at your fingertips.

A single Master Catalog makes the media management easy. You can check on the health of your files, and check for completeness of the Photo Library. You can upgrade your Lightroom version and transfer files to new drives simply and easily.

How many images can my Lightroom catalogs hold?

There is no hard limit to the number of images you can include in a Lightroom catalog. The limit is generally determined by your computer’s performance. At some point, a catalog may get so big that it really slows down. This may show up when you are opening and closing the catalog, or when you are browsing the Library thumbnails, or when you expand the Library Filter bar or the Keywording panel.

A catalog may outgrow the space you have available on your hard drive. This is a real possibility for catalogs stored on internal laptop drives. I’ll show you some tricks for keeping the preview size under control.

Most readers should find that catalogs of 100,000 images or more are perfectly usable, as long as there is enough hard drive space. The demonstration catalog used in this book has more than 70,000 photos and videos, and it runs acceptably fast, even with video recording software running at the same time.

YOU MIGHT BE WONDERING....

When should you make multiple catalogs?

If your Photo Library outgrows a single catalog, then you'll need to create additional catalogs. Only do this when you need to. Most Lightroom users can get by with one single catalog.

- Your Photo Library might outgrow a single catalog due to the number of photos or storage space available.
- You might need to use Lightroom on multiple computers.
- You might need a location-based workflow as well as a studio-based workflow.
- You might need to collaborate with others.
- You might want to save individual creative Projects as catalogs so that the settings never change.

There are five basic reasons to make multiple catalogs. In this book, we only cover the last of these possibilities, archiving Projects. If any of the other needs describe you, then I suggest reading *The DAM Book Guide to Multi-Catalog Workflow.*

Making Lightroom run faster

Lightroom may be running slowly because of catalog size, but it can also be hamstrung by inadequate RAM. If you have less than 16GB, and you can afford to upgrade, you should consider doing that. Storing your Lightroom catalog on a fast drive like a Solid State Drive (SSD) will also make a big difference. You'll also want to make sure there is plenty of free space on the drive that holds your Lightroom catalogs. And if that does not help, the only way to make it faster may be to buy a faster computer.

LIGHTROOM CATALOG STORAGE

When you first open Lightroom, a new catalog is created in your Pictures folder (Mac) or My Photos folder (PC). That's generally a fine place for the catalog to live, particularly for those with a single drive in their computer. It's possible that it will grow too large for this location and need to move to a new drive. And you may want to move it to a fast Solid State Drive for added speed.

Finding your catalog

If you are not sure where the catalog is stored, you can open the Catalog Settings. You'll find those in the *Lightroom* menu on Mac, and the *Edit* menu on PC. Choose the *General* tab and click *Show* to open the folder that holds the catalog.

Renaming a catalog

You can rename a catalog by renaming each of the parts. You'll need to close the catalog first, and then rename each of the elements using the identical root name.

Setting an identity plate

I suggest that you create a custom identity plate for your catalog. I use one that identifies the name of each catalog, but that's only because I need multiple catalogs for my large Photo Library. If you have a single catalog, as most of you should, you may want to set the identity plate to your name.

You can set the Identity Plate by choosing *Identity Plate Setup* in the *Lightroom* menu on Mac, or the *Edit* menu on PC.

Making a new catalog

If you need to make a new catalog, you can hold down the *Option* key on Mac (*Alt* key on PC) as you start Lightroom. This will bring up a dialog to open an existing catalog or make a new one. You can make a new catalog in this dialog and choose where to save it.

Finding existing catalogs

The dialog that comes up when you hold down *Option* (*Alt* on PC) while starting Lightroom will allow you to choose between any existing catalogs that Lightroom knows about. Note that Lightroom does not search your entire computer for catalogs. Lightroom simply remembers the ones it has used before. It will show you those catalogs if they are in the same place, with the same name.

To search more comprehensively, you can search the hard drive for .lrcat in the OS search tool. Note that this will show you backup versions of catalogs as well, and might be kind of difficult to sort out.

Moving your catalog

You can move your catalog to a new location just like any other file on your computer. If you are moving it to a new drive for additional speed or capacity, you'll probably want to delete the version in the old location once you see that everything has transferred properly. You could also change the name of the folder that holds the older catalog so that Lightroom does not inadvertently open the old version.

If you are moving the catalog so that you can get extra speed, you'll want to consider using a Solid State Drive for the catalog. You can also use a conventional hard drive. You get better speed if the drive that holds the catalog is not the same one that holds your Photo Library, especially if it's a conventional hard drive.

When you move a catalog to a new location, you typically want to move the entire catalog folder: the one that contains the .lrcat file, the Previews.lrdata, the Backups, Smart Previews, etc. And you will only want to move it when the catalog is not open in Lightroom, so there wil be no journal or lock files showing in the catalog folder.

Organize your catalogs by folder

If you ever need to make multiple Lightroom catalogs, it's best to keep these organized in folders. If you have legacy catalogs to merge, make a Legacy Catalogs folder to store them. If you want to export a Creative Collection to preserve Book or Slideshow settings, store that in a Project Catalogs folder.

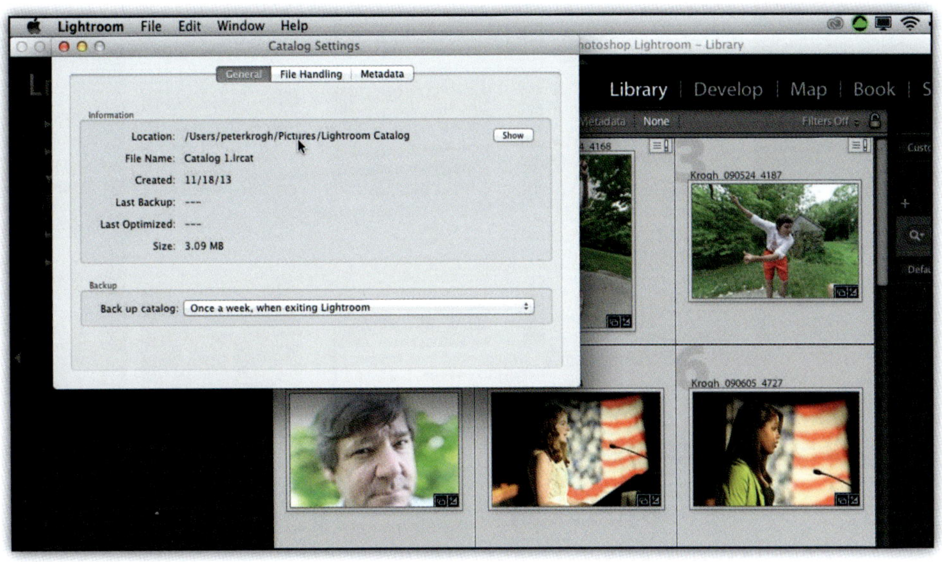

VIDEO 2-1 CATALOG HANDLING (5:52)
This video shows how to find, rename, move and set a custom naming template for your catalog.

WORKING WITH OFFLINE PHOTOS?

Lightroom allows you to make tags and do other organizational work, even if the Photo Library drive is not currently connected to your computer. You can browse through the images, create tags, search and filter, because the catalog keeps a record of the photos and all the metadata about the photos. All of this is accessible even when the photos are offline.

If you want to do any work to Develop your photos, or to output the photos while they are offline, you'll first need to build Smart Previews.

Smart Previews

Smart Previews are smaller, semi-raw versions of your original files that can be used when you are not currently connected to the Photo Library. You can make Develop adjustments to the files that will automatically be applied to the full-size versions of the files next time you're connected to the Photo Library.

These 2560-pixel-long Smart Previews can also be used for file export or email, as long as you can get by with the smaller file dimensions. The color and general image quality are pretty close to those of the original file, if you don't have to do a lot of severe adjustments. The video below shows how you can make and use Smart Previews.

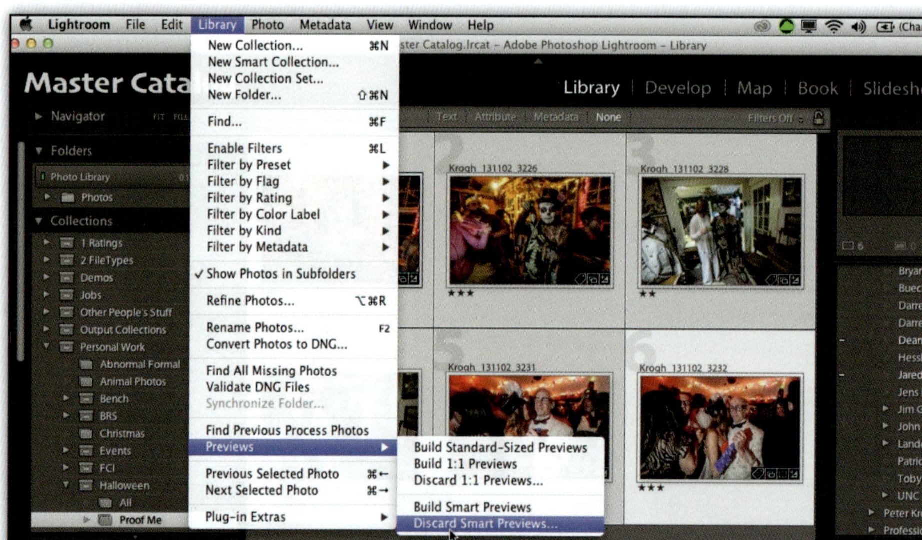

VIDEO 2-2 OFFLINE PHOTOS (3:44)
This video shows how to create Smart Previews.

MANAGING CATALOG SIZE WITH PREVIEW SETTINGS

The size of Lightroom catalogs is determined by the number of files in the catalog, the size of the previews file, and possibly the megapixel size of the originals. Once you've deleted your rejects, the best way to keep your catalog size under control is by managing the previews.

Each photo in a Lightroom catalog has a standard-sized preview in the catalog. This lets you see the photo, even if the Photo Library drive is not connected. You have control over the size and quality of these preview files.

You will also have full-size previews in the catalog. You may create these on import for faster full-size viewing. And 1:1 previews are always made when you open a photo in the Develop module. You can tell Lightroom how long to keep these previews in the catalog.

A catalog of 20,000 images with 1:1 previews may grow to 75 GB or more, while the same catalog with the smallest, lowest quality previews may be only 5 GB. You can customize these settings according to your needs, and according to the size of your available storage space.

Let's see how we can use the Preview Preferences to manage the catalog size.

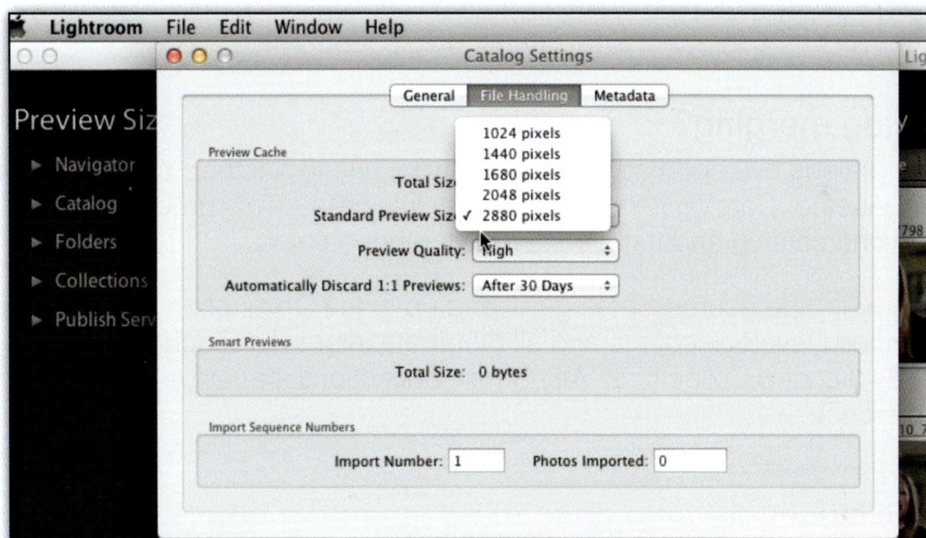

VIDEO 2-3 PREVIEW SIZE AND QUALITY (4:59)
This video shows how to use preview preferences to manage catalog size.

Here are the options:

Open Catalog Settings in the *Lightroom* menu on Mac, and the *Edit* menu on PC.

- Standard Preview Size determines the smallest preview size that Lightroom will keep.
- Preview Quality determines how much JPEG compression is applied to the preview. Lower quality is much smaller, but shows artifacting.
- Automatically Discard 1:1 Previews controls how long Lightroom will keep any 1:1 previews it makes for a file.

(Whenever Lightroom shows a file at full size in Library module, it will create a 1:1 preview. The Discard function can clean these out automatically.)

MERGING YOUR EXISTING CATALOGS

If you have only one single Lightroom catalog, you can probably skip this section. But if you have several different catalogs, then you'll want to pay attention here. We need to merge these catalogs into as few as possible. And we want to do this at the earliest possible opportunity, so the rest of our work organizing the Photo Library can be done as comprehensively as possible. Ideally, we'll get everything into one single catalog.

What is catalog merging?

You merge two catalogs by importing the settings from one to another. You do this with the Import From Another Catalog item in the Library File menu. This process takes all* the information from one catalog and transfers it into another catalog.

All photos that are "in" the Source Catalog will end up in the Destination Catalog. The images will appear with their Develop settings and all metadata intact. This includes History, Flags, Virtual Copies, Books, and Collections. Any Smart Collections that are in the Source will also be copied to the Destination.

***Warning:**

Publish Services are not included in the merge.
Any Publish Services will be left behind, and not transferred to the new catalog.

MERGE, OR START OVER?

You'll want to make some decisions about whether merging your catalogs even makes sense. For some people, merging can be a fast and neat process, and lots of valuable work can be brought together in the new Master Catalog. For others, the merging process may be far more trouble than it's worth. These folks would be better off starting from scratch, and re-cataloging everything.

Ask yourself these questions to help determine whether to merge your existing catalogs or start over. I've provided some insight for how your answers can guide your decision-making process.

Q: Have I done valuable work in my existing Lightroom catalogs?

Yes: If you've made Develop settings, tags or projects that you want to preserve, you'll want to consider catalog merging.

No: If your catalogs are filled with random settings that are not worth keeping, then it's best to start over.

Q: Do my file names and folder structure match the ones in the catalogs?

Yes: If the files and folders match, then catalog merging may be for you. (Check Library > Find all Missing Photos to see how many orphaned files there are in a catalog.)

No: If you've renamed lots of files, or moved files to a very different subfolder structure, merging can be a horrible and frustrating process. Renamed files are harder to reconcile than renamed/reworked folders are.

Q: Do each of my catalogs reference separate groups of photos?

Yes: If each of your catalogs references a specific group of photos, and there is very little overlap, it probably makes sense to merge your catalogs.

No: If the same photos are included in multiple catalogs, it can be a big mess to sort out. You'll only want to do this if you're pretty sure there is enough good work in the catalogs to justify the work of sorting between versions.

Q: Do I know which of my catalogs is the most recent version?

Yes: It's common for people to end up with multiple versions of the same (or similar) Lightroom catalogs. If you know which version is the best (usually the most complete, and/or the most recent), then you should consider catalog merging.

No: If you sometimes work in this version of a catalog, and sometimes work in that version, none of them may be fully up-to-date. You can still move ahead in this situation, but it's best to settle on a single version of a particular catalog. Do your merge with that catalog, and don't worry about trying to reconcile everything. Some of your tagging or Develop work may need to be recreated.

The following video outlines the decisions you might need to make when choosing whether to merge catalogs.

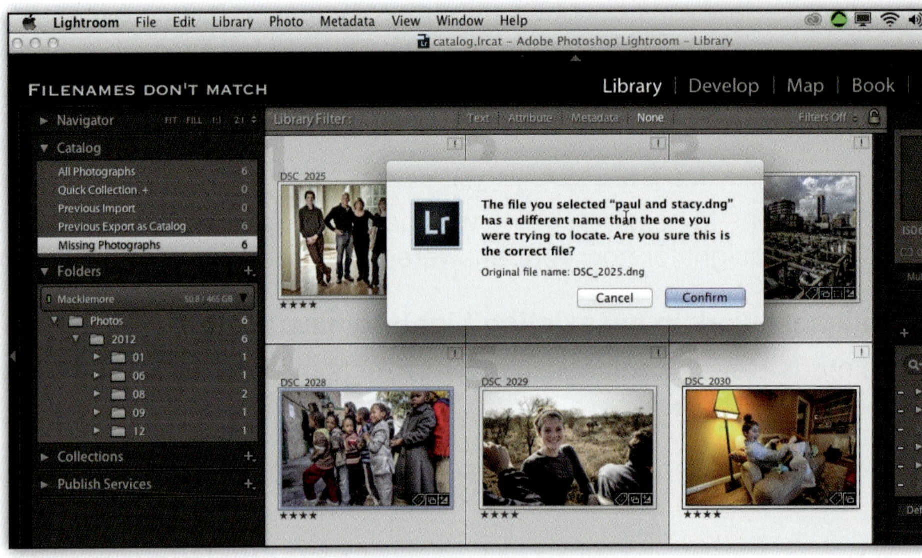

VIDEO 2-4 DECIDING TO MERGE (4:25)

This video outlines some of the factors you should use when deciding whether to merge your existing catalogs into a new Master Catalog.

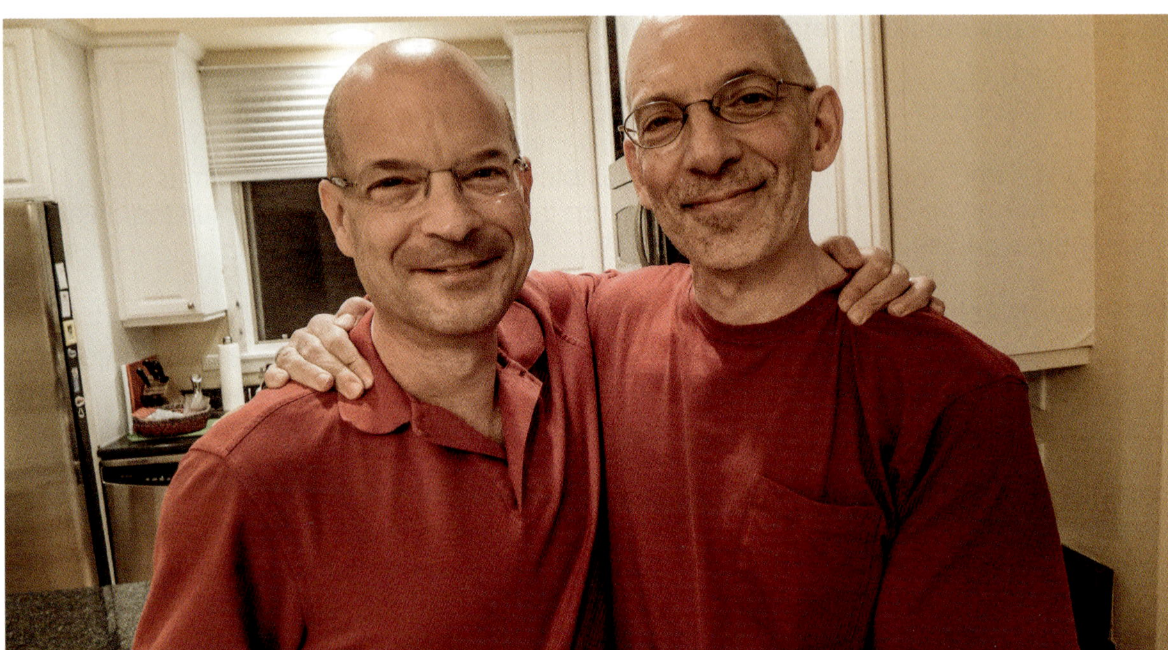

CATALOG MERGING WORKFLOW

If you read through the Q&A above, and you still want to merge, here's an outline of the process. These are general guidelines, but it's a pretty good work order for most people. If you have more than two or three catalogs to merge, you should probably track the process with a written list.

Preparation:

1. Identify the catalogs you want to merge, and bring them together in a folder called *Merge Me*.
2. Make sure all missing files are reconciled in each catalog before the merge.
3. See how much overlap there is between catalogs.
4. Decide which catalog "wins" in the case of duplication — winning catalogs should be imported first. Keep this list on a piece of paper, or some separate document.
5. Determine which catalog will be the new Master Catalog. Change the name and identity plate if necessary, or make a brand new catalog.
6. If you have a catalog with active Publish Services, that's the best candidate for the Master Catalog, since that information is not transferred through Catalog Import.

For each merge:

1. Do the process in an orderly way.
2. Open the Master Catalog, choose *File > Import from Another Catalog*.
3. In the Import dialog, under *New Photos*, choose *Add New Photos to Catalog without Moving*.
4. Unless you really need to preserve multiple versions of the same file, I suggest that under *Changed Existing Files* you *Do Nothing*.
5. Move each catalog to a ***Merged*** folder once it has been processed.
6. Check for missing files after each merge and reconcile them right away before the next merge.

After you've finished:

1. Throw the imported catalogs away once you have optimized and backed up the new Master Catalog.
2. Move all your files to your Photo Library, if necessary, using the *Folders* panel in the Master Catalog.
3. If possible, put them into a folder structure divided by year. If that's too difficult, you might want to place them in a folder called *Legacy* for now.
4. Choose the folders and run the *Synchronize* command. This will alert you to uncataloged photos and videos in the existing folders.
5. Add any uncataloged photos to the Master Catalog after the process has finished.

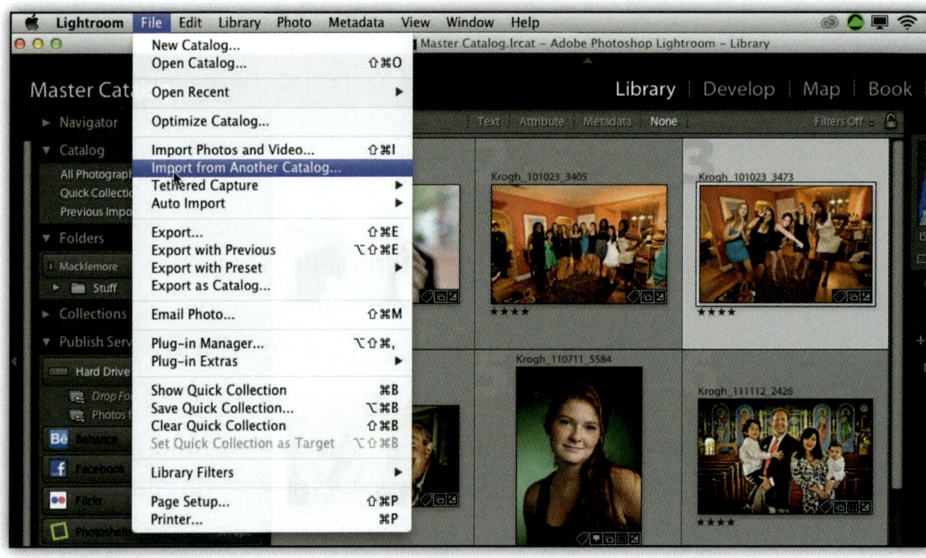

VIDEO 2-5 MERGE WORKFLOW (6:44)

This video outlines the process for merging existing catalogs into a new Master Catalog.

LIGHTROOM CATALOG BACKUP

The work you do to your photos is valuable work worth preserving — the Develop adjustments, the organization in Library, the creations you make in Book or Slideshow. It's essential to have a solid backup strategy in order to preserve that work. I suggest using two kinds of backup to make sure you protect this important information.

MAKE BACKUP COPIES OF YOUR CATALOG

It's possible (even likely, over time) that you'll have a problem with the hard drive that holds your Lightroom catalog. Drives can fail, and they can be stolen or lost. It's essential to regularly backup the catalog to another drive. I strongly recommend that you set this up with a backup program that runs daily. I use ChronoSync on Mac, and SyncBack on PC.

You only really need to backup the .lrcat file

Note that for data preservation, you really only need to backup the .lrcat file. It's not essential to include the Previews.lrdata file, since these can be recreated (as long as you still have the Photo Library). It's often a real time-saver to skip the previews as part of your regular backup procedure.

When you make a backup that excludes .lrpreviews, you protect all your settings information, but the backup catalog won't show you your photos until it has rebuilt the previews.

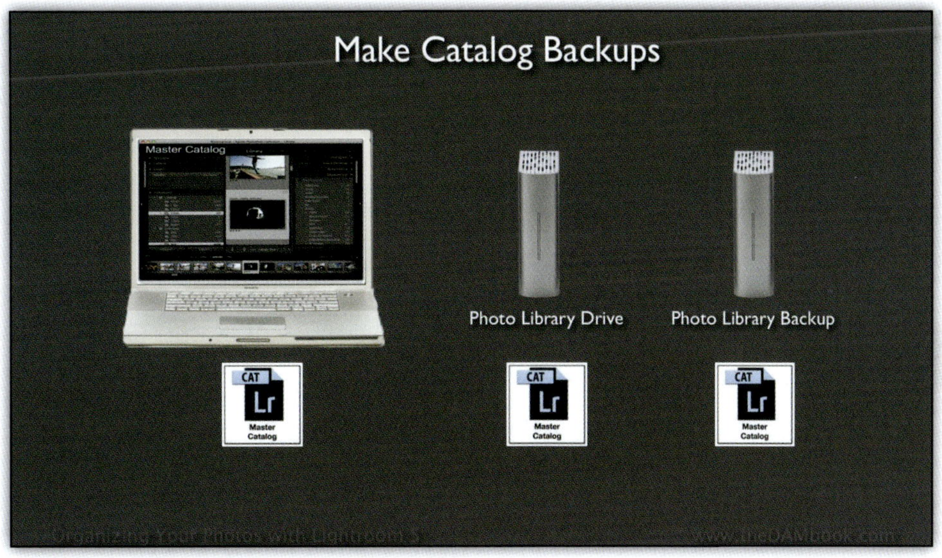

VIDEO 2-6 CATALOG BACKUPS (3:05)

This video shows how to make a daily backup of your Lightroom catalog, and to exclude the Previews file in ChronoSync on Mac and with SyncBack on PC.

MAKE BACKUP VERSIONS OF THE CATALOG

In addition to the backup copy of the catalog that is written to another drive, it's also important to make a backup version of the catalog. This is a secondary copy of the .lrcat file containing all the settings we've made. It's useful for a couple of reasons.

- It's possible that you may do something unwanted to the catalog. Perhaps you accidentally set all ratings to 0. Or perhaps the cat walks across your keyboard while the program is open, changing lots of settings and you don't realize it and close the catalog. In either case, you would want to roll back to a previous version of the catalog before the unwanted changes were made. The versioned backup makes it possible.
- It's also possible that a Lightroom catalog gets corrupted. This has only happened to me once, despite a long career of testing beta software and mistreating my catalogs. While the chance is small, it would be a huge bummer if it happened. So protect yourself by doing a versioned backup.

I suggest that you tell Lightroom to backup every time the software exits. Lightroom gives you the option to run it or skip it. You want this reminder to protect yourself against disaster, even if you don't always run it.

Always make a backup any time you add, move or rename files or folders

You don't always have to run the catalog backup on exit. If you've opened the catalog and not done any work, then it's fine to close without backup. Or perhaps you've only done minor work to a single file, and the loss of that would not be problematic. Fine, you can skip the backup.

However any time you've done file management tasks such as adding images, moving them, renaming images or folders or deleting folders, you'll want to consider running a backup. If you need to rollback to a previous version of a catalog and the files are in a different place, or the files or folders are named differently, it could be time-consuming to sort out the changes. Renamed files, for instance, will probably have to be reconnected one-by-one.

Optimizing during backup

When you close Lightroom and run the backup process, you have the option to optimize the catalog and check it for integrity. I suggest you do this whenever possible. This basic database maintenance will ensure that Lightroom runs at its fastest, and the catalog stays healthy.

Prune your backups every now and then

Lightroom will make a new copy of the .lrcat file each time you run the backup. Unfortunately, you can't tell Lightroom to remove old copies, so these can pile up. I suggest that you keep a few and delete any older ones periodically.

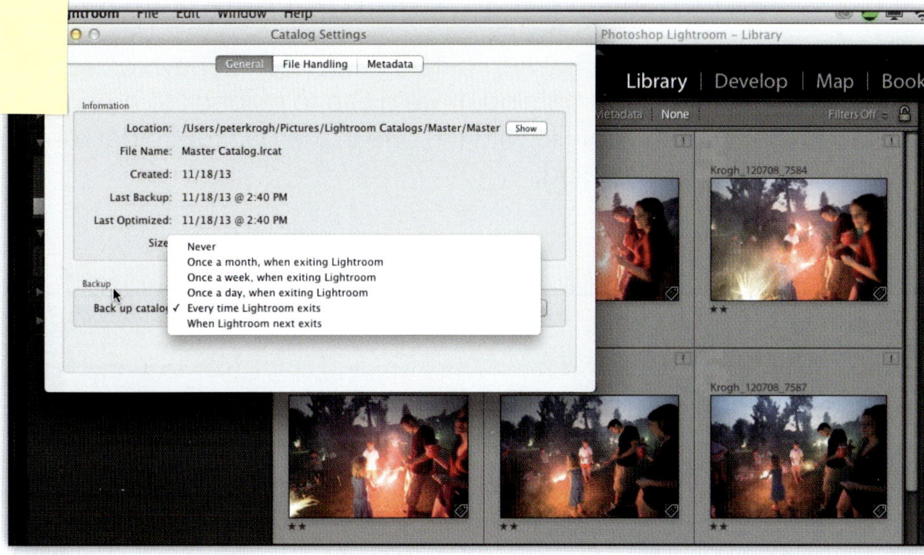

VIDEO 2-7 VERSIONED BACKUPS (3:10)
This video shows how to set up the catalog backup in Catalog Settings.

Here are the steps:

1. Go to the menu item *Lightroom > Catalog Settings*. (on PC, it's in the *Edit* menu).
2. In the *General* tab, set *Backup* to *Every time Lightroom exits.*
3. When you close a catalog, Lightroom will ask you if you would like to backup. If you've made any changes you'd like to preserve, and if time allows, run the backup.
4. Run the *Integrity Check* and *Optimization* as often as possible.
5. Prune the backups by throwing away older versions of the catalog backups.

USING THE BACKUP .LRCAT TO ROLLBACK A CATALOG

Now that we've outlined how to make a backup catalog, let's look at how to use one. Let's say we've done something unwanted to the catalog. If we'd like to rollback to a prior version, we need to simply replace the current .lrcat file with the one in the backup folder. All the images will revert to the settings in the backup catalog.

The video below outlines the process.

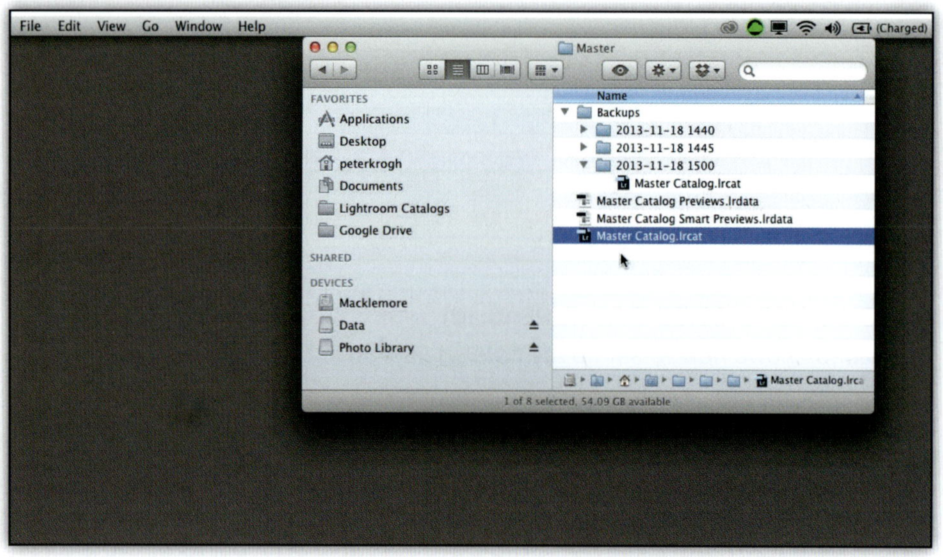

VIDEO 2-8 ROLLING BACK TO A PREVIOUS VERSION (4:14)
This video shows how to rollback a current Lightroom catalog to a backup version.

Here are the steps:

1. Make sure that the catalog is closed.
2. Put the current .lrcat file in a new folder labeled as *Trash Me* or some other descriptive name.
3. Take the most recent .lrcat out of the backup folder, and put it in the catalog's main folder.
4. Open the catalog and confirm that the content is correct.
5. You may want to rebuild previews so that they will be current to the state in the rolled back catalog.

METADATA WRITEBACK

As I've outlined above, all the work you do in Lightroom is "remembered" by the catalog itself. It's also possible to write some of these tags and other instructions back to the metadata of the file itself. If you write keywords back, then these can be seen by other programs, or by other Lightroom catalogs. The same goes with Develop settings.

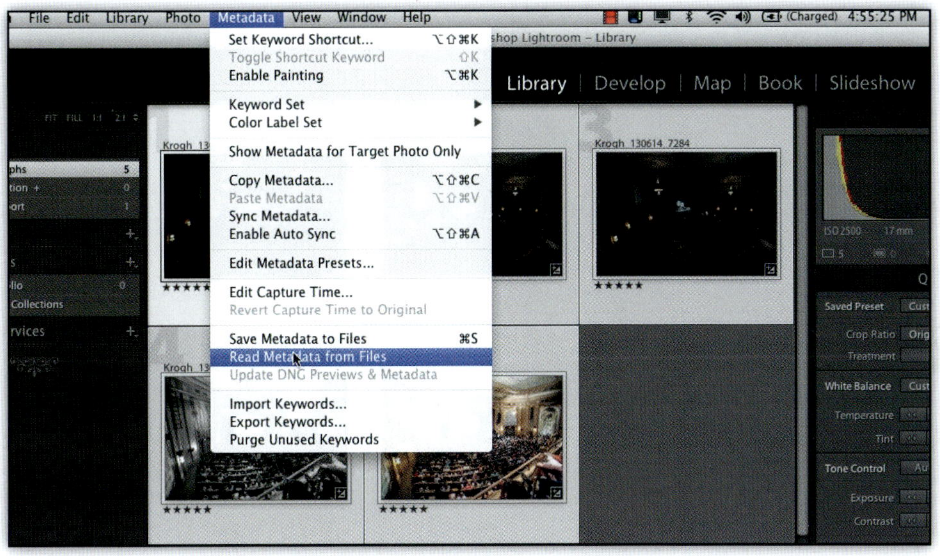

VIDEO 2-9 RESTORE FROM EMBEDDED TAGS (2:51)
This video shows how you can use Save Metadata and Read Metadata to function as a last-ditch backup.

This data written back to the file can serve as a last-ditch backup for the work you do in the catalog, since you can put the images in a new catalog and all embedded metadata will be extracted. While this is possible, I suggest that you do not rely on it. Instead, you need to make sure that you are following the backup process I outline above. Here's why.

Not all data is written back

While Develop settings and "regular"metadata is written back to the files, a number of important things are omitted. The Develop History is not written back. Nor are Flags, Virtual Copies, Collections, Book settings, saved Slideshows, or Publish Services. These are all really valuable additions that you make to the Photo Library, and you should preserve them.

Even more importantly, the saved catalog is a record of which files are in your collection. If you've lost your catalog due to a drive crash, then you will probably also want to check on the completeness of the collection. Preserving the catalog preserves a record of what files are supposed to be there. So, while it's possible to re-catalog all your files and create a new catalog as a last-ditch effort, you really want to try and keep yourself out of that last ditch.

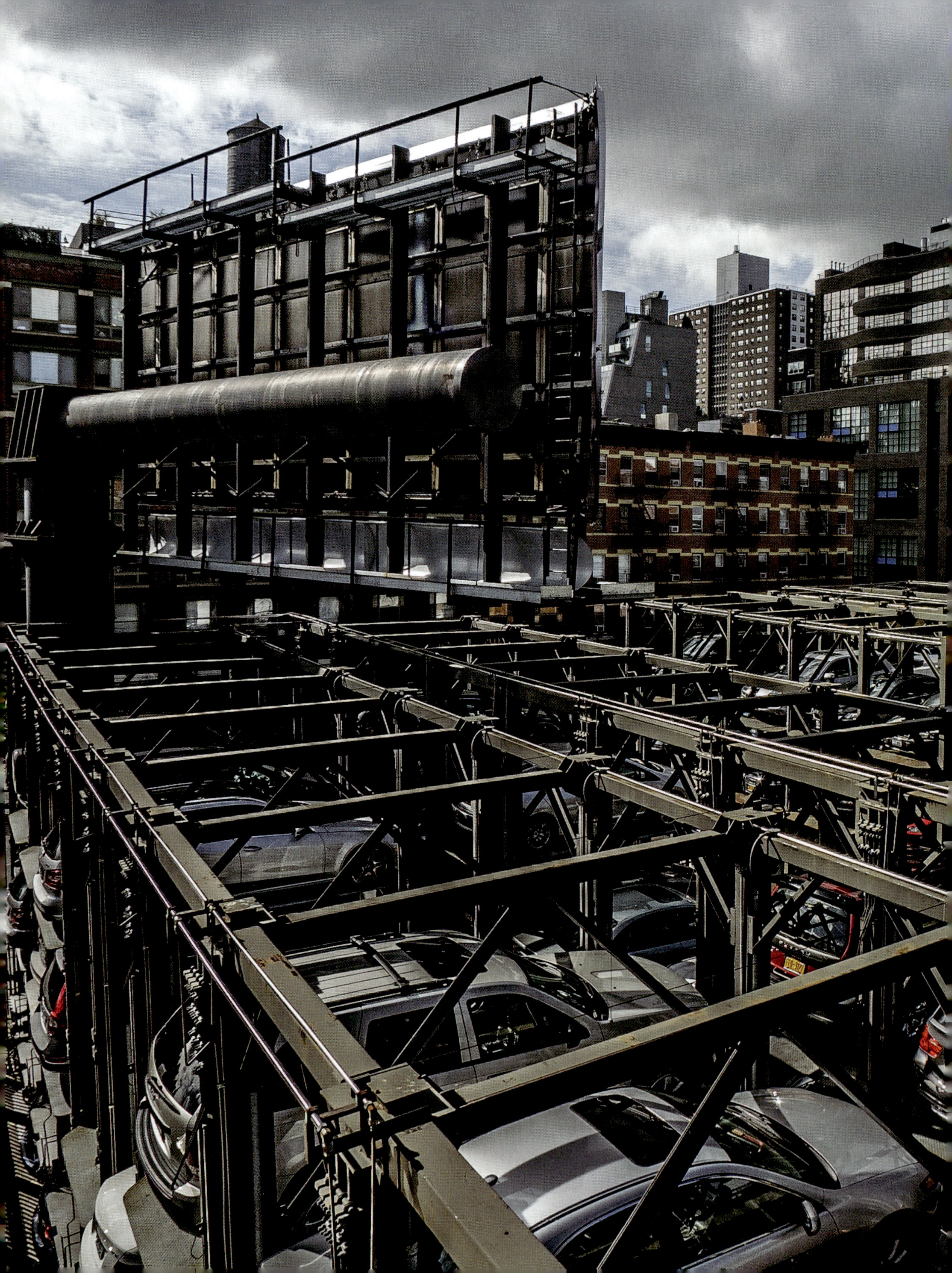

CHAPTER 3

PHOTO STORAGE

In the first chapter, I outlined the goals of the Storage Layer, and the main elements. In this chapter, we'll take a more in-depth look at each of those elements. Once we're done with that, we will move on to a demonstration of the storage controls in Lightroom.

OUR GOALS FOR FILE STORAGE

The goals for the Storage Layer are very straightforward. We want to preserve the images and make them accessible.

Our goal of preservation includes the ability to store the image files safely and to recover from hard drive failure, since this is all too common.

Access is an easier goal to achieve. All we need to do is make sure that Lightroom does not lose track of the files. We need to assign permanent names to the files, and we need to keep them in their folders. If you do need to rename files or move files, you'll want to do that with the tools in Lightroom, instead of using another program or the computer's operating system.

YOU MIGHT BE WONDERING....

What if you have a huge mess to sort out?

If you've already created a big mess by moving files around outside your existing Lightroom catalog, you have a couple of choices. You can try to find the files using some techniques mentioned later in this chapter, or you can scrap the entire catalog, and rebuild a new one from scratch.

THE ELEMENTS OF THE STORAGE SYSTEM

Listed below are all the parts of the Storage Layer. We will go through these in order in this chapter.

Photo Library storage: This section provides an overview of the different options for hard drives you can use to store the Photo Library.

Folder structures: We'll look at a couple of folder structures I recommend for storing your Photo Library.

File naming: I provide some recommendations for file names, and show you how to make a file renaming preset.

Backup procedures: This section outlines how to protect your files, and examples of a Mac and a PC program in action.

DNG: This section provides a quick overview of the DNG file format, and shows you how to convert your raw files to DNG.

File management tools in Lightroom: In this section, we look at some of the most useful tools for working with files and folders in Lightroom.

File verification tools: In the final section, we look at the tools Lightroom offers to verify that al the files are in the right place, and that they remain uncorrupted.

PHOTO LIBRARY STORAGE

Let's start with a discussion of the Photo Library storage. A Lightroom-based library has two primary components that need to be stored: the Lightroom catalog and the Photo Library files. These can be on the same hard drive, but they should be separated into different folders.

Basic storage arrangements

Let's outline how you may want to store these two elements, starting with the smallest and simplest arrangement, and watching it grow. (There are other more complicated arrangements that some professionals may want to use, and these are the subject of my Multi-Catalog Workflow book).

- In the beginning, it's possible for most users to keep both the Photo Library and the catalog on an internal drive of a laptop or other computer.
- As the Photo Library grows, you'll probably want to move it off to a dedicated hard drive while keeping the Lightroom catalog on your computer's internal drive.
- Very large Photo Libraries may require several drives for storage. For added performance, you may want to store your Lightroom catalog on a fast Solid State Drive.
- And finally, some people who travel will want to keep their Photo Library on an external drive that lives at home, while new shoots are temporarily stored on the laptop while traveling. Professionals will often take portable drives for the photo files, as well as backup drives for protection of new files while in the field.

The following flowchart shows you these different arrangements.

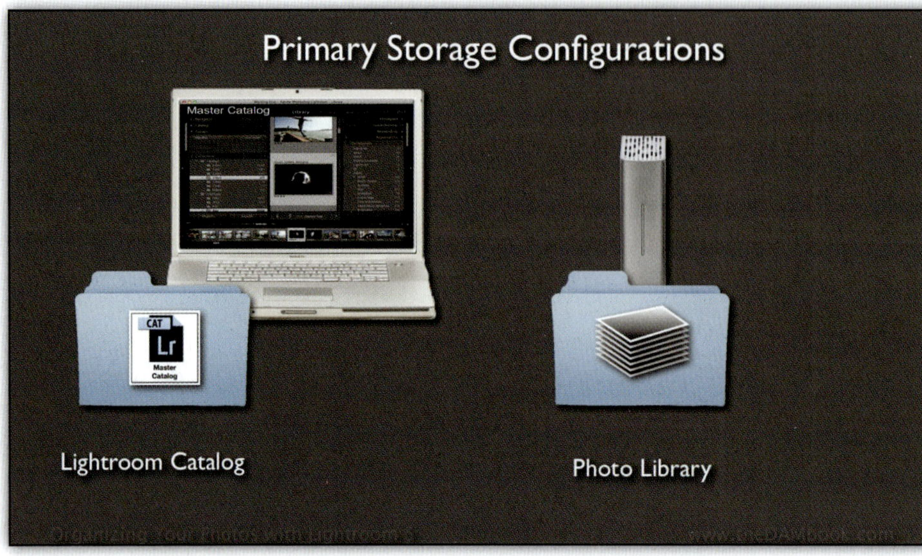

VIDEO 3-1 PRIMARY STORAGE CONFIGURATIONS (3:16)
This video outlines how you can store your catalog and your Photo Library on several different drive configurations.

HARD DRIVE TYPES

Let's take a quick look at some of the different types of hard drives you may want to use to store your Photo Library. I suggest that you keep your storage system as simple as possible. For most people, a single external hard drive will be enough. You can get them in sizes up to 4 Terabytes, which holds quite a few photos. For a very large Photo Library, you may need to move to one of the multi-drive devices. Here are the classifications:

Internal Drive: Most laptops and all-in-one computers have a single internal hard drive. It's good to start out, but may be filled quickly by a Photo Library.

Single Pocket Drive: These are easy to find at any electronics store. They are small, cheap and very portable.

Single Full-Size Drive: This is the larger version of the pocket drive. The drive is larger in size, and it will typically also have a higher capacity, at least for the same cost.

Multi-Drive Array: These devices hold multiple drives and can offer very large capacity and may also offer some protection against one of the drives failing. In most cases, I only suggest getting one of these because you are outgrowing a single drive for your library.

***Warning :**

Of course, no matter which of these you choose, you'll still need a backup drive, as outlined a bit later.

The video below outlines the choices you have for primary storage devices.

If you want more information on this, check out the Storage page at www.theDAMbook.com/oyp_resources.

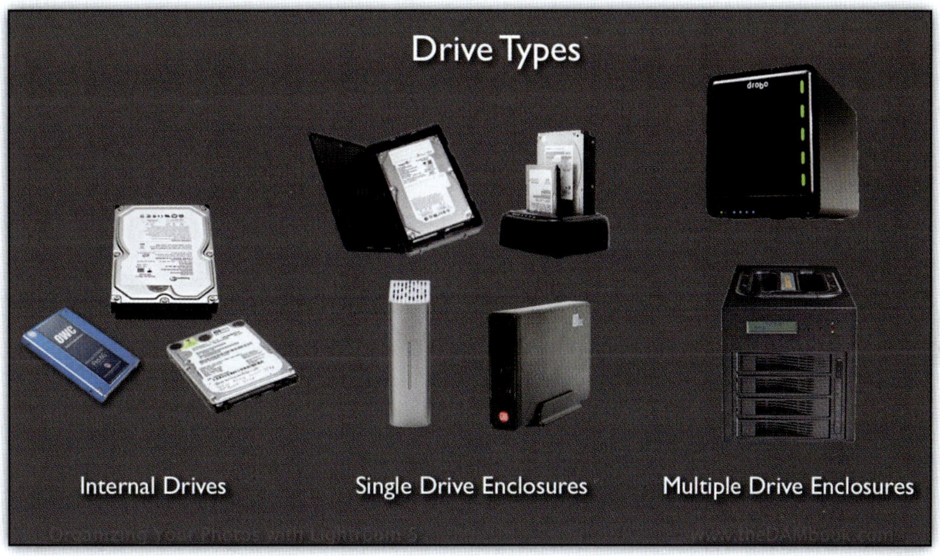

VIDEO 3-2 DRIVE TYPES (4:17)
This video outlines the different hard drive configurations you might use to store your Photo Library.

YOU MIGHT BE WONDERING....

How about the Cloud?

Cloud storage, like Dropbox, iCloud or Google Drive, can be a real blessing for photographers. These tools make sharing easy, and they can provide easy off-site backup of your files. They are well-suited to store stuff like your word processing documents, and your "greatest hits' images.

Most readers of this book will probably have a Photo Library that is too large to be entirely stored with one of these services. So we will treat these more as tools for sharing than as primary storage.

In Chapter 9, I'll show you some techniques for backing up your most important files to the cloud with Publish Services.

FOLDER STRUCTURES

In this section, we'll outline some recommendations for a good solid folder structure. Here are some basic principles for good folder usage.

Folders are best for storage, not organization

At my desk, I use folders for organizing my papers, as well as storing them. In the digital world, it's better to use folders mainly for storage, and leave the organization mostly to the metadata tags. We've already seen in Chapter 1 how tags can let us organize in lots of ways that are impossible with folders. The main job of the folders it to provide a place for you to stack up all your images as you download and save your photos, and to help you create a clean process for backup and restoration of the files.

Keep it simple

Folders should provide an orderly place to store the images. You need a simple, clean system for your folders that expands easily. And this simple structure makes it easy to backup the files and to restore from the backup in the event of a problem.

Always have a parent folder for your Photo Library

You always want to keep your Photo Library inside a parent folder. (That's a term that means the top level folder.) This makes it easy to backup the Photo Library, and it also makes it easy to restore from backup, or to move the Photo Library to a larger drive as the collection grows.

Your Lightroom catalog(s) should be stored outside of this parent folder. If you use more than one hard drive to store your Photo Library, then you need a parent folder for each drive.

Put files away and leave them there

The biggest headaches with Lightroom are caused by moving files and folders outside of the catalog. This can easily cause Lightroom to lose track of the photos, and may require a one-by-one reconnection. Our goal should be to get the photos safely stored in their permanent folder structure as quickly as possible.

And then leave them alone.

If you need to move to new folders, do it with Lightroom

Once image files have been cataloged with Lightroom, you generally only want to move them around using Lightroom's *Folders* panel, rather than using the computer's Operating System. This is certainly true if you want to move files between different folders.

There is one exception. If I need to move files from one hard drive to another, I'll move a folder with the OS, and then update the folder's location in the Lightroom catalog's *Folders* panel.

Don't blow up what you already have

Many people will be reading this book because they already have a bit of a mess on their hands. Maybe you have hundreds of small folders scattered around your computer, named in lots of different kinds of ways. As you move to a more organized system, make sure you don't lose the organization you may have already done with your folders. We'll look at that process a little later.

PARENT, YEAR, MONTH, PROJECT

The best folder structure for most people is based on the date the photo was made, along with a name for the shoot.

- At the top is the Photo Library parent folder.
- Inside that are folders for the year the photos were taken.
- Inside that are folders for the month the photo was taken.
- And inside that are folders for the name of the project or shoot.

What about photos that are not part of a real shoot?

Sometimes there is no real project name. In that case, I download into a *Misc* folder, which tells me it's a hodgepodge of images from different dates and locations. I don't spend time breaking these up into a lot of little folders, since our metadata tags let us organize this much more effectively than folders do. Remember, the folders are just for storage.

What about shoots that crossed over a month or year?

And sometimes a shoot or a trip will start in one month and end in another. What then? I suggest that you put the shoot folder into the month you downloaded, rather than creating a shoot folder in each of the two months. So if you start a project in April and finish in May, download the whole thing into a shoot folder that lives inside *May*.

The only time I might break this rule is when I have a shoot that crosses January 1st. I generally like to keep the files separated by year.

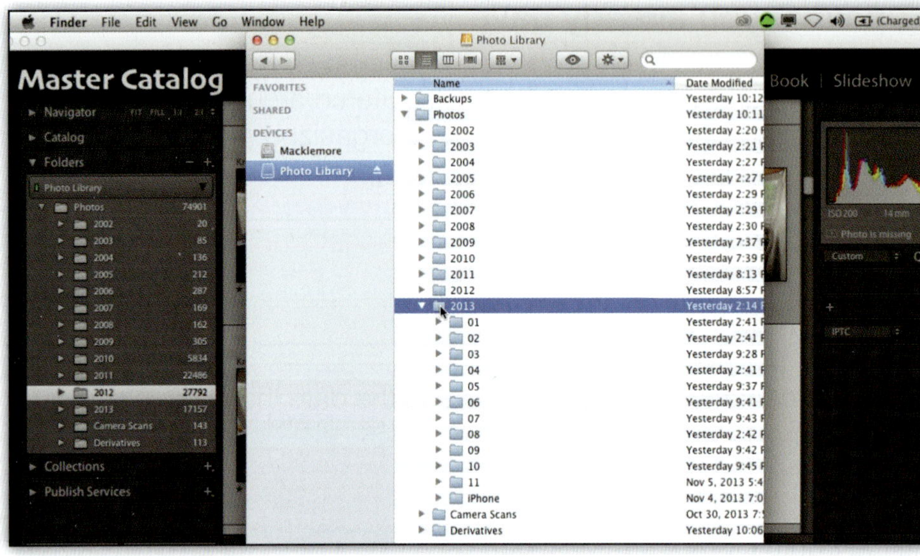

VIDEO 3-3 FOLDERS BY DATE (2:52)

This video shows how a Parent/Year/Month/Project folder arrangement can look.

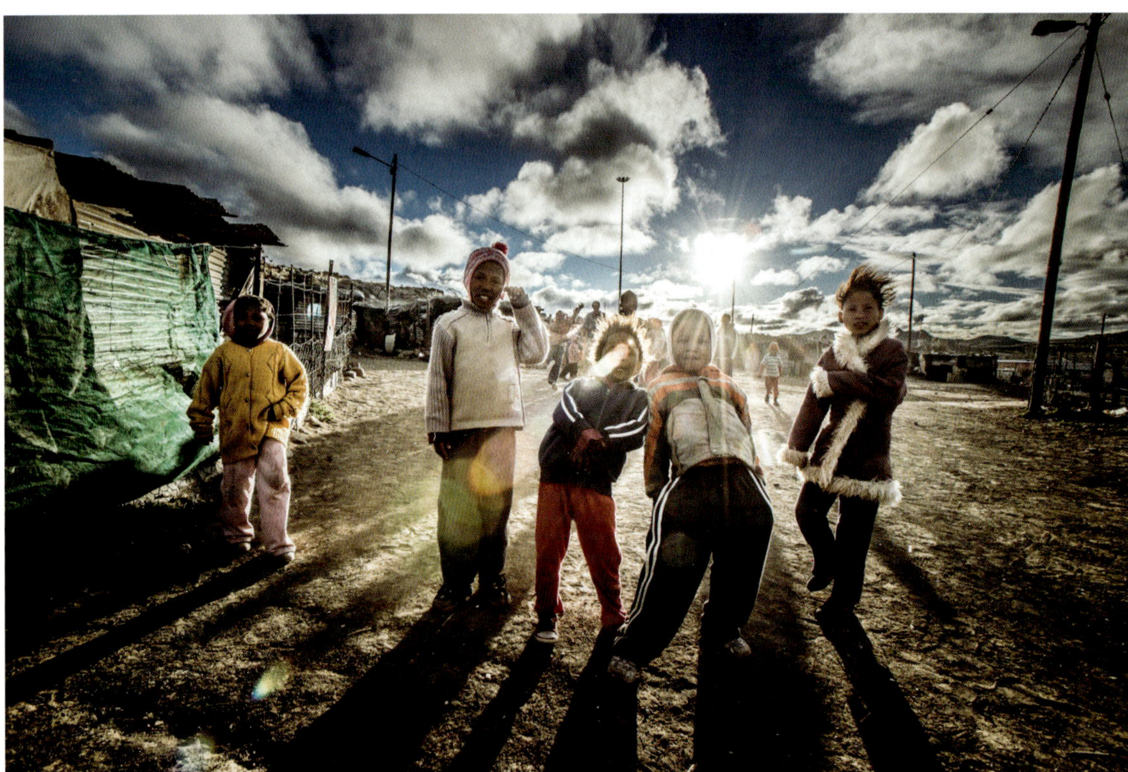

WHAT HAPPENS WHEN YOU OUTGROW YOUR PHOTO LIBRARY?

At some point, you're almost certain to outgrow the use of your current hard drive. When your Photo Library outgrows its current storage space, I suggest that you get a larger hard drive and transfer the Photo Library to the new drive. After you have done the transfer, you can tell Lightroom to find the files in the new location.

The video below shows how.

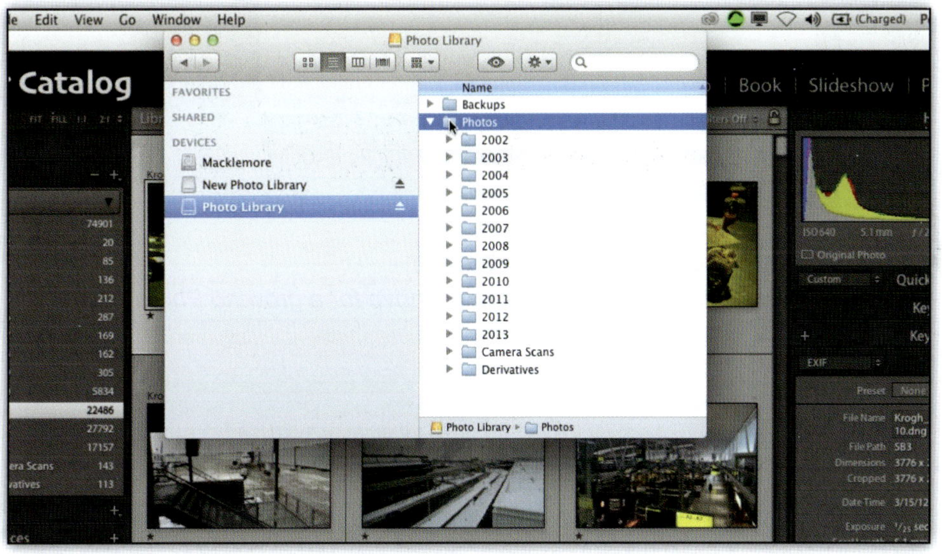

VIDEO 3-4 MOVING TO A NEW DRIVE (1:56)
This video shows how to transfer a Photo Library to a new, larger hard drive as it outgrows the current location.

Using two drives for primary storage

As you outgrow your current storage capacity, you may want to add a second drive instead of moving to a larger one. In general, I suggest using as few drives as possible, so I'm in favor of transferring everything to a larger drive, if possible. But Lightroom does allow you to split things up.

You'll want to set a breaking point for your files as you start using the new drive. It's probably cleanest to break between one year and the next, but you don't have to.

Of course, the new drive needs to have its own parent folder for the Photo Library that is stored there.

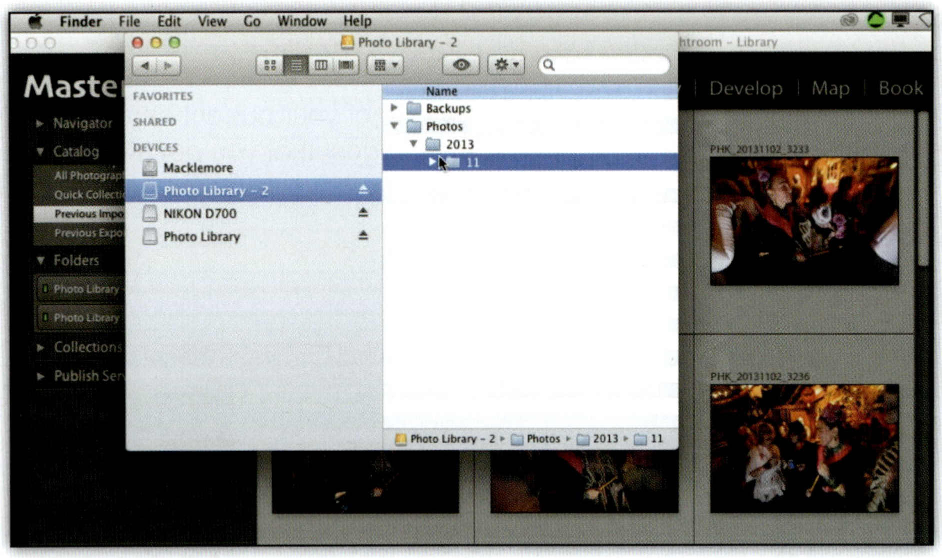

VIDEO 3-5 ADDING A SECOND DRIVE (1:53)
This video shows how to add a second hard drive for a growing Photo Library.

SIZE-LIMITED BUCKETS

Readers of *The DAM Book 1* and *2* are familiar with The Bucket System. In this configuration, storage folders are organized in a sequence instead of by Year/Month/Shoot. Each of these folders is the same size as an optical disc backup, such as CD, DVD and (in my case) Blu-ray. This allows for a backup system in which it's easy to correlate the primary folders to the backup discs.

CHANGES FOR DAM BOOK 1 AND 2 READERS

Moving away from buckets for DNG storage

I have moved over to the date system for my own work, because I can now check the health of all copies using Lightroom's DNG verification tools. This reduces the need for the use of optical discs. But many people still like the added security of an optical disc backup.

Here's what a folder structure of DVD-sized folders looks like.

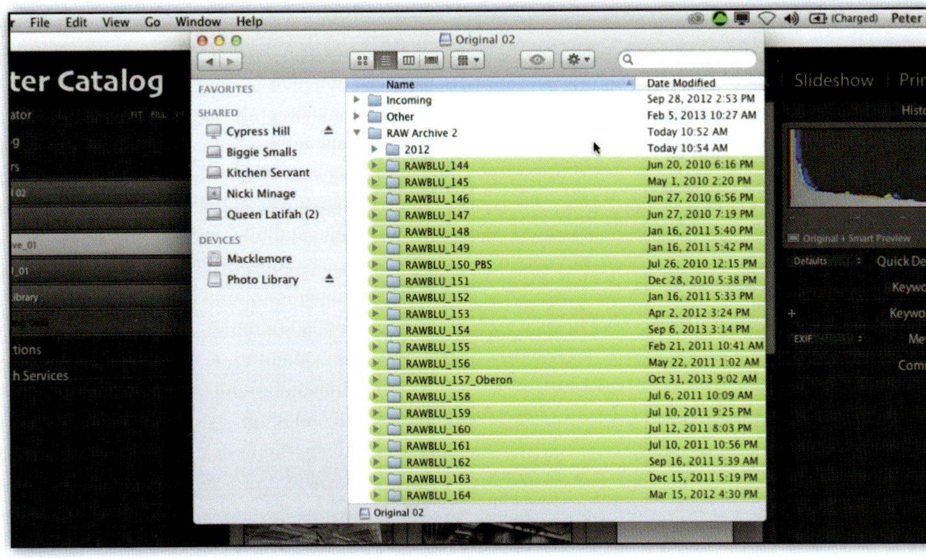

VIDEO 3-6 CHANGES FROM *THE DAM BOOK* (6:00)
This video shows a folder structure of size-limited "buckets " that correspond to Blu-ray discs. It also explains how I have changed my own workflow since the publication of The DAM Book *1 and 2.*

DIGGING DEEPER

Works-in-progress storage

Some people will need temporary storage of their images on the way to the Photo Library. This is particularly true for people who download on location, but it may also be necessary for others who like to keep recent shoots on faster hard drives.

If you need this temporary storage, I suggest making a dedicated folder on your Hard Drive for the storage of works-in-progress. Shoots can be stored there in Year/Month/Project folders, and transferred to the Photo Library at an appropriate time. Then you'll need to tell Lightroom to go find the files in the new storage location.

See the workflow in the video on the next page.

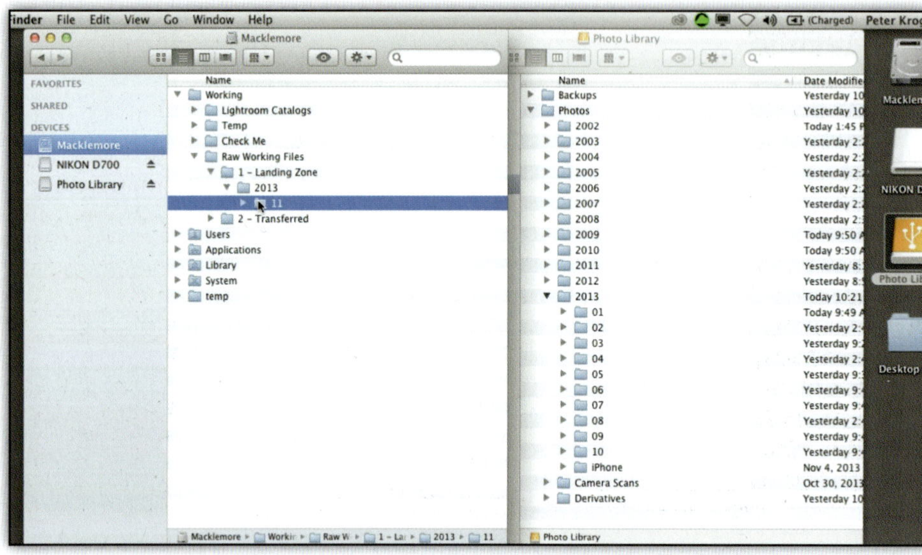

VIDEO 3-7 USING A WORKING FOLDER FOR NEW FILES (4:59)
This video shows how to move files through a temporary works-in-progress folder on the way to the Photo Library.

COLLECTING LEGACY PHOTOS

Many readers will have a bunch of images scattered around the hard drive in various folder arrangements. (That's probably why you bought a book on organizing your photos, right?) We'll want to collect those folders together as part of our organization process.

Let's start by collecting everything together in a folder inside the Photo Library parent folder. We'll name it *Legacy* and bring the old legacy folders together there.

- If the folders are already in your Lightroom catalog, let's use the catalog to help gather everything together. Move the folders with the Folders panel to the new *Legacy* folder inside the Photo Library folder.
- Folders that are not already in the Lightroom catalog can be moved in the OS and then added to the catalog.

At some point, you may want to rework the folder structure for these files, but let's not be in a hurry to do that. We'll want to make sure that we have transferred the information in the folder names into appropriate tags before we start moving stuff around between folders. The video below outlines how this can work.

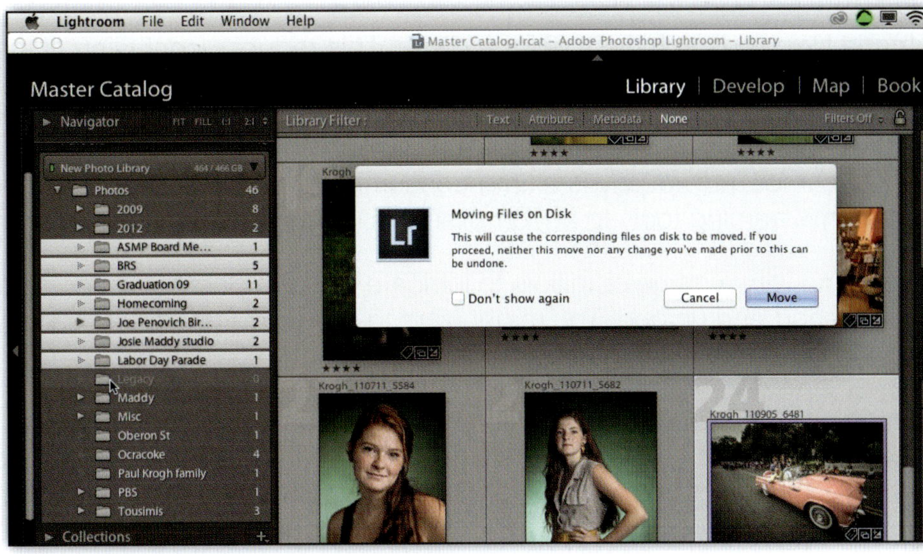

VIDEO 3-8 LEGACY FOLDERS (3:49)

This video shows how to gather legacy folders together inside the new Photo Library parent folder.

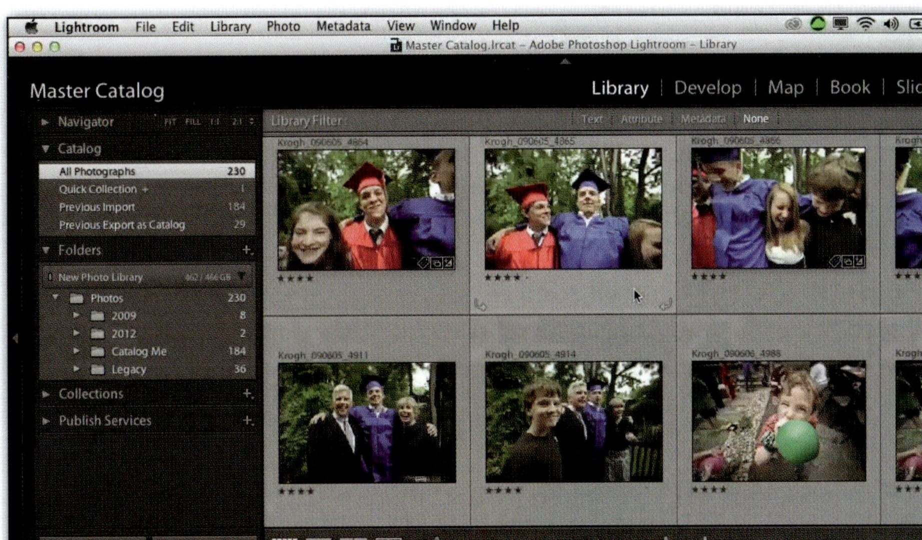

VIDEO 3-9 SORTING LEGACY PHOTOS (7:25)

In the second part of the legacy workflow, we'll sort through the newly imported files to find ones to delete. Once we're done, we'll move the newly imported folders into the Legacy parent folder.

FILE NAMING

Each original image file needs to have a unique name. This reduces confusion at many levels. It helps Lightroom to stay attached to the right photo. It keeps your computer from accidentally overwriting files. And it helps keep things straight when you send photos off to other people.

Creating unique file names individually is a time-consuming and unpleasant process. So we'll want to use Lightroom's naming tools to accomplish this. I suggest the following naming system.

Let's start the file name with a name or initials to indicate who the photographer is. I use my last name, because it is short and unique. You might want to use your first name (that's what my wife and my kids do). Or you might want to use your initials.

Then, let's add a date to help create unique names automatically. I suggest that you start with the year, then the month, and then the date (this helps all the files to line up in chronological order). In my system, that looks like 131007 for October 7, 2013. You might also want to use all of the year, which would look like 20131007. You could also put hyphens in the date, but that starts to make it too long.

And finally, I add a four-digit number to tell this photo apart from all the other photos I shot the same day. Typically, I pick this number up from the original file name that my camera creates.

Putting it all together, we get one of these options:

- Krogh_131007_1234.DNG
- Alyson_131007_1234
- PHK_20131007_1234

YOU MIGHT BE WONDERING....

What about putting the subject name in the file?

Some people like to put a word or a code into the file name to say what it's a picture of. I don't suggest doing this. First, it makes it difficult to assign names automatically. You would always need to examine the images and make a determination about the subject matter before you can put them away and back them up.

Secondly, while it would be easy for some things (my trip to China could use the word China), it gets tricky around the edges. Are the photos from JFK Airport labeled "China" even though they are shot in the US? How about the taxi ride to the airport? How about the photos shot out the airplane window? As we see in the next chapter, it's much easier to use metadata to sort this stuff out.

Let's keep the Storage Layer components focused on the storage issue, not the organizational ones.

MAKING A FILE NAMING PRESET

Lightroom lets you create a preset for renaming that can automatically assign text, dates and sequence numbers. You can apply a renaming preset when you first import the files, and you can also apply it after the files are in the catalog. You can also rename the files as you publish or export them.

In all cases, you'll use the renaming preset. This lets you set up a renaming system and run it automatically. You find this in the Library module in the Library menu under *Rename Photo.*

Once you've opened the Rename dialog, select *Edit* from the *File Naming* pulldown. You can use the "tokens" to set up your renaming system. The video below shows you how.

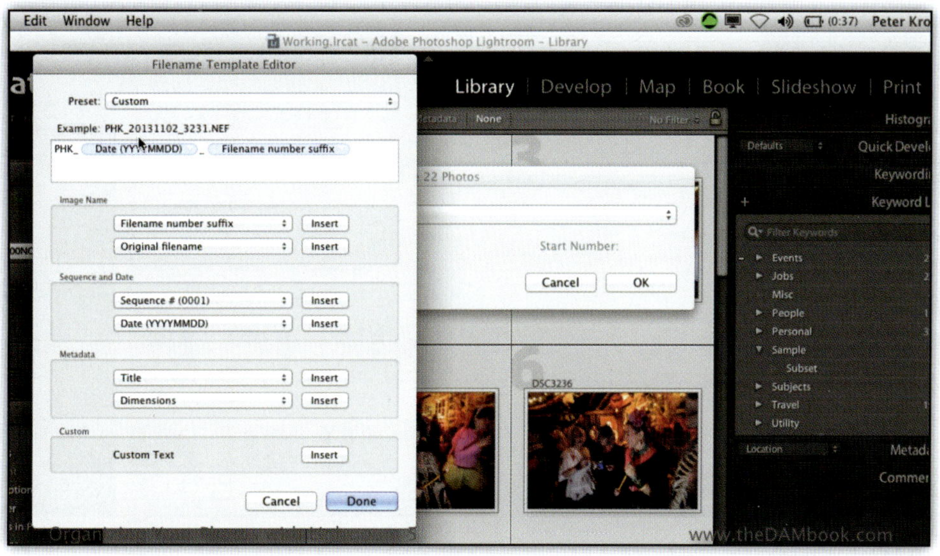

VIDEO 3-10 RENAMING PRESETS (3:37)

This video shows how to create and apply a rename preset.

DIGGING DEEPER

Renaming a two-camera shoot

In most cases, I suggest using the camera's original sequence number in the new file name. This can cause problems if you are using two cameras and the file numbers overlap. Since we want to always create unique file names, we'll need to fix this.

We can create a preset that lets us rename the files again once all of them have been downloaded. If you like, you can line them up in the order taken in the Library module, and rename the files with a new sequence number. The video below shows how.

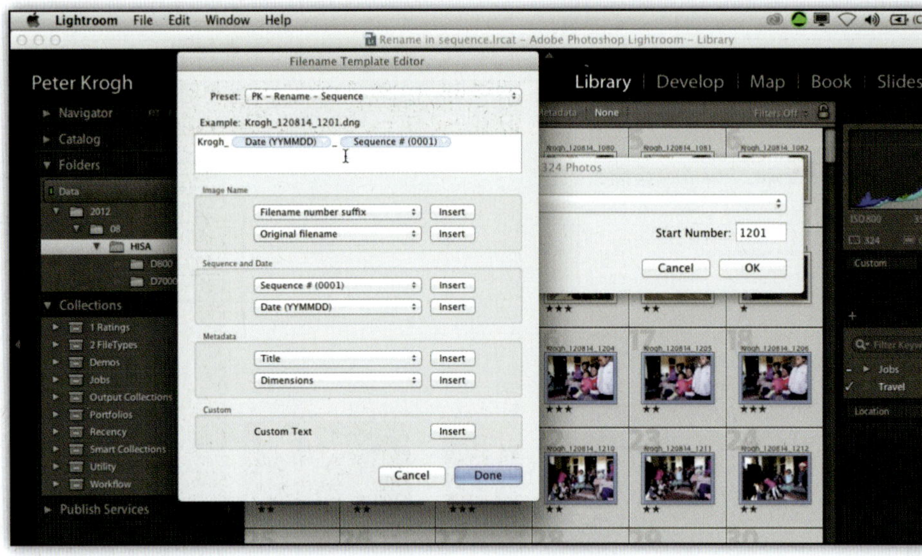

VIDEO 3-11 RENAMING A TWO-CAMERA SHOOT (6:30)

This video shows how to rename files from two cameras so there are no duplicate names.

Renaming on export

You may also want to rename your files when you export them. The most common scenarios for me are these:

Sometimes I want to export files to another computer or program, and I want them to keep the sequencing I've created in Lightroom. I can add some numbers to the front of the filename so that they show up in order when they are viewed on my iPad or when I upload them to a web service.

Here's the second scenario. When I take an image into Photoshop to make a master file, I'll add the term *Master* to the name. This lets me know that it's the one that has been edited in Photoshop.

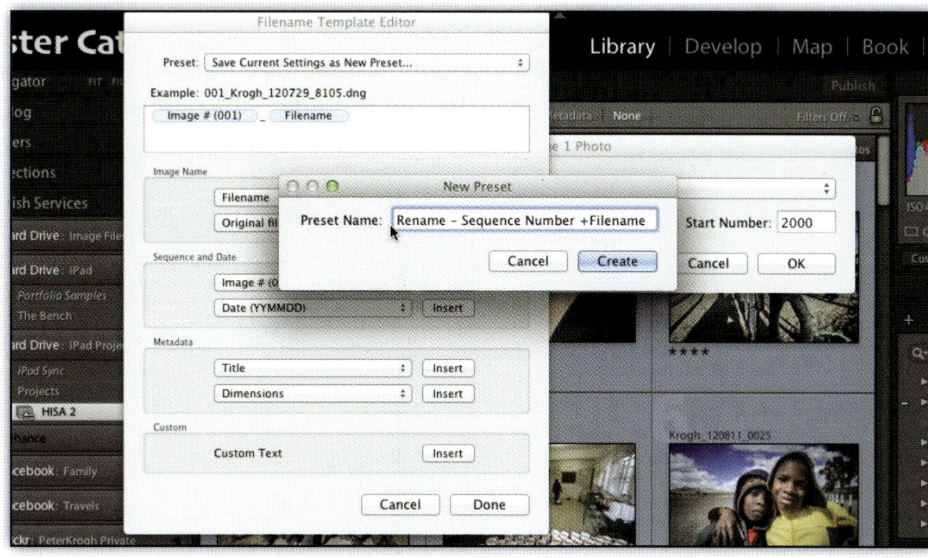

VIDEO 3-12 RENAME ON OUTPUT (4:41)

This video shows how to rename files on export.

FILE BACKUP

We can't talk about storage without talking about file backup. A hard drive can fail at any time, and we need to make sure we have another copy of the files on a separate device. In most cases, this can be easily done by copying the Photo Library to another hard drive.

For additional protection, you should also consider making a backup that you can carry to an offsite location. In most cases, you can do this with an external hard drive that connects to your computer by USB, FireWire or Thunderbolt.

For maximum protection, you should consider creating two backups. One stays near your computer and is updated very frequently. This helps to protect against the failure of your primary hard drive. A second backup can be made that lives offsite, and this protects against some catastrophe like fire or theft of all your computer equipment.

Make the primary match the backup

Most Lightroom users should be able to simply copy the Photo Library drive to an external hard drive. The backup should be updated any time you add new photos, or on some regular basis. Remember, any files that are not on the backup could be lost in an instant.

This arrangement provides excellent protection against the most common problem: hard drive failure.

On the Mac, I use a program called ChronoSync to backup my Photo Library and catalogs. On PC, you can use a program called SyncBack.

Make a second backup for added safety

Creating your second backup is just like creating the first backup, except that you save it to another hard drive. If you take this one off-site, your Photo Library will be very well protected.

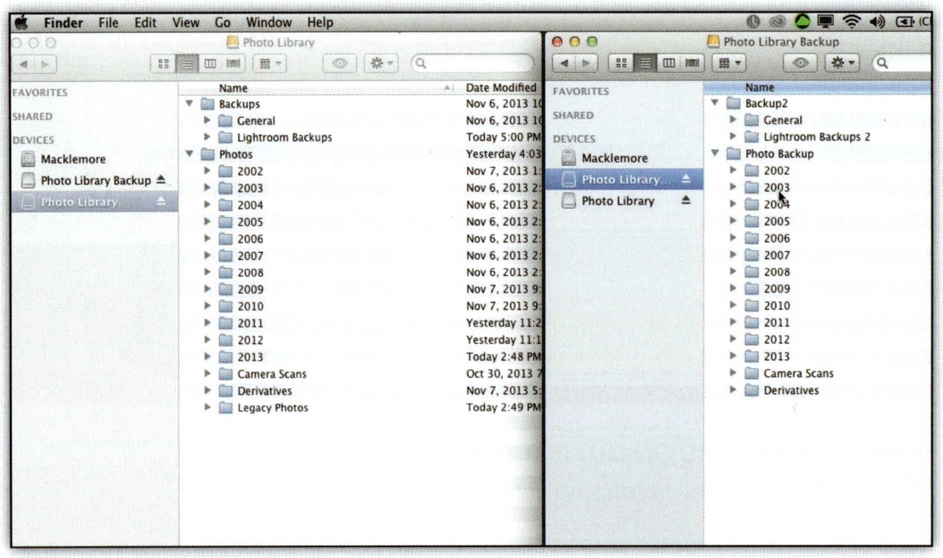

VIDEO 3-13 BACKUPS (2:25)
This video shows how to backup files with backup software.

CONVERSION TO DNG

Lightroom gives you the opportunity to save your raw files as DNG or Digital Negative files. DNG is a flexible and openly documented container format that holds the raw data as well as a bunch of other useful stuff. I have been using DNG for more than five years, and have found it to have far more advantages than disadvantages.

The main advantage for most readers is automatic file integrity checking. Due to some clever features in the DNG, it's possible for Lightroom to check on the health of an entire DNG Photo Library with a single click. This will tell you that the storage is working as expected and no file corruption has occurred silently in the background.

Here are the DNG settings I suggest you use:

For more information on the DNG file format, check out www.thedambook.com/oyp_resources.

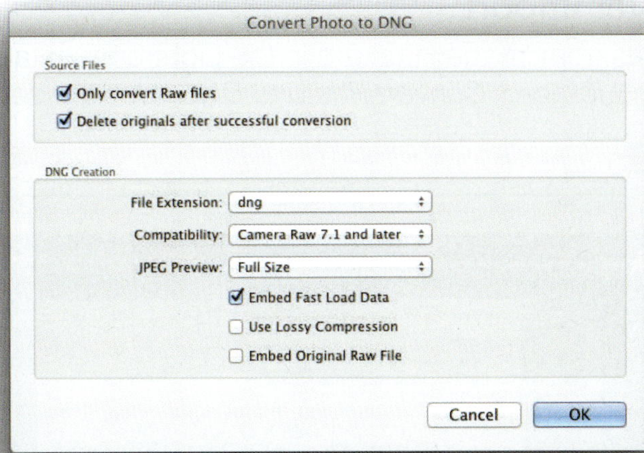

Figure 3-1 When you make DNG file in Lightroom, use the highest Compatibility in the list. I suggest you also delete files after successful conversion and embed Fast Load Data.

Converting to DNG on import

You can create DNG files as you download your images from the camera and import them into Lightroom. You can see how to do this in the video below.

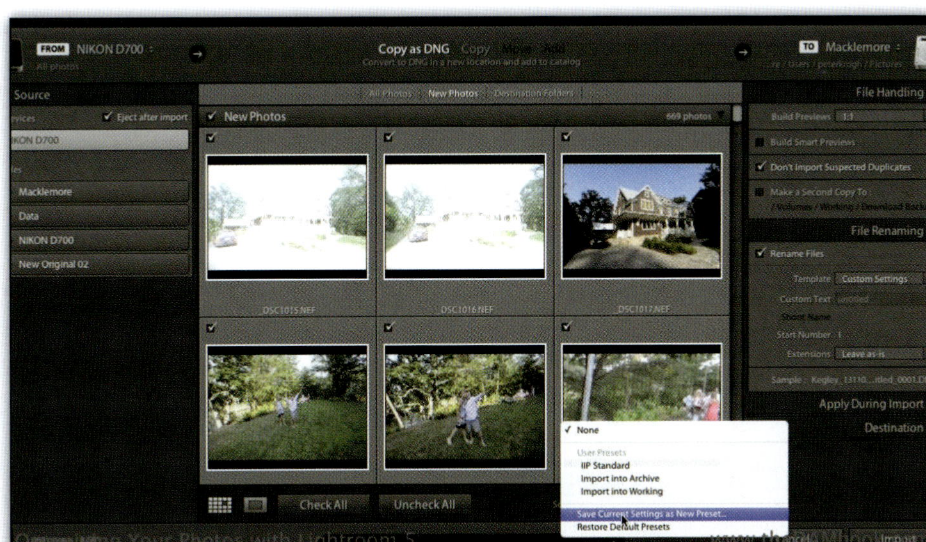

VIDEO 3-14 IMPORT AS DNG (1:18)

This video shows how to create DNG files as you first import your images into Lightroom.

Converting to DNG after import

You can also create DNG files from images that are in the Lightroom catalog. Select the files you want to convert, and choose *Library > Convert Photo to DNG.* Use the settings outlined in the video below.

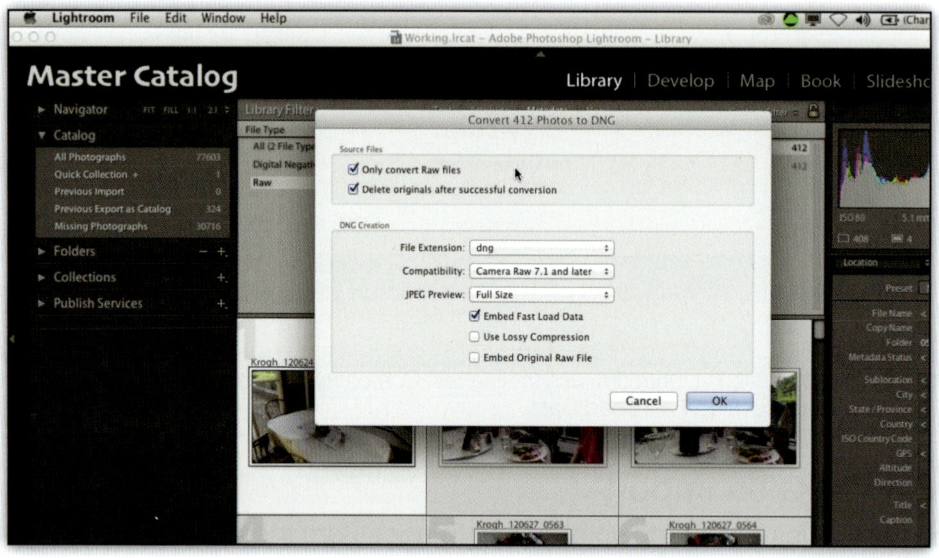

VIDEO 3-15 CONVERT TO DNG IN LIBRARY (2:15)

This video shows how to create DNG files for raw images you have already imported.

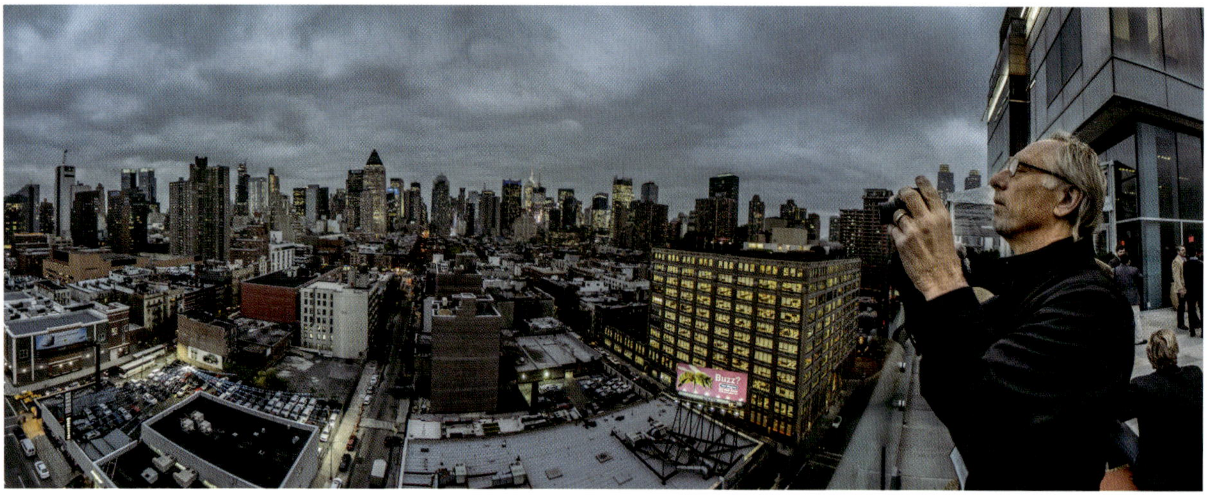

FILE AND FOLDER HANDLING IN LIGHTROOM

Now that we've covered the basics of a good storage system, let's take a look at the tools Lightroom has for viewing and working with images. Almost all of this happens in the Folders panel.

When images are imported into Lightroom, the catalog remembers where all the files live. You can use the Folders panel to select the folders and to move the files around, and to update folders to bring newly added photos into Lightroom.

Let's start by looking at the Folders panel interface.

For a full description of what every possible Folders panel menu command means, check out Victoria Bampton's *The Missing FAQ*.

The Folders panel interface

Inside the Folders panel is a listing of any hard drives that contain files that are in the catalog.

- The status light is green if the drive is connected and has plenty of room.
- It is yellow if the drive is getting full.
- It is red if the drive is totally full.
- And it is black if it is off-line.

You have a choice of what information is next to the drive name. I typically choose to show the drive's capacity and remaining open space.

Inside the drive, you can choose how the folders are displayed. I typically choose to show the folder name. I will then tell Lightroom to show the parent folders all the way up to the top level folder of the Photo Library.

You can rename a folder in the Folders panel by right-clicking and choosing *Rename...*

Finding a missing folder

If a folder is showing up in the Folders panel with a question mark, and it used to be on a drive that is currently connected to the computer, then the folder has been moved, renamed or erased. The first thing you'll want to do is figure out which of these things happened.

If the folder has been moved or renamed, the fix is really easy (if you can find the original files). Use the *Find Missing Folder* command and reset it to the folder.

If the files have been erased, then you'll need to find a backup copy of the files, or perhaps you will need to enter the expensive and uncertain world of data recovery. If the folder has been erased on purpose, then you can right-click and choose to remove the folder from the catalog.

The video below shows you what all this means.

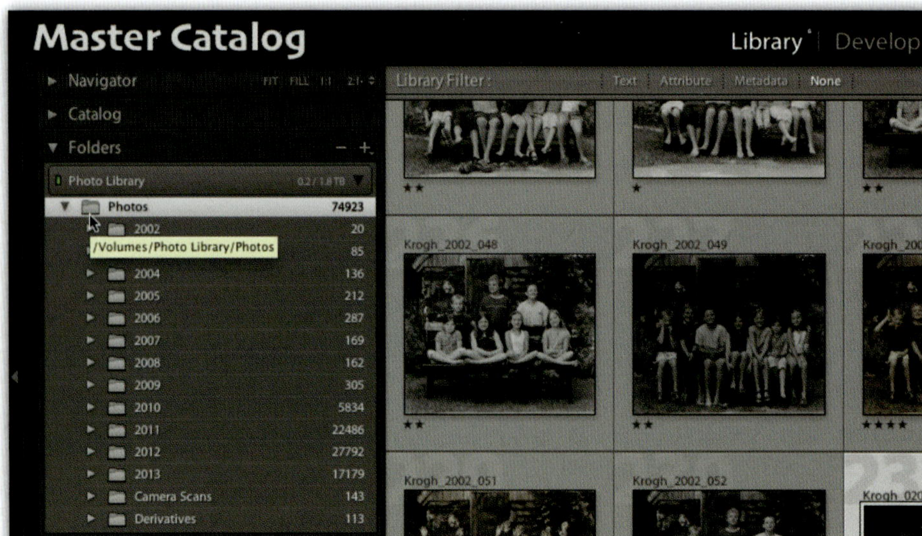

FIGURE 3-16 THE FOLDERS PANEL (5:10)

This video shows how to customize information display in the Folders panel.

Moving files

If you need to move files around to folders within a single drive, you'll want to do that from the Folders panel. This will keep Lightroom from losing track of the files. Simply select the files you want to move, and drag them to the destination folder. This will tell your operating system to move the files. You can move folders around the same way.

If you want to move some files or folders to another folder, and that folder is not present in the Lightroom Folders panel, you have to do a two-step process. You'll want to move something into that folder using the OS. Then you'll want to find the thing you moved, using the command *Find Missing.* From that point on, you'll see the folder in the Folders panel and can use it normally.

If you are moving files from one drive to another, I suggest moving the folder with your OS, and then telling Lightroom to *Update Folder Location.* There have been some reports of Lightroom having trouble doing this kind of move in the past, and I think it's safer to do as this two-step process.

The video below covers moving files.

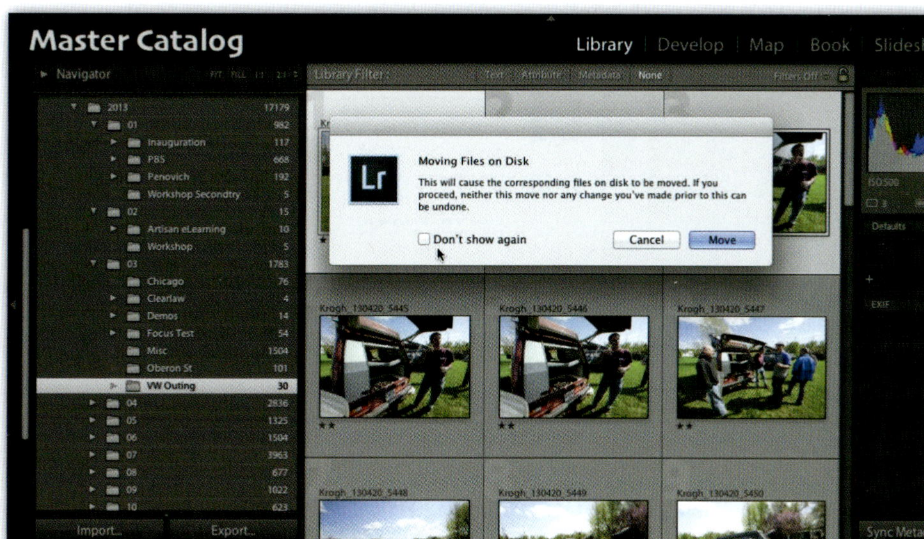

VIDEO 3-17 MOVING FILES (5:52)

This video shows how to move files, reconnect moved files and find files that were moved accidentally.

Syncing folders

The last tool I'll cover in the Folders panel is the *Synchronize* command. I use this one every now and then, and it feels a little mysterious until you see how it works.

When you right-click on a folder and tell Lightroom to *Synchronize* the folder, Lightroom will show you if new files have been added to the folder or if existing ones have been removed or updated. You can choose to have Lightroom update the catalog to match the condition of the folder.

I almost never use the *Remove missing photos from catalog* command, because I want to be sure exactly which ones are missing and are going to be removed. And I don't *Scan for metadata updates* because this is also a process I only want to do for some specific reason, rather than simply because there is a mismatch. However, I do use the first option, *Import new photos*. The video below shows how that works.

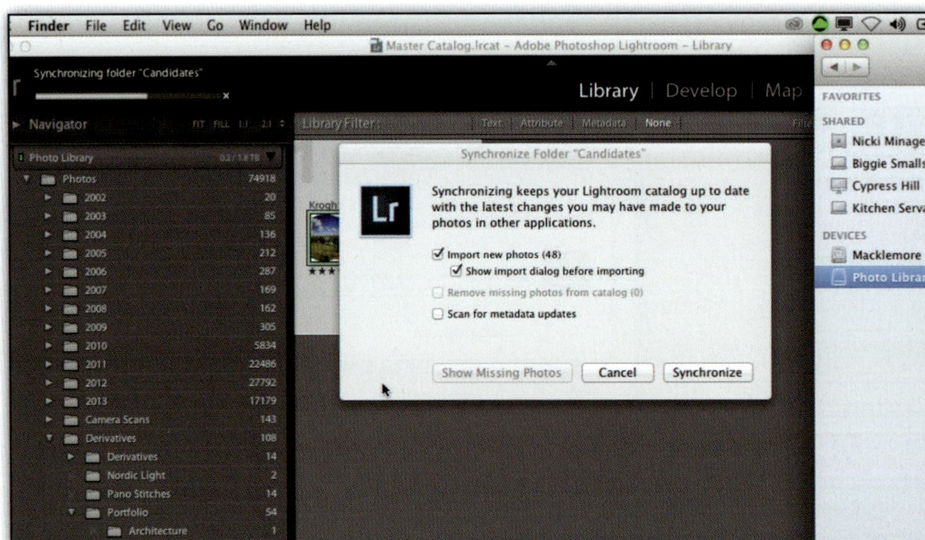

VIDEO 3-18 SYNCHRONIZE FOLDERS (1:39)
This video shows how to use the Synchronize Folder command to add new photos to the Lightroom catalog.

CHECKING COMPLETENESS AND INTEGRITY OF THE LIBRARY

The last two things we'll look at in this chapter are the tools Lightroom offers to check on the general status of the image files.

Checking for missing files

In the course of normal events, no files should go missing from the Photo Library or from the catalog. As long as you don't move files around with the OS, Lightroom will know where everything is. Sometimes, as they say, stuff happens. You may accidentally move, rename or throw files away. Or you may have a drive failure and need to restore from backup.

Even when nothing strange has happened, it's a good idea to check on the completeness of your Photo Library from time to time. Fortunately, Lightroom make it really easy to do. You'll want to make sure all necessary hard drives are connected to the computer and that they show up in the Folders panel. Then, choose *Find All Missing Photos* from the *Library* menu.

If the Library finds missing files, it will create a new item in the Catalog panel and show you which files it can't find. I suggest resolving the problem as soon as possible. If you've moved or renamed something, fix that. If files are missing, try and restore from backup. If you've thrown them away on purpose, then remove them from the catalog. Check it out in the video below.

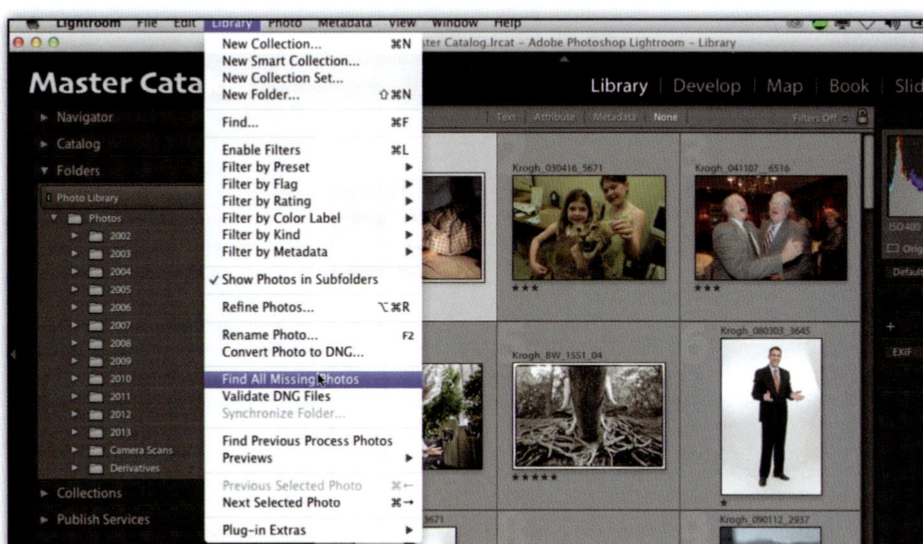

VIDEO 3-19 LOCATING MISSING FILES (2:57)
This video shows how to check for missing files.

Checking up on your DNG Files

You can use the DNG Validation check to make sure that your DNG files have not become corrupted while stored on your hard drive (This might happen because of any number of computer malfunctions.)

Simply select a group of DNG files to check, and choose *Library > Validate DNG Files*. This is a good thing to check after you have moved DNGs from one drive to another, or any time you feel uneasy or suspicious that there is something amiss. You'll also want to check this any time that Lightroom tells you there is a problem with a DNG file opening, developing or building a preview.

If everything is fine, Lightroom will tell you once it's finished checking. If there are any problem files, it will also tell you that, and it will make a new item in the Catalog panel showing them You'll want to see if any of them open, and check for visible corruption if they do. If they don't open, you'll want to restore them from your backup.

Here's a video showing the process.

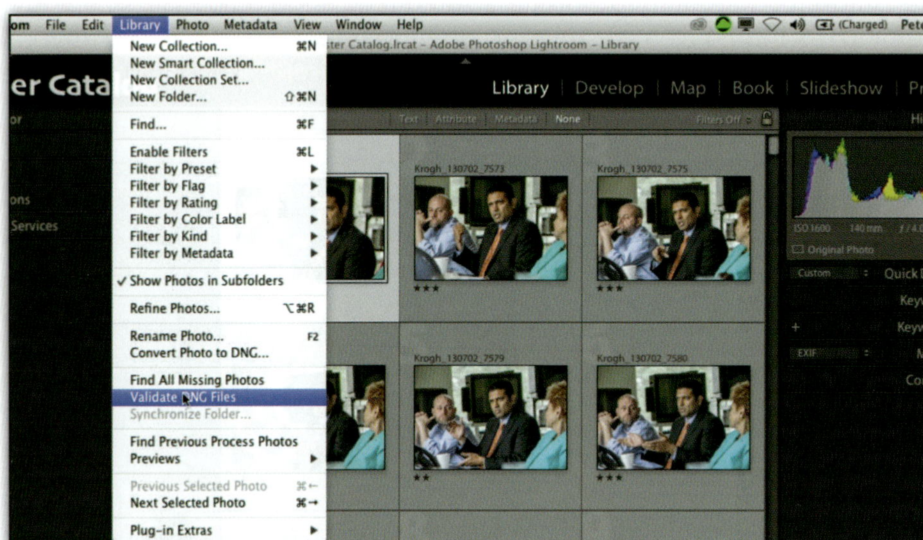

VIDEO 3-20 VALIDATE DNG (3:26)
This video shows how to check integrity for DNG files.

DIGGING DEEPER

Checking on other file types

The Validation command only works on DNGs, and won't tell you anything about raw, JPEG, TIFF, PSD, etc. While you can't get the kind of rock-solid reporting that DNGs offer, you can do some basic checking on these other file types. Here's the workaround hack. (Of course, the *Find Missing* command works the same for all files in Lightroom.)

You need to first change the *Standard Size Previews* settings in the *Catalog Settings*. Any change is fine. Once you've made the change, you can select all files (or some subset of the files) and choose *Library > Previews > Render Standard Previews*. Lightroom will attempt to read all the files and create new previews for the catalog. If it can't read a file because of a corruption, it will alert you at the end of the process. You'll get a message saying that preview generation failed for some images, and it will show you a list.

The video below shows it in action.

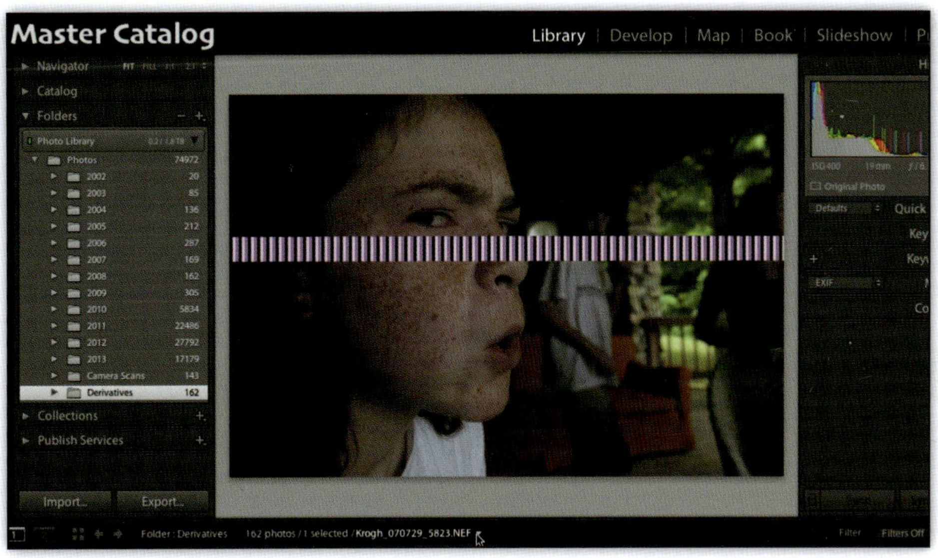

VIDEO 3-21 VERIFICATION OF NON DNG FILES (2:52)
This video shows how to rebuild previews to get a basic integrity check for non-DNG files.

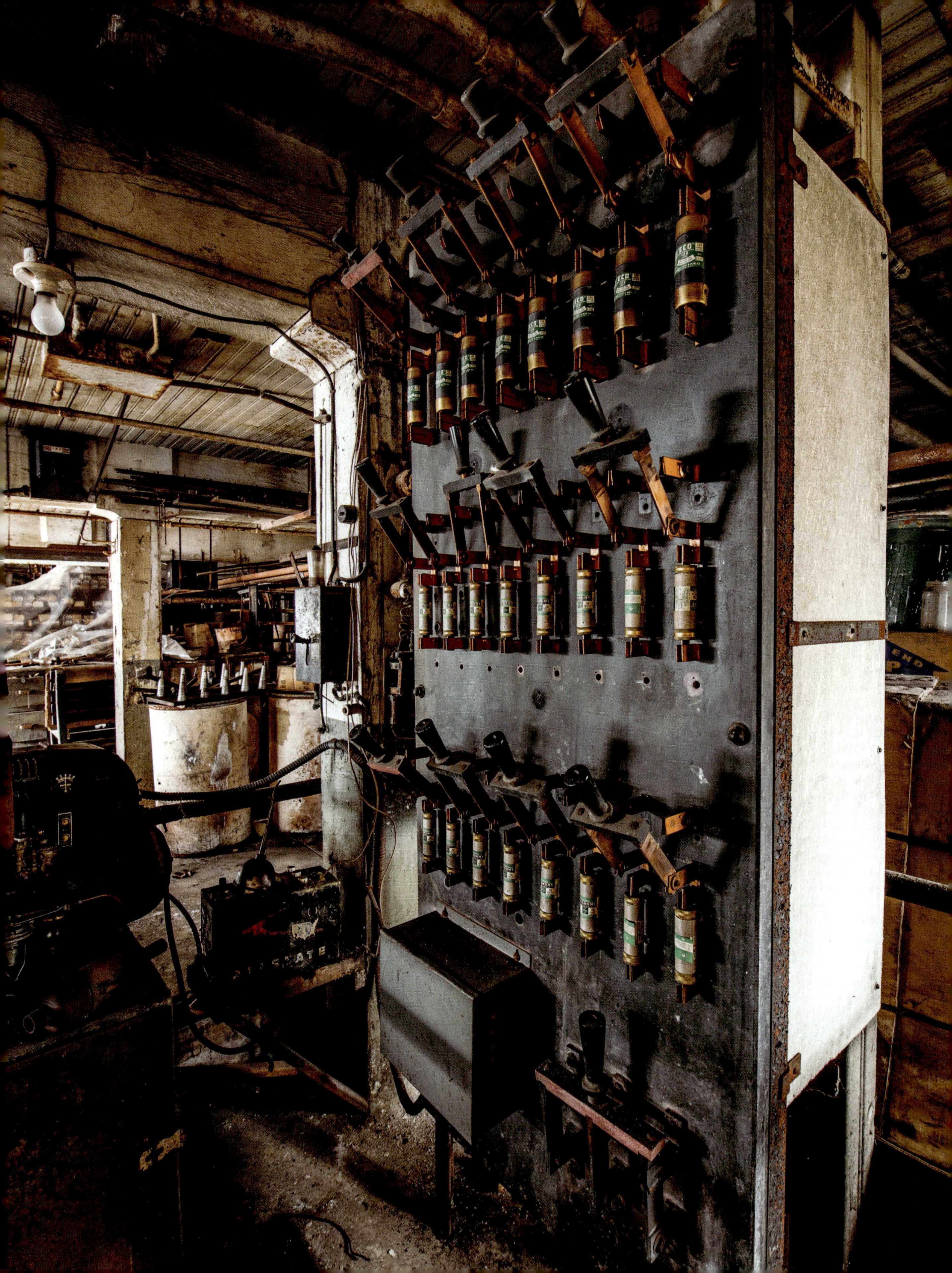

CHAPTER 4

FINDING & FILTERING WITH TAGS

Now that we have outlined the Storage Layer, we'll move up to the Organizational Layer. As outlined in Chapter 1, the primary goal of the organizational tags is to make it easy to find images in your Photo Library. In this chapter, as well as the following three chapters, we'll explore the creation and use of tags.

We'll be making these tags all through the workflow. New shoots should get a few tags as they are imported. And existing photos that don't have tags should get a handful as soon as possible. And, over the lifetime of your photos, you'll probably be adding new tags as you sort back through images for some purpose.

CREATING USEFUL TAGS

As we start to discuss tagging, we need to keep a few things in mind.

Do what's useful for you

Above all, the tags you create need to communicate useful information about **your** collection and the ways you use the photos. If you are the family's photographer, then names, locations and special events may be the most important tags. If you are a wildlife photographer, then locations and animal species may be most important. If you do professional events, then the client name and event name may be most important.

It's not hard to come up with a list of the most important classifications you'll want. Spend a little time thinking about what will be most useful to you in the future. Of course, you'll also be able to create these classifications as you simply add keywords to the catalog, so you don't have to do too much advance planning.

Remember the difference between organizing and creating

The tags we are working with in this chapter are about classification of the pictures. These tags help us find a photo according to where it was shot, what it's about, or how much we like it. Let's keep this process as targeted as possible, and not confuse it with the creative projects that we make later in the book. With the exception of ratings, almost all these tags are simply descriptions of facts about the photo.

If you keep this tagging as simple and objective as possible, it will be quick to create the tags, and really useful to filter with them. And the easy access to the photos will be invaluable when it comes time to make some projects later.

Let's start at the finish line

The real power of metadata lies in its ability to help you pinpoint an image or a group of images easily. So, before we dive into the creation of metadata, let's examine how it can be useful. The easiest way to show that is through finding and filtering. We'll see how Lightroom tags help you to find just what you're looking for. In later chapters, we'll see how easy it is to make these tags.

WHO, WHAT, WHEN, WHERE, WHY AND HOW (GOOD)?

If you use them wisely, a handful of metadata tags can make any image easy to find, even in a large collection of images. You can use tags to help define the 5Ws + H. This helps you to find images by the date taken, the location, the client, the event or other subject matter.

Some of this information is assigned automatically by the camera, and some can be assigned to an entire shoot with a preset. And some of it, such as the ratings, must be assigned by the photographer one-at-a-time.

When? Date tags

This is the easiest question to answer, at least for digital camera photos. The time and date of the photo is recorded into the camera metadata when the photo is taken. Lightroom pulls this information out, and lets you see it in the Library Filter bar. Lightroom also lets you use this information to create unique file names, as we saw in the last chapter.

If you set your camera's clock incorrectly, you can also use Lightroom's tools to fix the date.

Where? Location tags and map coordinates

Although it's possible to use keywords to specify where a photo was taken, I think it's much better to use the tags that were built for the purpose. The location tags have a natural hierarchy of Country, State/Province, City and Location. These tags can have their own column in the Library Filter bar.

You can also attach GPS coordinates to your photo. Many smartphone photos already do this automatically. GPS tags are useful, but I generally find that location names are easier to assign manually, and more useful for filtering.

Chapter 7 provides an in-depth look at the techniques you can use for location tagging.

Who, What, Why? Keywords and Labels

For most people, the tagging process will be centered around keywords. This is the place in Lightroom to create a tag structure that is customized for your Photo Library. It's quick to make big groupings of people, for instance, and to subdivide them later as necessary. And you can make tags for events you photograph, trips you take, clients, assignments, ongoing subjects and more. The entire next chapter is devoted to making keywords that work for you.

You can also use color labels to help with your image classification. I find it very useful to create labels for images that are parts of multi-sequence captures like HDR and panoramas. I'll also use labels for other image sorting tasks. We'll see more of this later in this chapter.

Taken together, keywords and labels can help you tag an image for who is in it, what it shows, why you shot it and more.

How Good? Ratings and flags

The ratings stars and the flags let you tag pictures according to how much you like them. When ratings are used consistently, they allow you to narrow your filtering or search to just those images that you have decided you like the best. You can control how tightly or loosely you want to filter any search with ratings.

Lightroom allows two kids of flags: Pick and Reject. I typically only use the Reject flag. I'll use this to designate files to delete.

Instead of using the Pick flag, I suggest using a temporary label or *Set Target Collection*. I'll show you those in the Collections chapter.

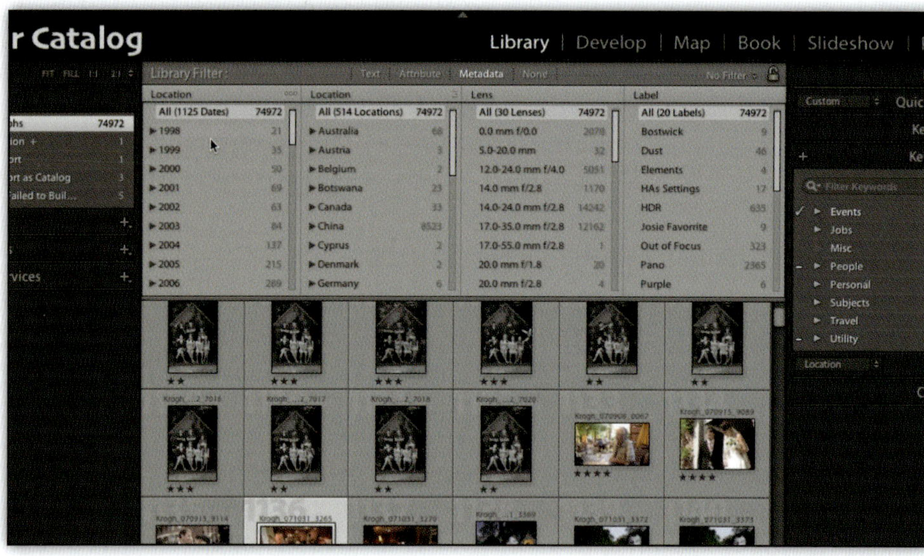

VIDEO 4-1 5W'S AND H (5:19)
In this video, we'll see how we can tag images for the 5 Ws + H.

CHOOSING A SOURCE TO FILTER

Before we get into the mechanics of filtering in Lightroom, we'll need to say a little about what you are applying the filter to. In order to see any images in Lightroom, you need to choose a source in the left-hand panel. This could be one of the entries in the Catalog panel, the Folders panel, the Collections panel, or the Published Collections panel.

Any filters that you use are applied to this source. If you don't choose any filters, then you'll see everything in the source you've chosen. If nothing in the source matches the filter, then you won't see any images. Until you understand that, the filter process may seem a little confusing and unpredictable.

Lightyroom lists the source name and a count of how many images are in the source on top of the filmstrip near the lower left corner of the screen. You can click on the source name here to navigate to recent sources.

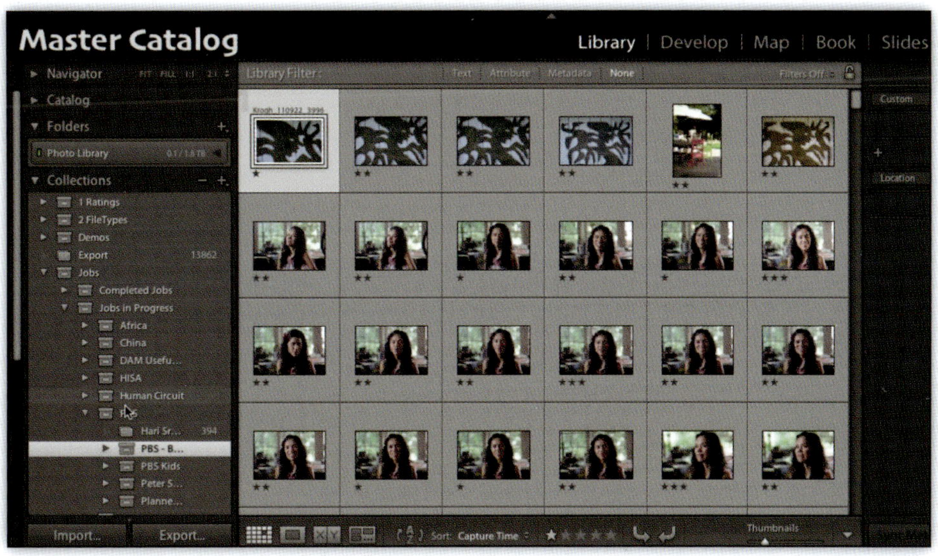

VIDEO 4-2 CHOOSING A SOURCE (2:19)
Whenever you are filtering images, you must first choose a source in the left-hand panel.

USING THE LIBRARY FILTER BAR

We've seen how the Library Filter bar allows us to find images simply. In this section, we will explore how the Library Filter bar works. I have found nearly every function on the Library Filter bar to be useful at some time, so I want to be pretty thorough.

Basic Navigation

Let's start by examining the basic functioning of the Library Filter bar. We'll outline each of the main elements and see how to show and hide each.

- The Library Filter is always filtering the source that is selected in the left-hand column.
- The top line allows you to show and hide the different filters. You can also save and choose filter presets here.
- The Text Filter allows you to search on any piece of text. Typically, I use this to find a file by searching on a piece of the name, or I search on all metadata.
- The Attribute Filter allows you to filter for Flags, Ratings, Labels or Virtual Copy status.
- The Metadata Filter allows you to filter on any of the selectable fields.
- Flags, Ratings, Labels and Presets are also available just above the filmstrip on the lower right-hand side.

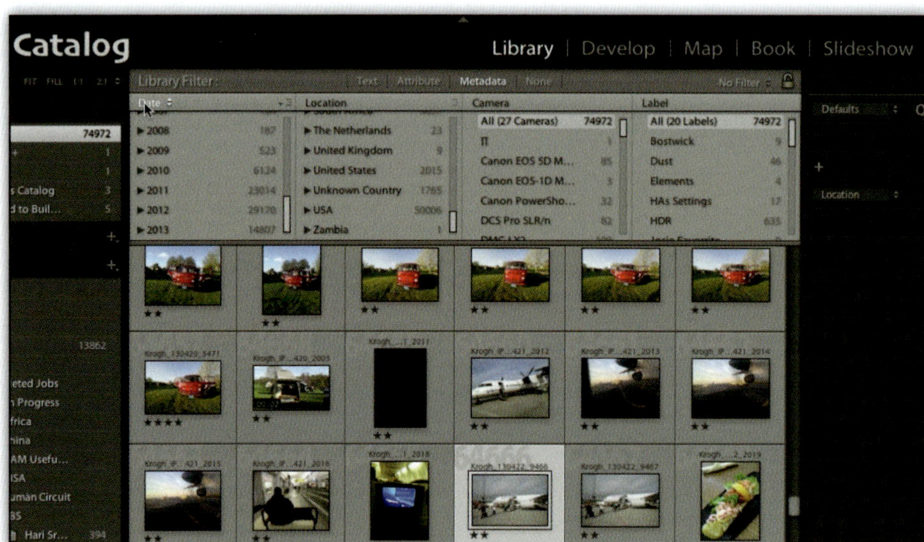

VIDEO 4-3 FILTER BAR BASICS (3:22)

This video outlines the basic navigation of the Library Filter bar.

The Metadata Filter

There is a lot of power in the Metadata Filter. Not only does it allow you to filter the tags, but it also allows you to know what tags are used in the catalog.

When you click on a source, the only tags that show up in the column are ones that are present in the source. This allows you to see that a certain camera or keyword or location is tagged in the source images. So the Metadata Filter actually lets you **discover** what's in the source.

The Metadata Filter columns are recursive, moving left-to-right. As you filter a column, tags are hidden that are not in the filtered group. (This one is a lot easier to show than to explain, but basically it allows you to further explore the contents of any particular source).

You can customize the Metadata Filter.

- You can change which tags are shown in a column. This means you can also change the sequence of the filtration, which is useful for discovery.
- You can add or remove columns.
- You can change them from ascending to descending.
- And you can show some columns in a hierarchy, if the field is one that supports hierarchy, such as Date, Location or Keywords.

Using the Metadata Filter

In the course of normal work, I use the Metadata Filter for filtering and to examine the tags in a group of images. I can see the dates, locations, keywords and other tags that are assigned to a group of photos.

In my normal workflow, I frequently filter by date or by location. I also use the Library Filter bar to see what labels may be assigned to a group of images and to filter those as well. Sometimes it's important to confirm that a set of images all have Smart Previews, location tags or GPS data.

I also make specialized searches on the Photo Library that make use of camera information. I have used the Camera and Lens columns to let me check the focus accuracy of certain lenses and then make adjustments to the camera's autofocus fine-tuning.

I'll also use the recursive filtering to help me remember stuff, like the year I might have taken a certain trip. The video below shows how all this works.

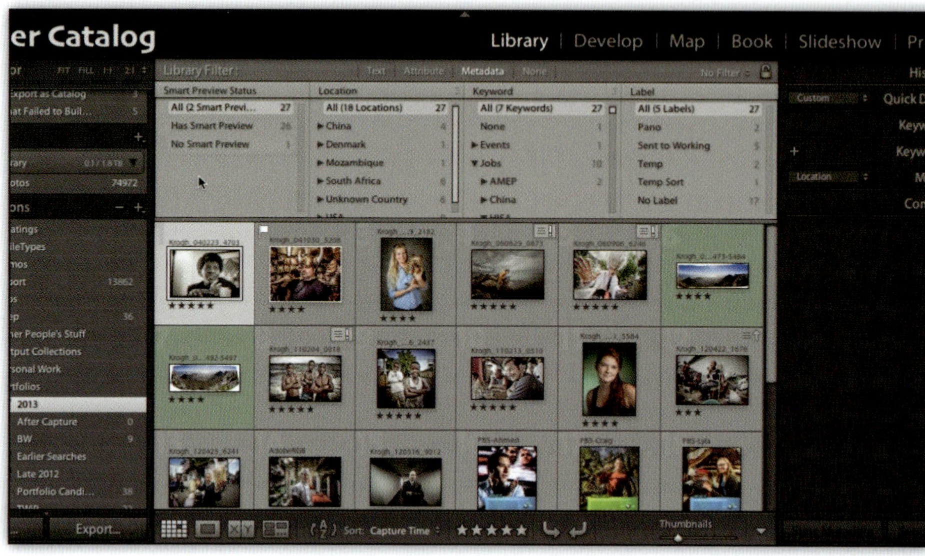

VIDEO 4-4 METADATA FILTER (4:21)

This video outlines the features of the Metadata Filter and some of the ways I find it to be useful.

Selecting Keywords changes the Source to *All Photographs*

When you select a keyword in the right-hand panel as a filter, you are really telling Lightroom to set the first column of the Metadata Filter to *Keyword* and to set the source to all photographs.

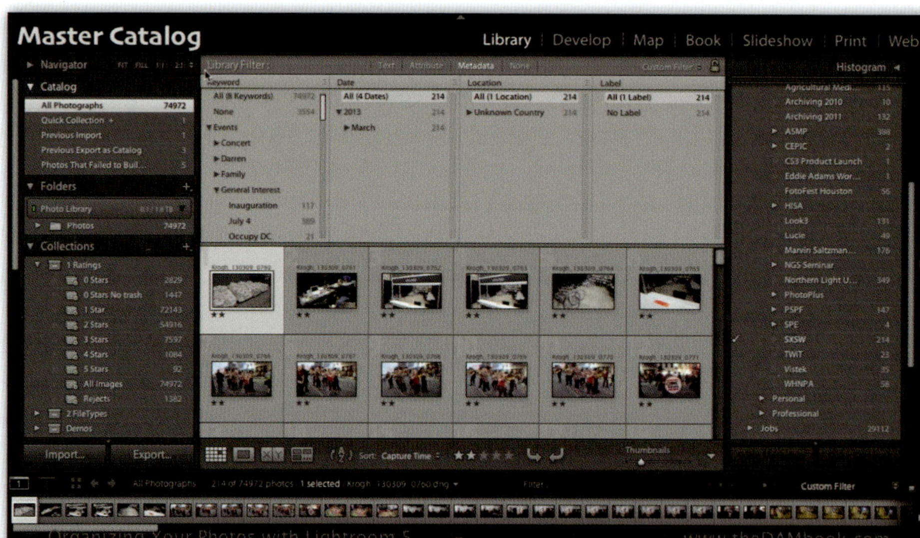

VIDEO 4-5 KEYWORDS FILTER (2:41)

This video shows how selecting Keywords actually changes the Source and Metadata Filter.

USING RATINGS AND FLAGS

Ratings are used to tag images for levels of quality. There are 5 levels; 6 if you count "zero stars" and 7 if you count the reject flag (I do). The 5-star designation is designed to be used for the highest quality images. I suggest that you come up with a collection-wide definition for each rating, and try to use it as consistently as possible. (Actually, I suggest that you adopt my definition.)

Of all the tags in Lightroom, ratings are the most subjective. Only you know what makes a picture "good" in your opinion. Some people hate any photo that's blurry, and others use blur as an element of their photographic style. Ratings can be used to measure the quality of an image according to what you like in a photo.

Ratings make for a particularly powerful filter. They allow you to hide lower-quality images without having to delete them.

Here are some suggestions for assigning and using ratings.

- Don't use ratings stars to mean anything other than "levels of goodness".
- Use ratings as consistently as possible. They are more valuable if they are used across your Photo Library to mean the same thing.
- Don't agonize too much over assigning the ratings tags. It's mostly there to allow you to hide the lower-quality images.
- Ratings are most valuable in making the best photos "float to the top".
- When in doubt, give an image a higher rating. That will keep it from getting lost.
- Use the Reject flag to mean "Delete me".
- I like to browse through my mid-level rated files every now and then searching for overlooked gems.

My ratings definitions

I assign ratings according to the following set of definitions. You don't have to use mine, but I suggest that you create a simple set of guidelines that you use when applying ratings to your images.

Reject flag = Delete. Can be deleted with no further review.

Zero stars = Not yet Rated. When images are first imported into Lightroom, they don't have any rating. Eventually, all images need to either get one or more stars, or they need to get the reject tag. A zero-star image means "unreviewed".

1 star = Save: Don't delete, but typically keep hidden. I assign 1 star to images that are panorama, time lapse or HDR elements or that may be useful in image compositing or some administrative task. I also assign this rating to photos that are scouting photos or that simply help me remember what something looked like.

2 stars = Show: Show to the Client (even if the client is me). I assign this rating to all images that I would put in a web gallery for a shoot, for instance.

3 stars = Recommend: Recommend to the client (even if the client is me). I use this rating to tag the best images from a shoot. If it's a commercial shoot, I use this to tell the client which images I think they should use for the project. I use it for personal work in the same way.

4 stars = Best: Best of Photo Library. I use this designation to float a good image above the shoot itself, and make it visible whenever I'm searching the whole library for the best images. Many Portfolio images will be drawn from this group.

5 stars = Hero: I use this to designate a handful of images that I think are my very best. Some people like the term "Hero", some like the term "Signature", and some would simply call them the very best.

The ratings pyramid

I suggest that you envision a ratings pyramid as shown in the video below. There should be very few images with the highest rating, since these should be your very best photos. As you go down through the pyramid, most people will have more images at each level.

Depending on what you shoot and what you like to keep, the 1-star designation may be the widest category, or it may be slimmer than the 2-star rating

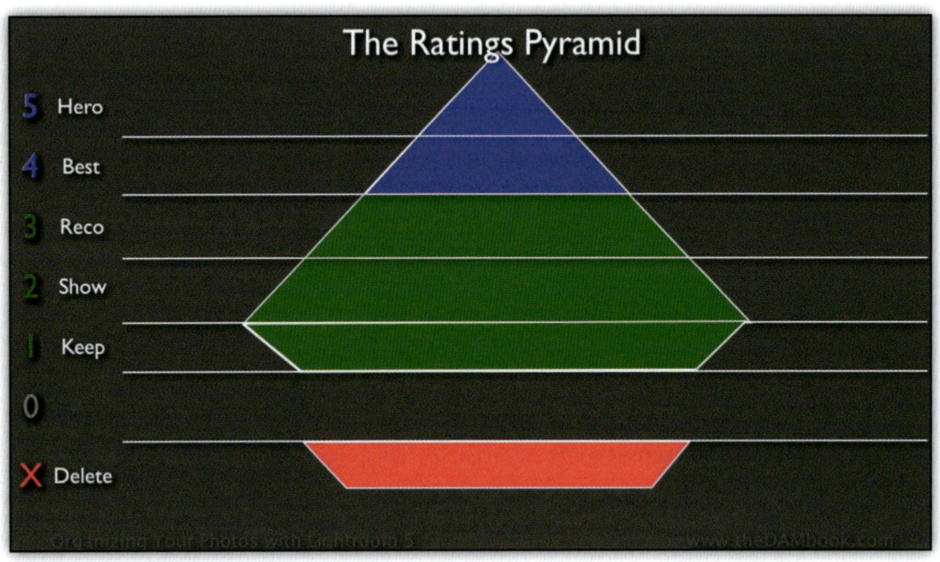

VIDEO 4-6 THE RATINGS PYRAMID (4:55)

This video shows the ratings pyramid.

Lifting the best photos to the highest ratings

I suggest that ratings should be used to "float" the best pictures to the top of the Photo Library. I reserve the 4-star and 5-star tags for images that are not simply the best of a shoot, but are best in the Photo Library. Every now and then, I'll look through the catalog to identify images that should get a higher rating.

Sometimes I will have overlooked 4-star photos because I was just focused on getting the shoot out on time. I also have a lot of photos from the early days of my digital photography. These were edited and archived before ratings stars even existed.

What should be deleted and when?

Let's talk for a second about deleting photos. Some photos should definitely be deleted. Blank pictures and fuzzy sports shots with no action are pretty clear examples of files to throw away. But what about photos on the margin? If I shoot 200 photos at an event, but only 20 are really good, shouldn't I throw away the rest?

The problem with deleting is that it's gone forever, and a photo may have hidden value that you don't know until later. Even poor photos may help you remember who was at an event in the years to come. Or perhaps an outtake photo shows your friend's cool car that was later lost in an accident. Or maybe Photoshop will be able to rescue fuzzy photos with image processing magic. (This just happened with Photoshop CC's Shake Reduction.) And other photos might be useful in slide shows and other animations.

As you are deciding what to delete, you may need to consider a lot of things, including unknown future events. Fortunately, ratings allow you to simplify the decision. You can filter out the worst photos and concentrate on the best photos without having to throw stuff away that you might want later. This saves you time in the editing process.

Of course, if you are looking through a lot of similar images from a portrait shoot, it may be obvious that a large percentage of them can be deleted. In this case, tag with the reject tag, and throw them away once you're comfortable doing so. For many shoots, I delete the reject photos during the first edit. For high-value shoots, I may wait until the client has accepted the final images and paid the bill before deleting.

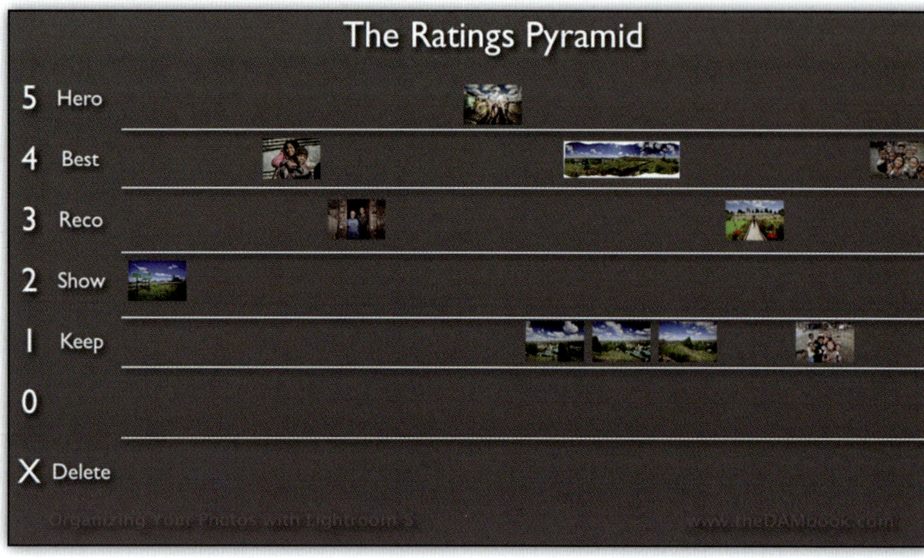

VIDEO 4-7 RATING A SHOOT (3:31)

This video discusses the process of rating your shoots.

Filtering by ratings and flags

Once you've made the ratings, you'll want to be able to use them to filter the collection. Again, Lightroom offers several ways to do that.

- You can make Smart Collections that filter by ratings on a catalog-wide basis.
- You can also use Smart Collections to combine ratings with some other tag filter.
- You can create filter presets that can be used to filter on any Source.
- You can use the Attribute part of the Library Filter bar to filter any source.

The video below shows how this works.

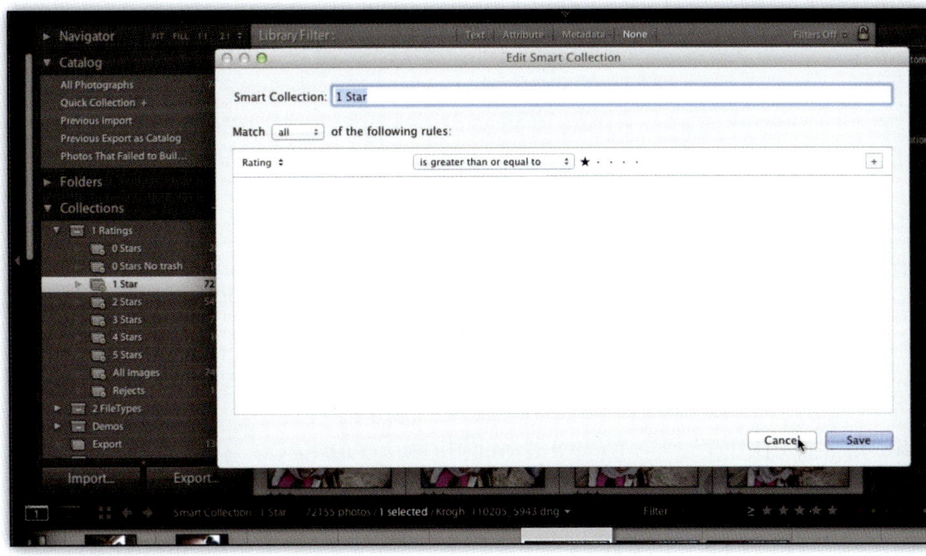

VIDEO 4-8 FINDING RATED IMAGES (1:53)
This video shows you can filter by ratings.

Assigning ratings and flags

Lightroom gives you half a dozen ways to assign ratings and flags. You can use the keyboard shortcuts, the *Photo* menu, metadata templates, the Painter, the toolbar and the thumbnail target. More than 90% of the time, I use the keyboard shortcut, so that's the one I'll concentrate on in the video below.

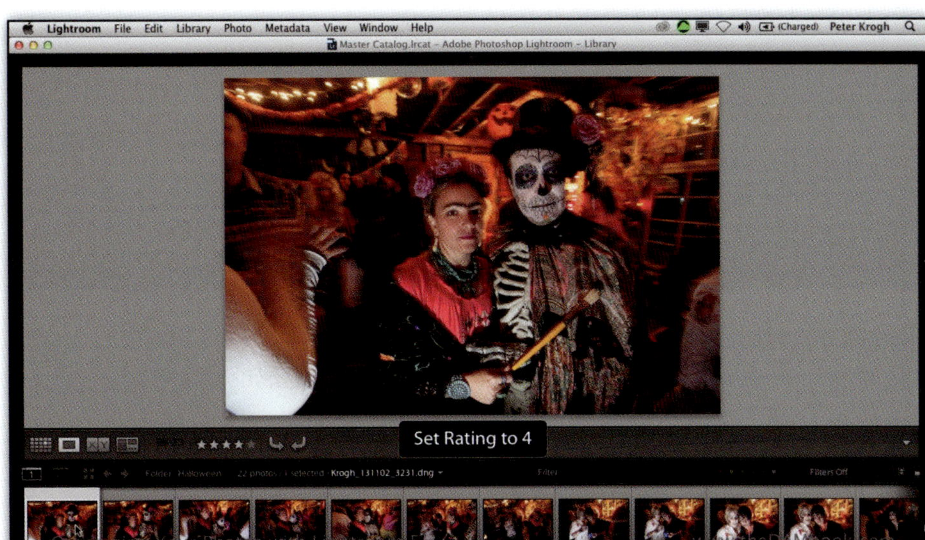

VIDEO 4-9 RATING A SHOOT PT.2 (4:38)
This video shows you can assign ratings with the keyboard shortcut.

CHANGES FOR DAM BOOK 1 AND 2 READERS

Isn't this a change from *The DAM Book*?

Readers of *The DAM Book 1* and *2* may notice that I am using ratings differently than I did previously. I have shifted my star ratings definitions up a notch. What used to be 1 is now 2, what was 2 is now 3, etc. What gives?

I have long said that I am reserving the 5-star rating for expansion of the system. Now I have 10 years of digital photography and half a million images in my Photo Library. I can see that 1-5 stars plus the reject tag will be sufficient to rate the collection. I don't ever anticipate the 5-star designation getting so crowded that I will need another star.

By shifting everything up, I'm able to get a workflow advantage. The 0-star rating now tells me that an image has not yet been rated (something I used to tag with labels). This simplifies the system.

The video below shows how I changed my existing ratings system to the new one.

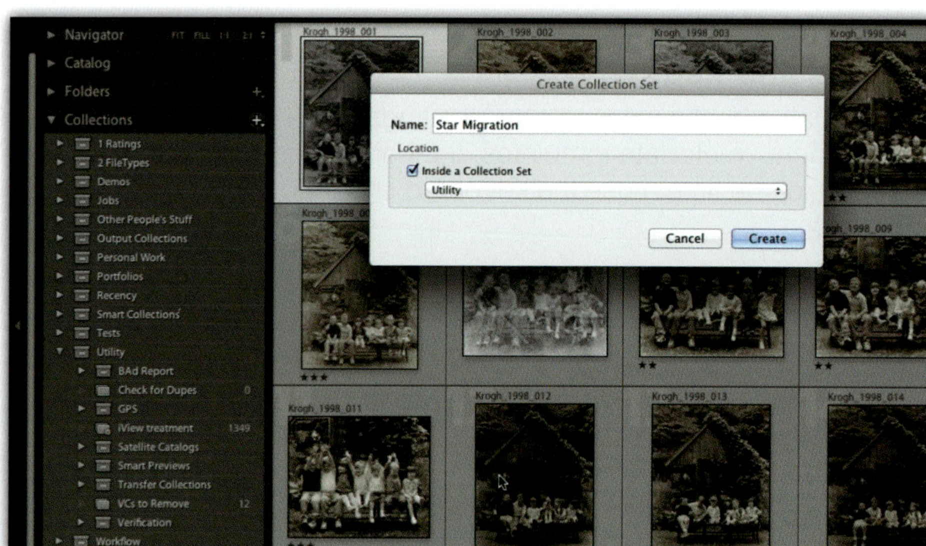

VIDEO 4-10 STAR MIGRATION (3:45)
This video shows how I changed the ratings I have been using.

MAKING FILTER PRESETS

You can make presets for the Library Filter bar for your frequently-used settings. You can also use these presets to save your column setup in the Metadata Filter. Note that all filter presets include the metadata filter, so you can't use these in conjunction with the keyword list. Here are the presets that I find useful to have:

_None: This removes all filters.

1 Star (etc): I make one for each rating star level.

Rejects: This shows any files with the reject flag.

Everything Rated?: This help me determine if I have fully rated a shoot for stars and rejects. It hides all images that have a star rating or that have the reject flag.

Reject Not: This hides Rejects.

Peter's defaults: This one sets up my Metadata columns the way I like it: Date, Location, Keyword and Label

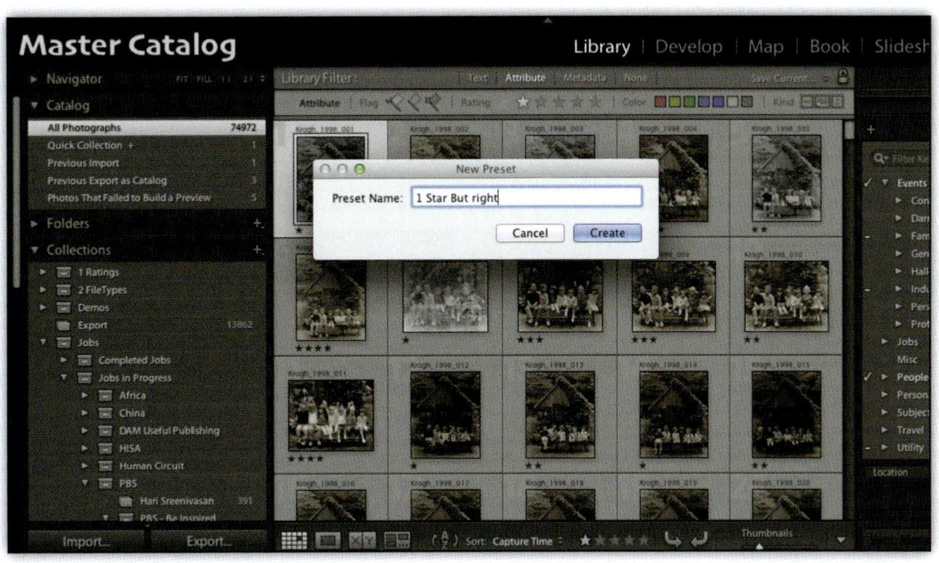

VIDEO 4-11 FILTER PRESETS (5:37)

This video outlines how to create and use filter presets.

USING SMART COLLECTIONS

Smart Collections are not really collections at all. Instead, they are filters. When you make a Smart Collection, you choose the criteria you want to filter to, and save it. These are particularly helpful for filtering certain attributes like ratings or file formats. They are also helpful for keeping repeating subject matter close at hand. (This could include a particular location or keyword, such as "best photos taken at my house" or all images for a certain client.)

Here are some tips for using Smart Collections.

- Use Collection Sets to keep your Smart Collections organized.
- Name your Smart Collections appropriately.
- If you find yourself filtering on a particular keyword or location a lot, it's time to think about making a Smart Collection for that tag.
- Smart Collections don't remember the sequence of the images, so it's not a good place to do your creative organizational work.

Attribute Smart Collections

One of the best uses of Smart Collections is to filter your Photo Library by some kind of attribute. This includes ratings and file formats, as well as Smart Previews and GPS data. In the video below, I show you how to create a set of Smart Collections for these most common types of filtering.

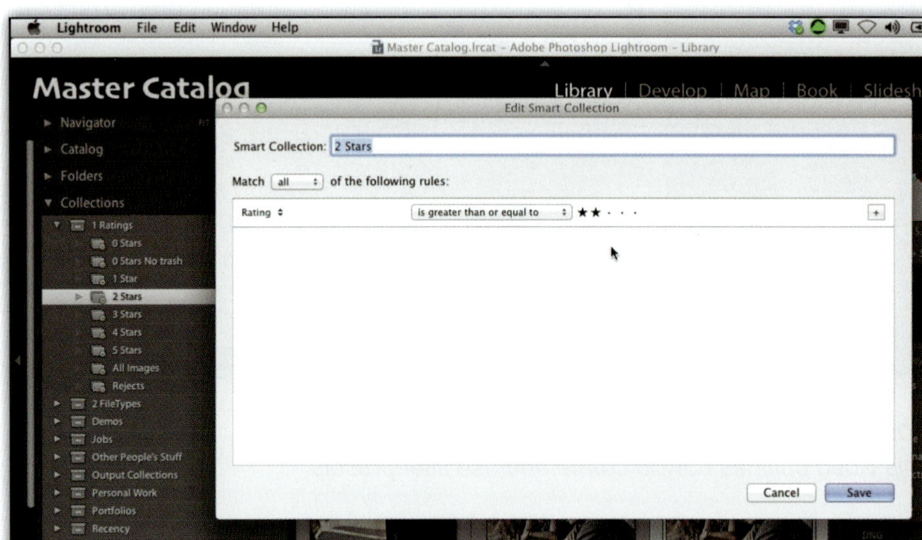

VIDEO 4-12 SMART COLLECTIONS (3:55)

This video shows how to create Smart Collections that group your images by attribute.

Commonly-used subject matter

If you want to keep some images right at your fingertips, then making a Smart Collection may be just the answer. For example, you can make a Smart Collection to show all images tagged with your home location, or anything tagged with the keyword *Family*. You can add ratings to the criteria and only show the best from each of these categories, if you like. The video below will give you some ideas for this.

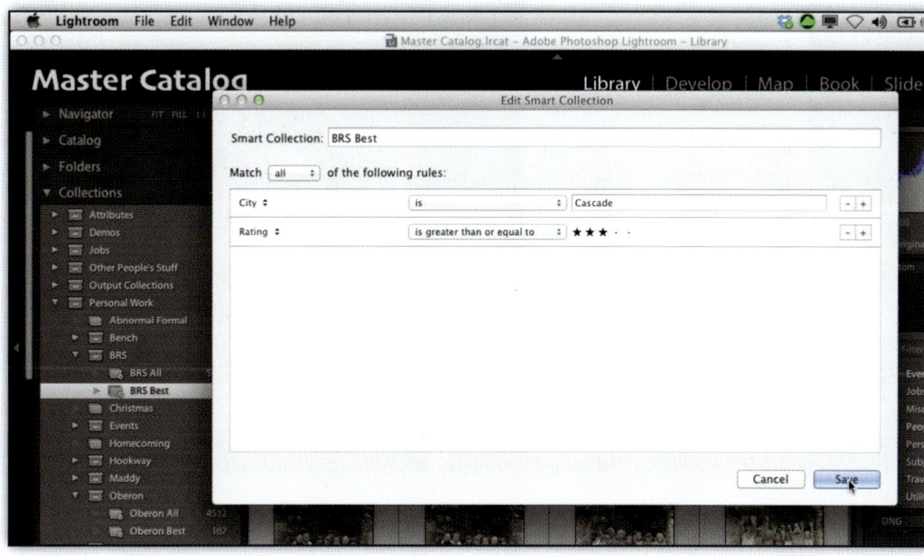

VIDEO 4-13 SMART COLLECTIONS PT. 2 (3:35)

This video shows how to create Smart Collections for repeating subject matter.

Importing Smart Collections

Whenever you import from another catalog, you will also import the Smart Collections that are in that catalog. The video below shows how.

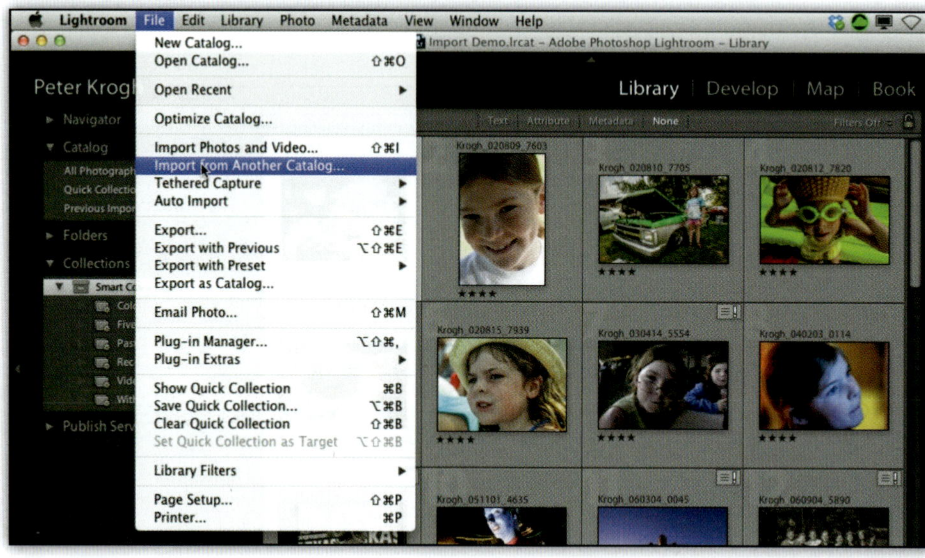

VIDEO 4-14 IMPORT SMART COLLECTIONS (4:25)

This video shows how Smart Collections can be imported from one catalog to another.

BONUS - DOWNLOADABLE SMART COLLECTIONS

I've created a set of Smart Collections like the ones you see above, and posted it online. If you download it and import it into your catalog, all these collections will be created automatically.

You can find the download file at www.theDAMbook.com/oyp_resources.

USING LABELS

Labels are a great tool to use for quick tagging in Lightroom. Color labels can be assigned with a number key as quickly as you can assign a rating. And colors jump out from a group of thumbnails more than any other kind of tag, so you can easily see which ones have the tag. Lightroom allows you to make multiple different Label Sets, so you can use them for different tasks you might be working on.

Labels do have a downside, however. Since they are so easy to assign, they are also easy to erase. A photo can have only one label. If you assign a label to a photo, you will automatically remove any existing label. And you can do this without even realizing it, because you don't always see the color, depending on which Label Set you are using.

Therefore, I suggest that you think of labels as a kind of a temporary tag. After you have applied the tag, you'll probably want to use another kind of tag that makes the information more permanent. So when I label images as panoramas, I'll also put the keyword *Panorama* on the image.

Making labels and finding labeled files

Let's start with a video that shows the nuts and bolts of using labels. We'll look at how we assign labels and find labeled images with the Library Filter bar.

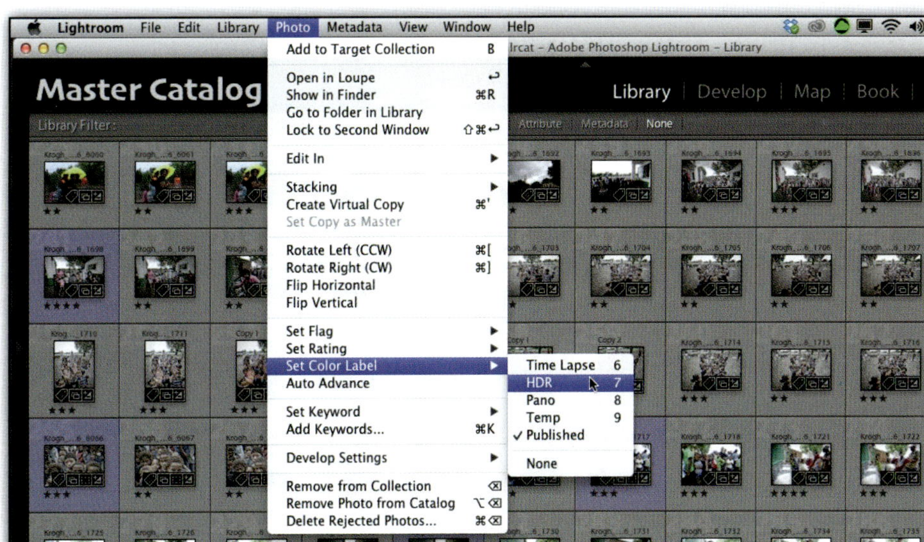

VIDEO 4-15 LABELS (5:53)

This video shows how to add labels to photos and find labeled photos with the Library Filter bar.

Using labels

In this video, I'll show you how I use labels most frequently. I use them to identify sequence types, such as panorama, HDR and time lapse. And I also use temporary labels to help me visually sort through a group of images. Labels can help you sort out duplicate downloads, for instance, because you can quickly identify images from each group.

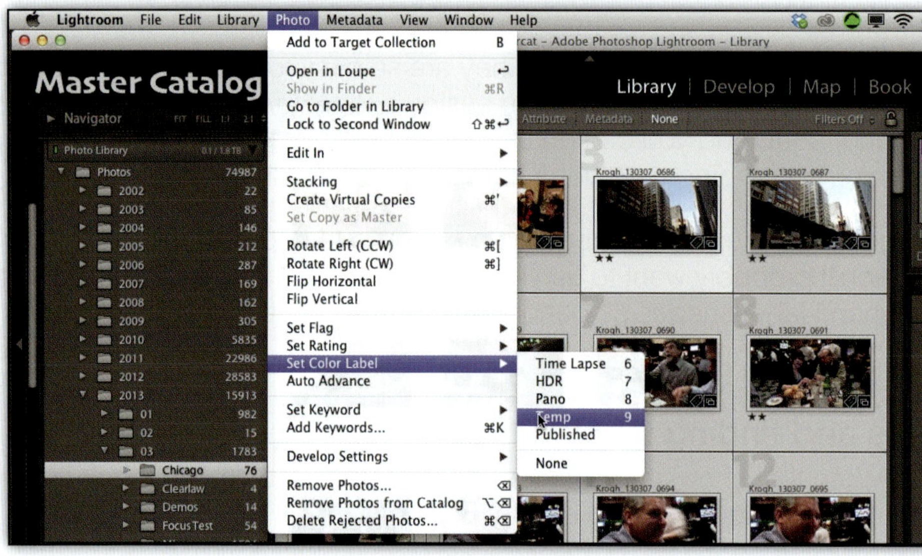

VIDEO 4-16 USING TEMPORARY LABELS (5:17)
This video shows how I suggest using labels.

Label sets

You can create Label Sets with totally different label names. This may be helpful if you need to do an alternate kind of tagging to a set of photos. But you'll want to watch out that you don't accidentally remove labels that belong to other sets.

The following video shows how to make new Label Sets, and how you might accidentally use these to remove labels invisibly.

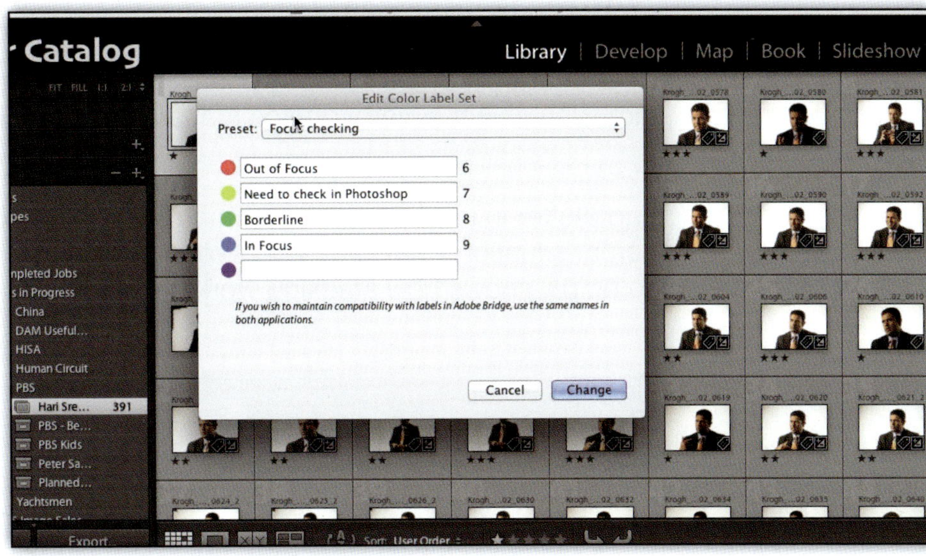

VIDEO 4-17 LABEL SETS (2:34)
This video shows how to make Label Sets.

STACKING

In Lightroom, you can create a stack of images that are a set. The main reason for stacking is to tidy up the grid view. To create a stack, you select several photos that are all stored in the same folder or Collection and right-click.

This is a useful technique for reducing clutter in large shoots. You can group images together in stacks for easy viewing of the different situations in a shot, and expand the stacks when you want to see all the photos. The video below shows how stacking works.

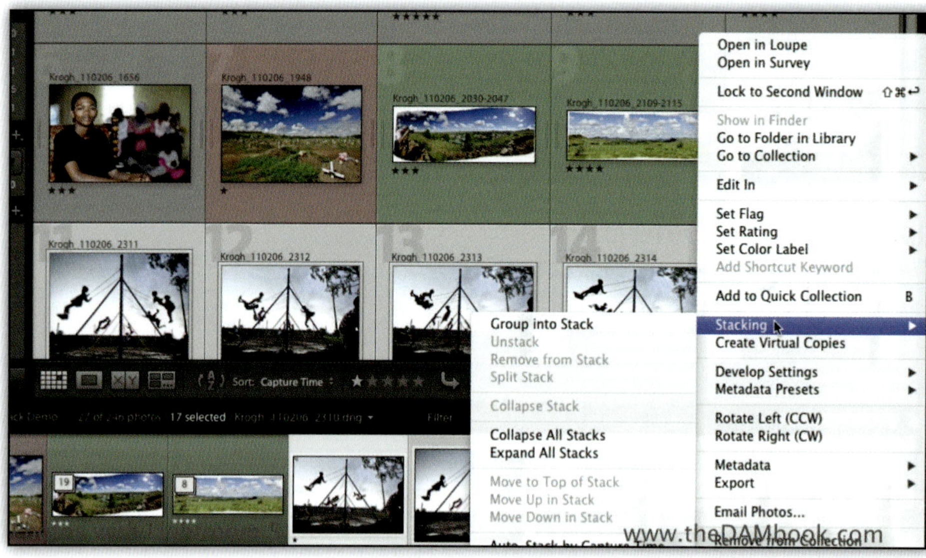

VIDEO 4-18 STACKS (4:14)
This video shows how to use stacking to reduce clutter in grid view.

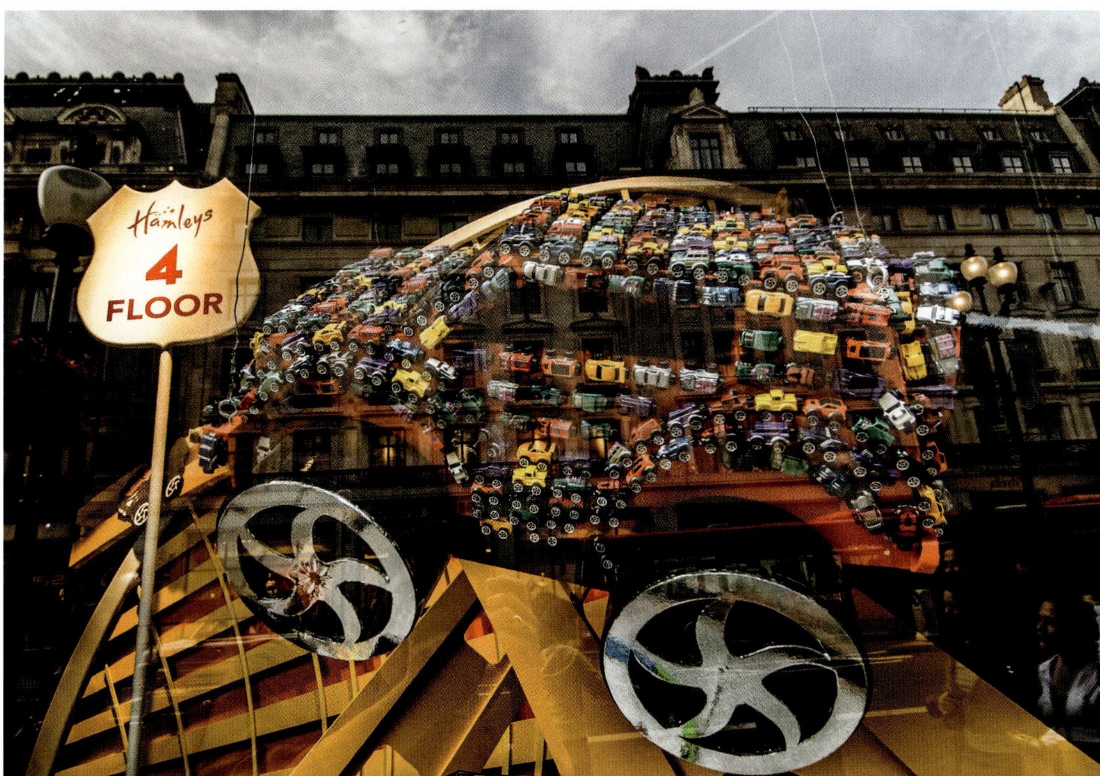
Hamleys
4
FLOOR

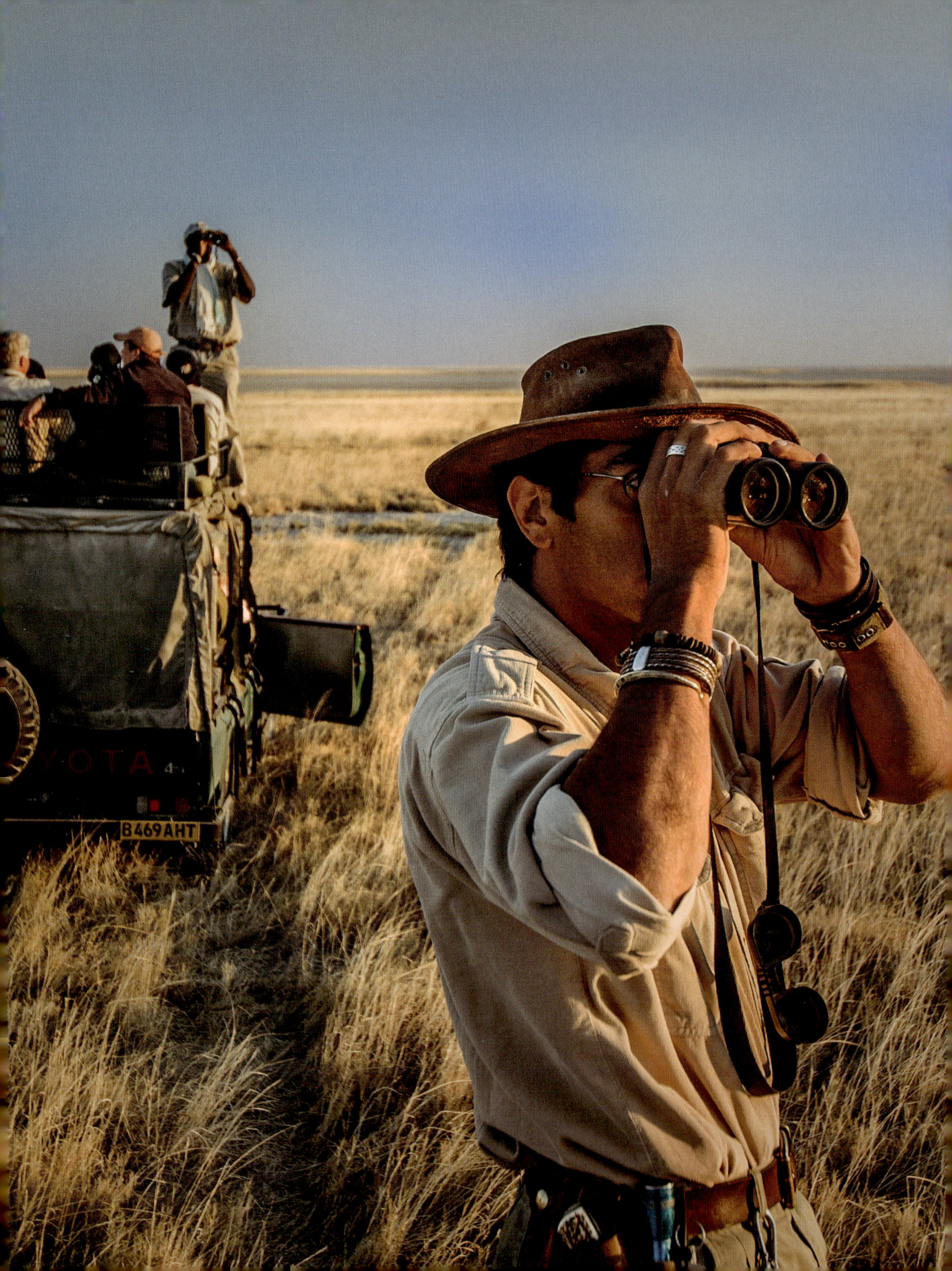
B469AHT

CHAPTER 5

KEYWORDS

Keywords are the most powerful organizing tool in Lightroom. You can use these tags in a simple way to start, and they can grow as your collection gets larger.

Many people are paralyzed because they over-think keywords. You don't have to start with a big and complex system of classification. You can start off with a few keywords that help you make sense of your images. Do only what's useful, and no more. And spend a few seconds tagging new shoots as you import them. You will be surprised how quickly the Keyword List will grow.

And remember, you can always make changes to your keyword structure. You can move them around into different hierarchies. You may decide to split your *Friends* keywords into *Childhood Friends, College Friends* and *Work Friends*. And you can change the keyword itself with a single click. If your childhood friend gets married and you want to change her name in the keywords, go ahead.

The way you organize with keywords will definitely evolve over time. You'll shoot new subjects, meet new people, and get new clients. Keywords can change with you in ways that folders should not. (Remember, we want our folders to be really stable and not to change over time.)

So go ahead. Get started. It's easy and fun.

USING KEYWORDS

Keywords are used for classification of a photo. They can describe the subject matter, event shown, person photographed, or any other characteristic of the photo you might want to filter for.

I've placed this chapter after the Filtering Chapter because I want you to think about the organizational keyword tags as a filtering tool. These tags allow you to easily show "just these images and no others."

While some people may like to tag images for every little characteristic, I don't have time for that, nor do most people I know. You need to make keywords that are appropriate for your Photo Library and the kinds of subject matter that interests you.

The most basic functions of keywords are the classification of your images, and the ability to filter to find those images. We'll start by looking only at the Keyword List panel, because I think that's the most useful for each of these tasks.

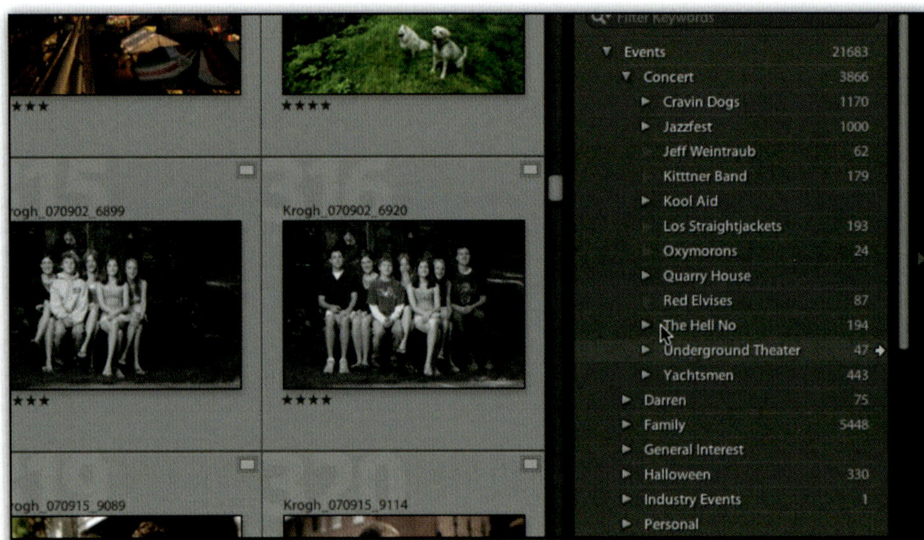

VIDEO 5-1 KEYWORDS OVERVIEW (4:38)
This shows how you can make keywords and put them in a hierarchy, and how you can find images by using that hierarchy.

BUILDING YOUR KEYWORD STRUCTURE

Your keyword structure will reflect the images in your Photo Library, and your interest in using those images.

If you love dogs, you may want to tag every image in your collection that shows a dog. If you don't care for dogs, then this might be totally irrelevant to you. You might want to make a tag for all animals, and put the dogs and cats in there together (watch out for fights). But if you are unlikely to need animal photos for any usage, then it's probably a waste of time to make that tag.

Your keyword structure should be a natural reflection of the subject matter you photograph, and the way you need to filter the images. Let's break the process down.

Start big and subdivide

Your keywords will be easiest to use if you create a handful of top-level hierarchies and organize your keywords within these. This makes it much easier to make good tags, and to find the right images with those tags. Good top-level keywords might include *People*, *Events*, *Projects* and *Subjects*. If you are a professional, you will want to create a category for your assignment work. It can be helpful to make one for Locations as well, but we will see in Chapter 7 that the location information should end up in the Location fields.

Inside each of these top-level keywords, you can make child keywords. These are used to subdivide the top level into useful subsets. So inside *People*, you may put *Family*, *Friends* and *Colleagues*. These can be further subdivided as necessary.

Remember that the point of making these keywords is to filter down to a manageable set of images when you make some kind of creative work, or when you need to choose images for output. Lightroom makes it easy to look through the filtered results pretty quickly. This means you probably don't have to get too specific with your keywords.

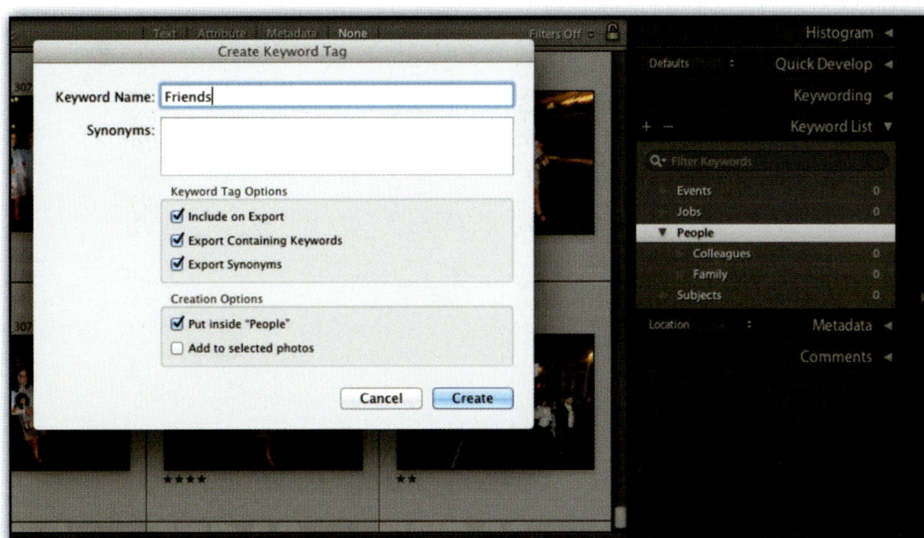

VIDEO 5-2 BUILDING YOUR HIERARCHY (3:04)
This video shows how you can create a generalized keyword hierarchy and use that to filter. You can subdivide the keywords whenever you find it useful.

Organize any of your existing tags

If you've already got some keywords in your catalog, then you'll want to start by organizing them into a hierarchy. You can drag them into a hierarchy using existing keywords, or you could make new top-level keywords to keep everything organized.

Sometimes these top-level keywords will only be useful as an organizational tool. The keyword *Subjects* is really useful for keeping your subject keywords organized, but it's pretty useless as an independent keyword. Later in this chapter, I'll show you how you can set these keywords to stay in the catalog and not be exported.

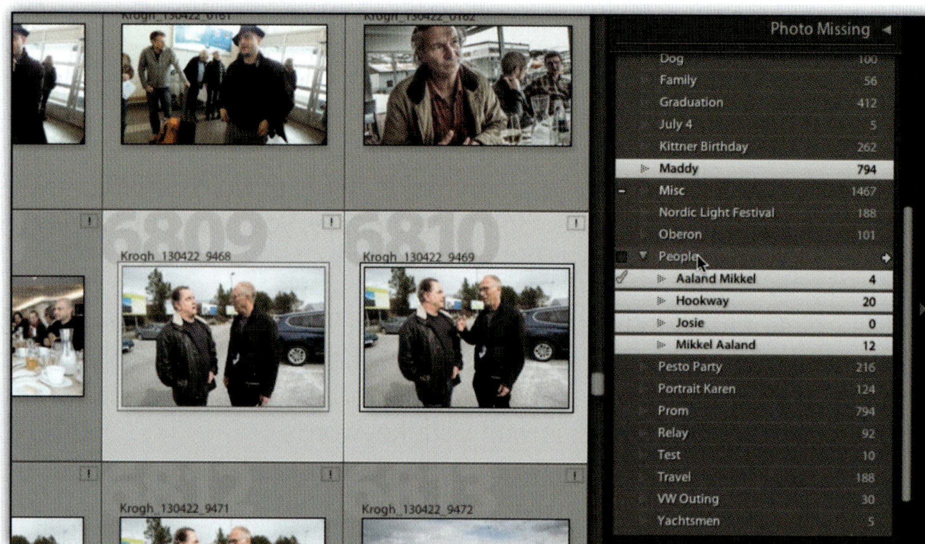

VIDEO 5-3 ORGANIZING EXISTING KEYWORDS (3:38)

Here we see how to reorganize your existing tags into a new structure.

GETTING STARTED

Once you've started to build your list, it's time to start tagging your Photo Library for the most common subjects. In this step, we want to make some really big divisions within the collection. If you're a pro, then you might need to divide between ***Assignment Work*** and ***Personal Work***. An enthusiast might divide between ***Family Photos***, ***Photo Projects***, and the ***Kids' Sports Teams***. Make top-level keywords for each of these terms.

These big divisions will help you find and filter the images more easily. And, for many people, this can be done pretty quickly. Consider how you might want to usefully divide up your Photo Library, and make keywords for each of those divisions.

Run through the collection assigning top-level keywords

Once you've made the keywords, it can be very quick to assign them to many images. Set your *View* to Grid and show All Photographs. Open the Keyword List on the right, and give it a lot of room. Set the *Sort* to *Capture Time* so everything lines up in the order shot. Run through the images using *Click, Shift-Click* to select groups of images, and assign them to the keyword. Even a large collection can be organized like this pretty quickly.

TRICK

The disappearing images trick

Let me show you a trick that can help make this process even easier. You can use a Smart Collection to make images disappear once they are assigned to one of the top-level keywords. This allows you to tag the large groups first, and to leave the stragglers for a later session.

We need to make a Smart Collection that shows all images that do not have a particular keyword or keywords. Set the Smart Collection criteria to *Other Metadata > Keywords > doesn't contain > Assignments* (or whatever the top-level keyword is you're assigning). When the keyword is assigned to the photo, the image disappears from the Smart Collection.

You can add a second criteria: *Keywords> doesn't contain > Personal* (for Personal Work), and set the Smart Collection to *Match all.* This will now hide all images that are assigned to either ***Assignments*** or ***Personal***. You should be able to divide up a collection pretty quickly into one of these two groups.

Note that the trick works even when the images are assigned to a child keyword. So you don't have to limit yourself to adding the top-level keyword.

The video below shows this trick in action.

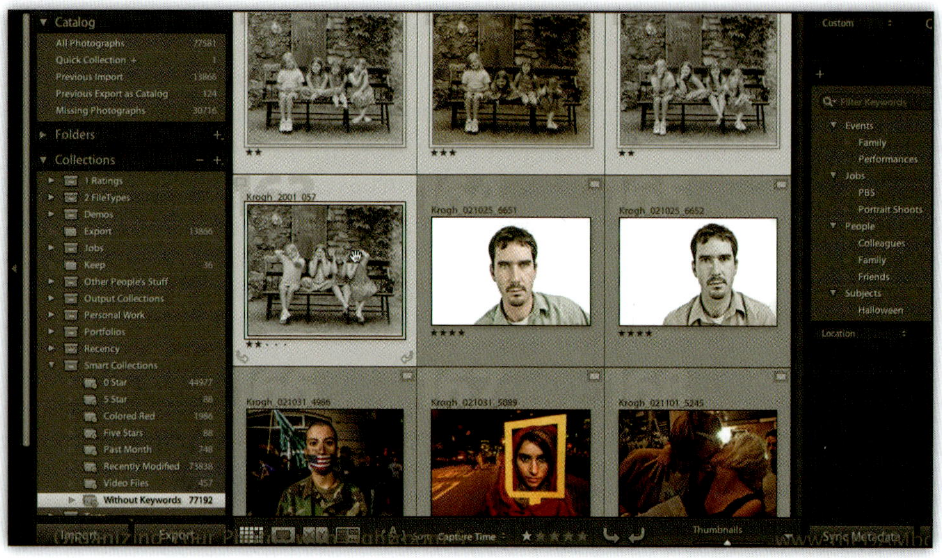

VIDEO 5-4 TAGGING A BIG COLLECTION (3:49)
Here we see how to assign a lot of top-level keywords to a large collection.

That's it. It's really easy to get started and to begin to divide your images up. In the next section, we'll take a look at a simple strategy for tagging shoots.

TAG YOUR SHOOTS

Once you've started building a keyword structure, you'll want to do a little work to each group of newly imported files. If you keep up with this, your Photo Library will become nicely organized without a lot of work.

Shoot tagging strategy

Like any use of keywords, the tags you assign to your shoots will reflect what you shoot and what you want to know about the photos. Here are some tips on creating a shoot tagging strategy.

- Try to tag the shoot as soon as you download it, when the information is still fresh in your mind.
- Most shoots only need a few top-level tags. This could be an event name, the client name or some other description of the subject matter.
- For large shoots, like a magazine story or a week-long vacation, you may want to divide the shoot keyword into smaller keyword subsections.
- Make sure you are creating some kind of location tag. Ideally you will do this with the

dedicated Location tags. But keywords are fine as a stopgap. You can transfer the information from keywords to Location tags later.

- Make Metadata Presets for repeating subject matter in order to speed up the keywording (and other tagging) of these images.
- If you download a card of mixed photos that don't belong to any one single shoot, work through them as time permits. You'll want to assign the most relevant keyword for each group. Metadata Presets (covered in the next chapter) can help you do this.

The video below shows these suggestions in action.

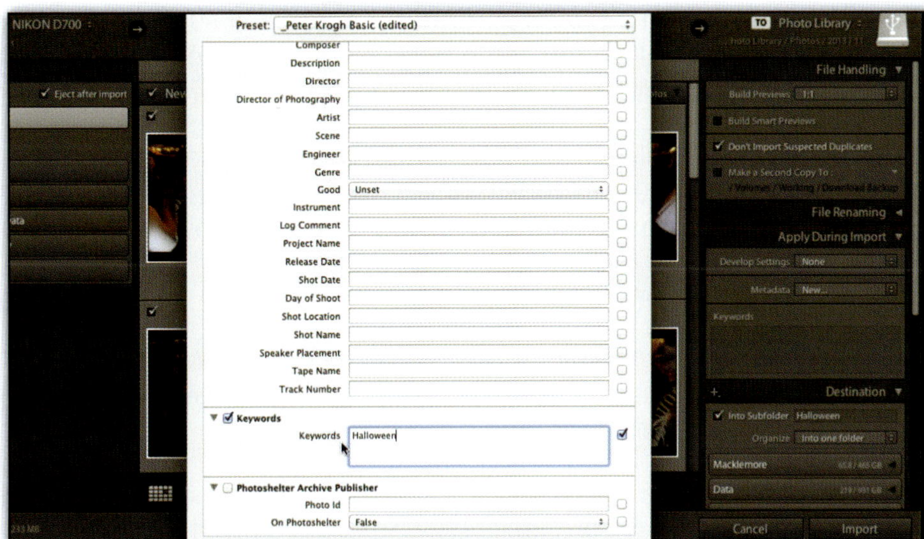

VIDEO 5-5 KEYWORD SHOOTS (6:43)
This video shows some strategies for keywording shoots as they are downloaded.

ADDING KEYWORDS WHILE YOU SEARCH

Adding a few keywords for a shoot is a great way to build up the "intelligence" of your tags. Over time, your catalog "knows" what the pictures are about. Here's another way to add intelligence to the Photo Library.

There are times when you will want to find a particular subject within your collection. You might want to find the best photos of Josie for a slideshow, or you might want to find the best landscape photos for a portfolio. In many cases, you won't already have every image fully tagged for this subject matter.

Instead of starting this process with a bunch of random searches, I suggest you do some comprehensive tagging. Spend a little time at the beginning of the process tagging **all** pictures of Josie or **all** landscape photos, and you'll be able to use these keywords again and again.

Most of the time, these searches will be recurring needs. If you are making a slideshow of Josie, it's probably because she is important to you, and you'll probably want to search this same set of pictures for some other project in the future. The tagging you do now will help you out later.

You can approach this tagging a few ways.

The brute force approach: You can run through the entire Photo Library looking for these images. Just sit down and slog through the whole collection. If you have not made many tags yet, then maybe you want to take this approach.

Make a parent tag for the subject: If you are new to keywording, then you might want to take this opportunity to do a little additional organization. You could start the process by making a keyword for *Family* and dropping all the family photos into that keyword. Then run through these photos looking for all photos of Josie.

In many cases, this is the best way to begin. By bringing all possible images into this keyword, you can do a rough search that casts a very broad net. The second pass through just the *Family* photos feels quicker and more rewarding. And, of course, the keyword *Family* will be very useful when you need to make the next family slideshow.

Search within the hierarchy: If you have made a hierarchy of keywords where the *Josie* photos or the *Landscape* photos are likely to be found, you may be able to confine your search to these areas.

Search highest rated photos: If you have been diligent about rating your photos, you may be able to save yourself some time by searching only through the highest rated photos.

The video below shows how each of these searches works.

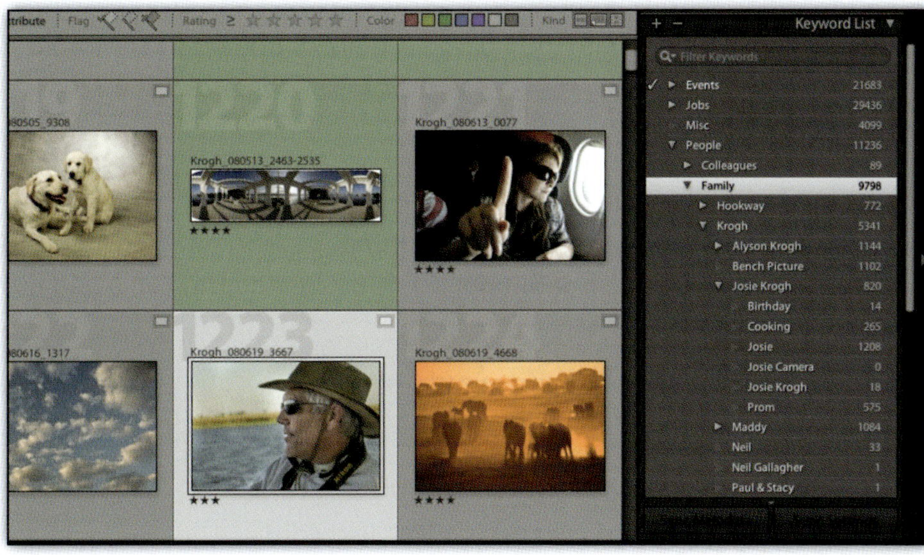

VIDEO 5-6 ADDING KEYWORDS WHILE SEARCHING (6:31)
In this video, we see some approaches for comprehensive tagging.

THE KEYWORD LIST

The rest of this chapter deals mostly with the nuts and bolts of putting the keyword tools to work. Lightroom has a lot of different ways to create and view keywords, but the *Keyword List* is my favorite by far. Let's take a look at how it works.

General features of the Keyword List

In the first section, we'll outline the basic functions of the Keyword List. This includes the creation of keywords and hierarchies, and the basics of assigning and removing keywords for a particular image.

Here are some of the basic features of the Keyword List.

- The Keyword List shows all your keywords in alphabetical order.
- You can drag images onto a keyword to assign that keyword.
- You can make a new keyword by clicking on the + next to the words Keyword List.
- You can delete keywords by selecting any number of keywords and clicking on the – next to the words Keyword List.
- You can add a child keyword by right-clicking on a keyword and choosing *Create Keyword Tag inside "..."*
- You can change a keyword's name by right-clicking on a keyword and choosing *Edit Keyword Tag...*
- You can drag the keywords onto each other to make a hierarchy, and you can drag them out to remove the hierarchy.
- All images with a parent keyword will show when you click on the child, even if the parent keyword is not assigned to all the images.
- Generally, you will want to assign the parent term to all keywords that are contained as children.
- You can only delete one keyword at a time with a right-click. If you select multiple keywords and click the minus sign at the top of the Keyword List, you delete all selected keywords, You can also delete multiple keywords by dragging them inside a parent keyword and deleting the parent.

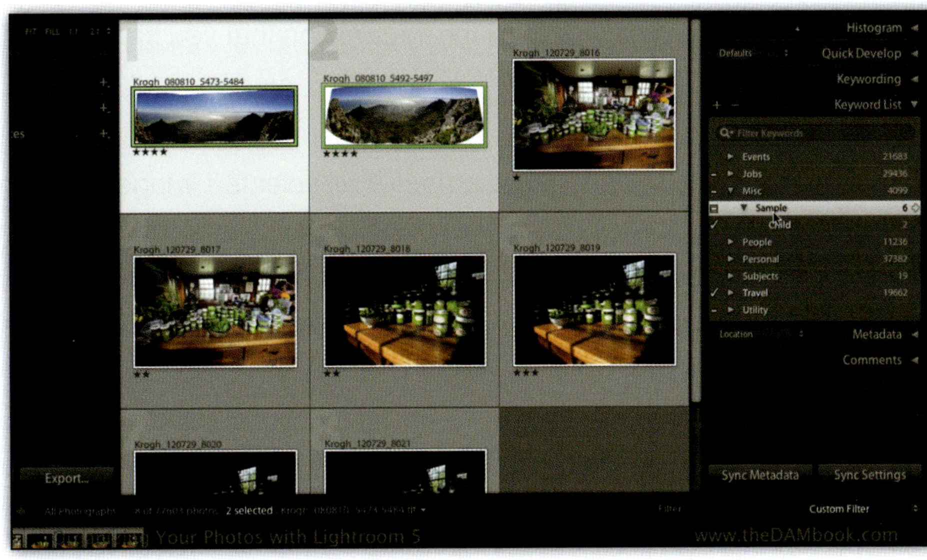

VIDEO 5-7 KEYWORD LIST (5:32)

In this video we see the basic functions of the Keyword List.

Checkboxes and other line info

In this section, we will look at the behavior of all the information that you can see on a line with a particular keyword.

- To the left of the keyword, you will see a checkmark if all selected images have that keyword assigned.
- If only some of the selected images have that keyword, you will see a dash.
- If you select some files and click on that box, it will assign the keyword. Click again to remove the keyword.
- If you see a triangle to the left of a keyword, the keyword has child keywords inside. Turn it down to show them.
- To the right of each keyword is a count of the number of images that have that keyword. This count does not include the child keywords which are not directly assigned to the parent.
- If you click on the arrow on the far right, that keyword will be chosen in the Metadata option of the Library Filter, and the Source will be set to *All Photographs*.

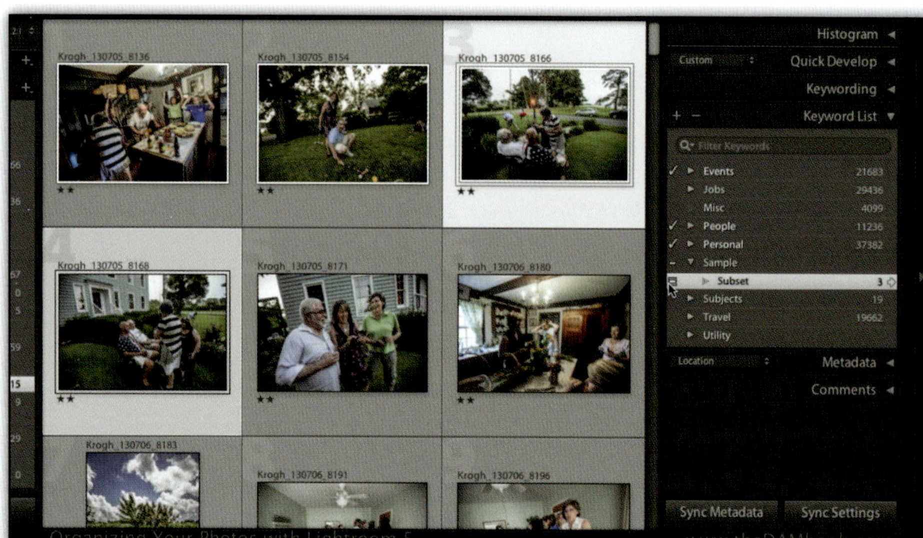

VIDEO 5-8 KEYWORD LIST PT. 2 (5:02)

This video shows all the functions on a line in the Keyword List.

The Keyword List Filter

As your hierarchy gets larger and more complex, you may lose track of where you've placed certain keywords. You can use the Keyword List Filter to find all instances of a keyword without having to dive through the hierarchy. It's useful to find all instances of a keyword. It's also useful if you forgot where you put the keyword inside the hierarchy. If you can't remember if *Halloween* is inside *Events* or *Personal Work*, you can simply search for the keyword *Halloween*.

- You can filter down to any keyword by typing in the Filter Keywords box.
- When you filter, you will see the entire keyword hierarchy that is above the filtered term.
- You can also show all child keywords by clicking the dropdown option Show All Keywords Inside Matches.

The video below shows how all of these functions work.

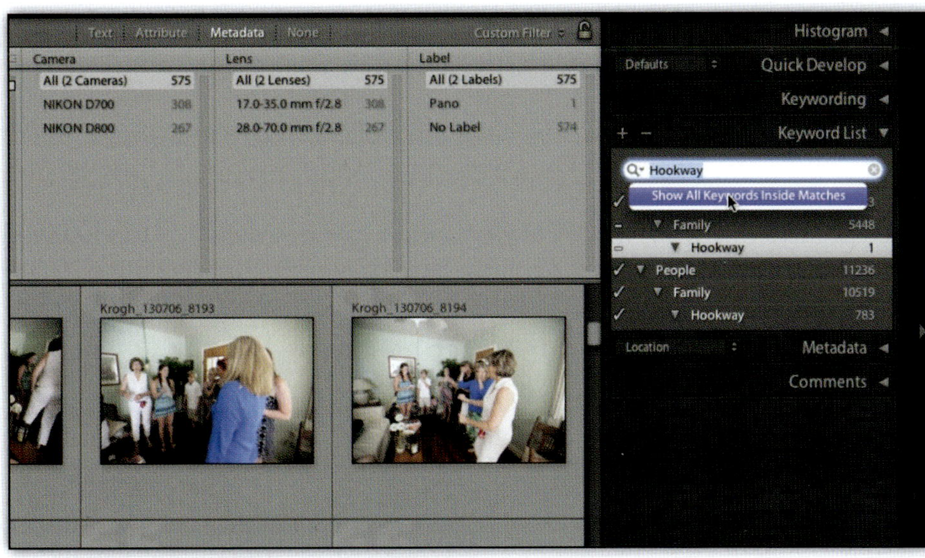

VIDEO 5-9 KEYWORD LIST FILTER (2:07)
This video shows how the Keyword List Filter works.

THE KEYWORDING PANEL

The Keywording panel allows you to add keywords and to see what keywords are assigned to any selected images. In my normal workflow, I generally use it to see what keywords have been assigned to an image.

Typically, I find that it's much quicker and easier to use the Keyword List than to add them in the Keywording panel, so I typically don't do much keywording here. But some people really like it.

The Keywording panel pulldown

In the top part of the panel, you can set the pulldown to one of three settings.

Enter Keywords: When it is set to *Enter Keywords*, you can see what keywords are assigned to the selected images.

- You can type new keywords into the box, and you can remove keywords from selected images here.
- Any keywords with an asterisk are only assigned to some of the selected images.
- Keywords without an asterisk are assigned to all selected images.

Keywords and Containing Keywords: If you set the pulldown to *Keywords and Containing Keywords*, the panel will show you what keywords have been assigned, but you can't edit them.

Will Export: If you set the pulldown to *Will Export*, you'll get a preview of the keywords as they will appear in any exported files. This will exclude any keywords that are not set to *Include on Export* and it will include any Synonyms. (Both of these are covered later in this chapter.)

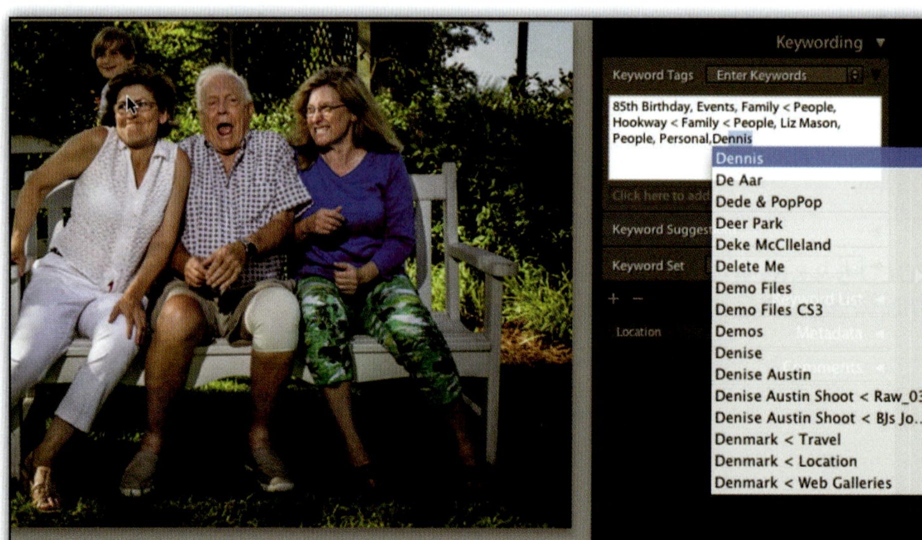

VIDEO 5-10 KEYWORD PANEL (3:09)

This video shows how the top part of the Keywording panel works.

Keyword Suggestions and Keyword Sets

The Keywording panel also has some other ways to assign keywords. The Keyword Suggestions and Keyword Sets allow you to push buttons or tap numbers to assign keywords to selected images. And the Keyword Sets tool allows you to make a group of keywords to populate the buttons with.

While I don't use these tools much, some people do. I'll show you one example that is frequently used by Wedding Photographers.

The video below shows how the lower part of the Keywording panel work

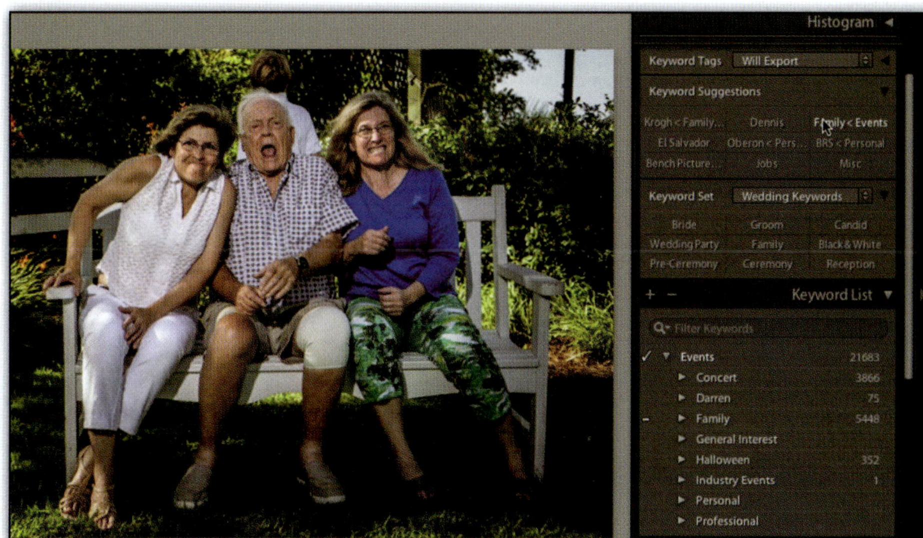

VIDEO 5-11 KEYWORD SUGGESTIONS AND SETS (2:44)
This video shows how the Keyword Suggestions and Keyword Sets function.

FINDING IMAGES WITHOUT KEYWORDS

One of the sample Smart Collections that comes with Lightroom can help you find images with no keywords. The Smart Collection is called ***Without Keywords***. If you double-click on it, you will see the criteria *Keywords > are empty*. This filters down to any images that have no keywords.

You can use this Smart Collection to keep track of any images that still need keywords.

The video below shows how this works.

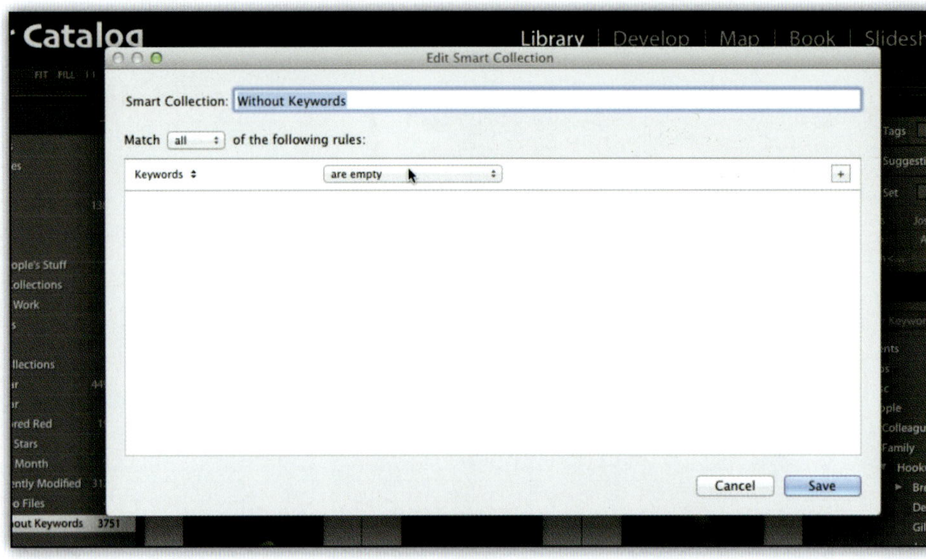

VIDEO 5-12 FINDING PHOTOS WITH NO KEYWORDS (1:31)
This video shows how to find images that don't have keywords.

DIGGING DEEPER

Advanced keyword settings

In most cases, the keyword strategies outlined above will serve all your keywording needs. There are a few advanced settings that will be useful to people with more specialized needs.

Private keywords

Any keywords you attach to an image may be embedded in the file when you export a derivative file, such as a JPEG file for email. It's possible to tell Lightroom to remove certain keywords from the exported version. You might do this because you don't want people to see the keyword, like the name of a model. You also might want to mark a keyword as private because it is a top-level keyword like ***Subject***, that has no real meaning and is only used to organize your other keywords.

You make a keyword private by unchecking the *Include on Export* checkbox in the *Create Keyword Tag* dialog or the *Edit Keyword Tag* dialog. You can confirm what keywords will export by looking in the Keywording panel and setting the pulldown to *Will Export*.

Using Synonyms for searchability

Sometimes it's hard to determine exactly which word you want to use as a keyword. If you shoot pictures of a friend before she is married as well as afterwards, you may have trouble deciding which name to use. And people tagging animals by species may want to search for a common name or the Latin name. In these cases, you should consider using synonyms.

A synonym is a hidden keyword that is assigned alongside a visible keyword. So ***Mary Beth Ralston*** could be a synonym for ***Mary Beth Bankson***. You won't see the synonym keyword in your Keyword List, but it will show up on search. You can also choose to tell Lightroom to make the synonym a "regular" keyword when it exports the file. This can make the keyword available in other programs.

Synonyms are frequently used in the stock photo business. The keyword ***Cow*** may have the synonym ***Cows***, ***Farm Animal***, ***Dairy***, ***Cattle***, ***Bovine***, etc. The keyword lists that contain these synonyms are often considered proprietary secrets because they provide the "intelligence" in a stock photography collection.

The following video shows how private keywords and Synonyms work.

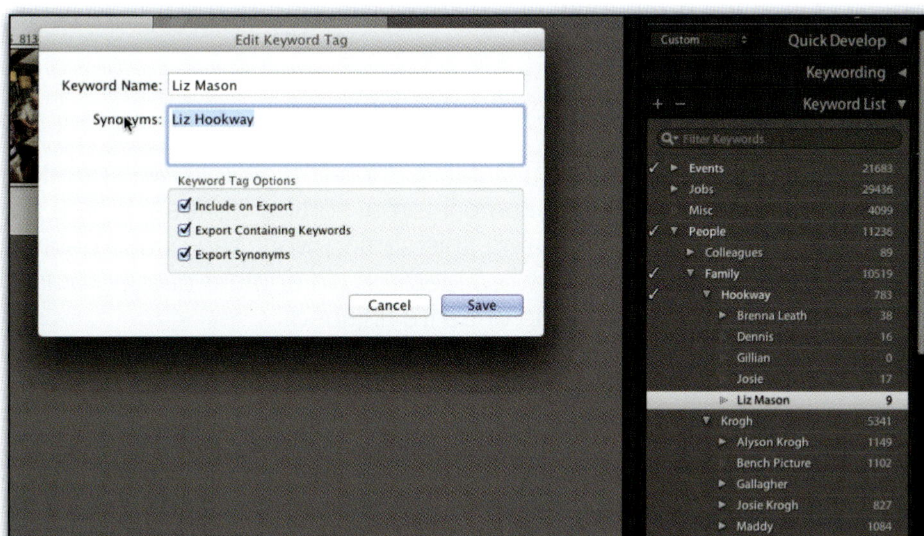

VIDEO 5-13 ORGANIZING EXISTING KEYWORDS (6:17)

This video shows how to set keywords to not export and how to review an image before to see what keywords will export.

DIGGING DEEPER

Keyword text lists

Lightroom allows you to both export and import a list of keywords from a text file. This is useful if you want to make use of a controlled vocabulary list as shown in the next section. It can also be useful if you want to use the same keywords in two catalogs. And finally, it can be used to speed up the creation of a new Keyword List in a large catalog.

You export a Keyword List by choosing *Export Keywords...* in the Metadata menu of the Library module. This creates a text file that can be edited by a program like TextEdit on Mac and Notepad on Windows. In the list, you can see keyword hierarchy, synonyms and keywords that have *Include on Export* checked. The following illustration shows the relationship between four sample keywords: ***Parent***, ***Child 1***, ***Child 1 Synonym***, and ***Grandchild***.

```
[Parent]
	Child 1
		{Child 1 Synonym}
		Grandchild
```

- Square brackets like those around [Parent] indicate a keyword that will not export.
- The tab inset indicates a child keyword, so ***Child 1*** is a child keyword of ***Parent***.
- The curly brackets indicate a synonym of the keyword it is underneath. So {Child 1 Synonym} is a synonym of the keyword ***Child 1***.

You can edit the text list and then import it back into Lightroom.

If you have a lot of images in your Lightroom Catalog, then it can be slow to create a lot of new keywords. This is because Lightroom does some internal sorting work each time a keyword is made. If there are a lot of images in the catalog, this sorting work can cause delays. In these cases, it may be easier to create a new keyword hierarchy in another catalog or in a text editor and then import it back into the main catalog once it's finished.

DIGGING DEEPER

Using keyword vocabularies

You can import comprehensive lists of keywords into your Lightroom catalog. These lists are called Vocabularies or Controlled Vocabularies. They provide a whole system of classification that is ready-made.

Most non-professional users, and many professional users simply don't need these. They will include thousands of keywords, most of which are unlikely to be relevant to any one person's Photo Library.

There **are** some instances where Keyword Vocabularies can be really helpful. In the video below, I show how a Keyword Vocabulary of bird names can be shared and imported, saving a lot of work. And if you are a stock photographer, one of these lists may be valuable. If you are making your photos available on a tool like Flickr or PhotoShelter that does not have its own list, one of these lists can get you started. If your stock photo distributor requires that you use their Controlled Vocabulary, then a third-party list may not help you much.

The video below shows how you can do that.

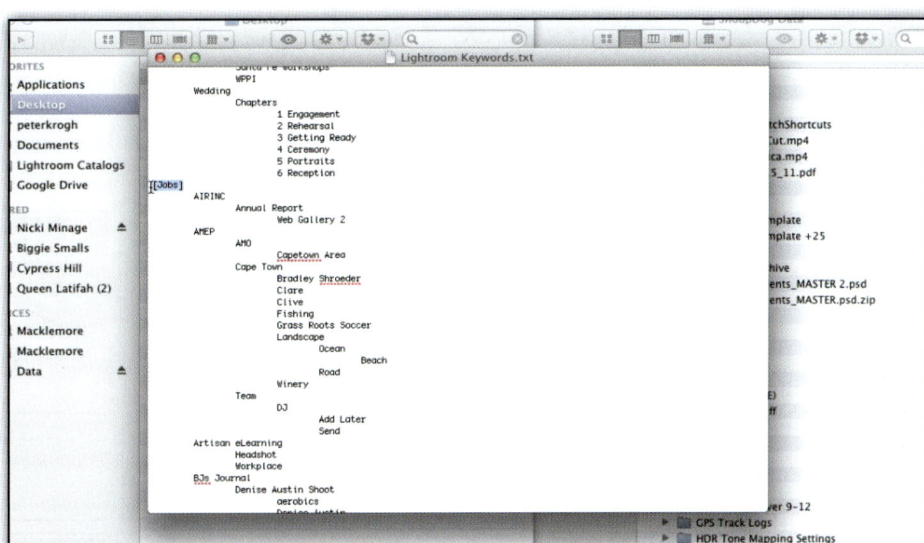

VIDEO 5-14 KEYWORD TEXT LISTS (5:04)

This video shows how to work with Keyword Text Lists, including Controlled Vocabularies.

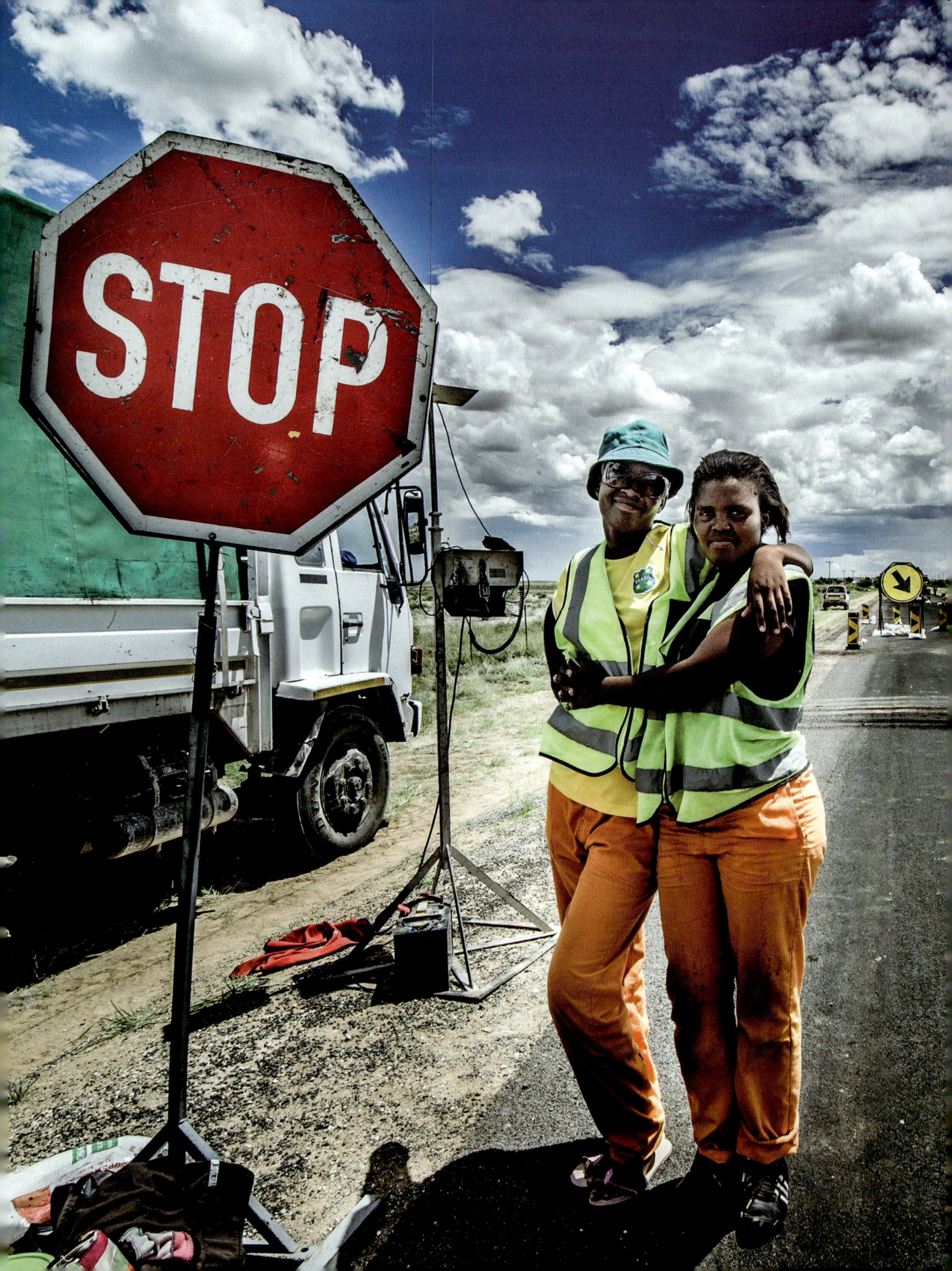
STOP

CHAPTER 6

METADATA PRESETS

In many parts of Lightroom you can create presets that help you to save time. The Metadata Presets are one of the most useful examples of this. You can create saved sets of tags that can be applied to many images simultaneously.

Metadata Presets are helpful for tagging your images with your identity, copyright and contact information. And they are particularly helpful for tagging images with recurring subject matter such as location or keyword tags.

You can apply Metadata Presets as part of the Import process, and you can apply them to images that are already in your catalog. They can save lots of time and help you keep your collection in order.

Let's get started.

YOU MIGHT BE WONDERING....

What's the difference between presets and templates?

I use the terms *Preset* and *Template* interchangeably, because they mean the same thing. Many programs, including Photoshop and Bridge use the term *Templates* to describe a group of saved settings that can be reused. Lightroom has opted for the term *Presets*.

METADATA PRESET BASICS

You can create and apply Metadata Presets in three different places. You'll find them in the Metadata panel on the right-hand side of the Library module. And you'll also find them in the Apply During Import panel of the Import module as well as the right-hand panel of the Map module. Each of these places refers to the same set of stored presets.

You can create a Metadata Preset by choosing the *Edit Presets* item from the Metadata Preset pulldown menu. In the Import module, you also have an option to create a new preset.

You apply a preset by selecting one or more photos and choosing a preset from the pulldown list. When you do this, all the tags in the preset are applied to the images.

For tags that can only have one entry (such as Creator), applying a preset will replace existing tags with any that are included in the preset. Some tags can support multiple entries (such as keywords). When you apply a preset that has keywords, it will add to any existing keyword tags without erasing them.

I suggest that you create presets for each photographer that is included in your catalog, and for locations that you shoot at repeatedly, and for other repeating subject matter.

The video below provides an overview of the process.

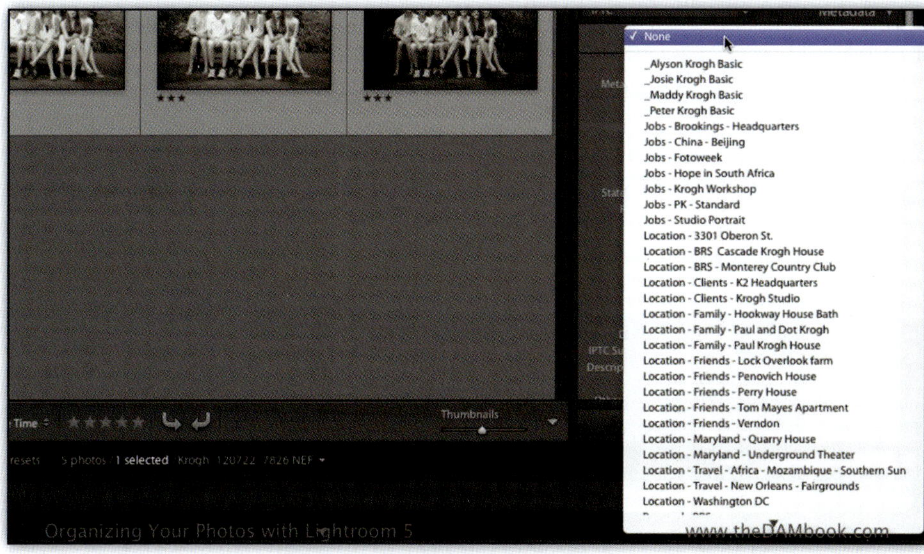

VIDEO 6-1 METADATA PRESETS (2:59)
In this video, we see the basic functions of the Metadata Presets.

PRESET STRATEGY

I have found it really helpful to make several different kinds of Metadata Presets and to name them according to type. Sometimes you will want to keep these templates around indefinitely. Sometimes you'll only need them for a short time. You can clean them out periodically to keep the list from getting too long.

Types of presets

Here are some of the types of presets I make.

Photographer: I make a preset for the photographers in my catalog. For me, that means each of my family members, and sometimes an assistant who is helping me shoot. These presets only include information about the photographer and no more.

Clients: I make presets for my repeat clients. These include my photographer information, the name of the client as a keyword tag, and a statement of rights if I have a standard agreement in place.

Jobs: When I have a job that will require repeated downloads, I can make a preset for that assignment. This includes all the information described in the *Clients* preset above, along with location information and a tag or two that will identify the assignment.

Personal: I make these presets for ongoing personal subjects. The ones I use the most are created for photographs shot in my own home, and in other places I frequently go, such as close friends' houses. These presets include my photographer information, some location tags and a handful of appropriate keywords.

Location: I make presets that include location information only. I make these for places I visit repeatedly. Some of these are for an entire city, and are helpful for my *Miscellaneous* downloads. Some of these are for very specific locations like my brother's house, and include GPS data as well as location tags.

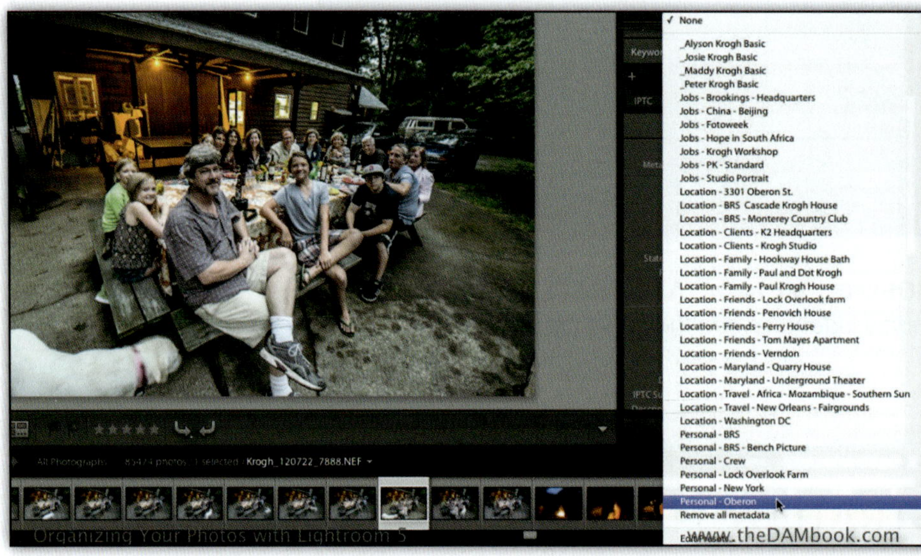

VIDEO 6-2 PRESET TYPES (3:17)
In this video, we look at several types of Metadata Presets to see what information is included.

CREATING CUSTOM PRESETS

Making the presets is easy, but it takes a little attention to detail. For your first one, it's easiest to select an image with no information and then open up the Preset editor.

I suggest first making a preset for you as a photographer. Enter your name, address, contact information, etc. Make sure that there are checkboxes to the right of each field that you fill in, and that there are no checkboxes checked for empty fields. Save it with an appropriate name.

Build on your basic preset

You can use this preset to build any other presets you need (whenever the photographer information is the same). You can select the photographer information preset in the Preset editor and all the tags will appear. Then you can add whatever new tags you want for the next preset and save it with a new descriptive name.

Naming your presets

Whenever you make presets in Lightroom, you'll want to name them in a way that helps you find them easily. I suggest that you start with the most general term and then get specific. This makes them line up together in the pulldown and makes them easy to find.

The terms I use for my presets are *Photographer, Location, Jobs, Clients,* and *Personal*. Each of these words is followed by terms that make it more specific.

Deleting presets

You can delete a preset when you no longer need it for new photos. Deleting the preset will not delete the tags from the photos.

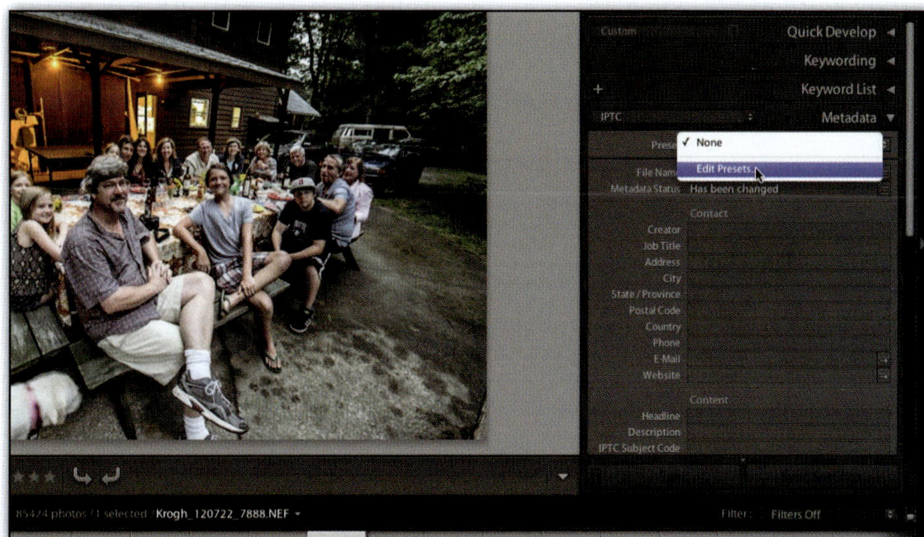

VIDEO 6-3 CREATING PRESETS (6:35)
In this video, we see how to make and name custom presets.

MAKE LOCATION PRESETS

Let's take a look at a specialized type of preset that is used to tag for location information. This is very useful for adding location information to a Photo Library that does not have any yet. Like any presets, this is most useful for repeating tags. If you have only been to a place once, and you don't expect to go back any time soon, you don't need a preset.

You can make location presets that tag for any level of location.

If you don't have many location tags on your images yet and you need to do some catch-up, it may be helpful to make some city-level locations to apply to large numbers of images.

For specific repeating locations, such as your home or the homes of friends and family members, you may want to add GPS location data to the preset. We'll look at location tagging in depth in the next chapter.

In the meantime, you can see how to use location presets in the video below.

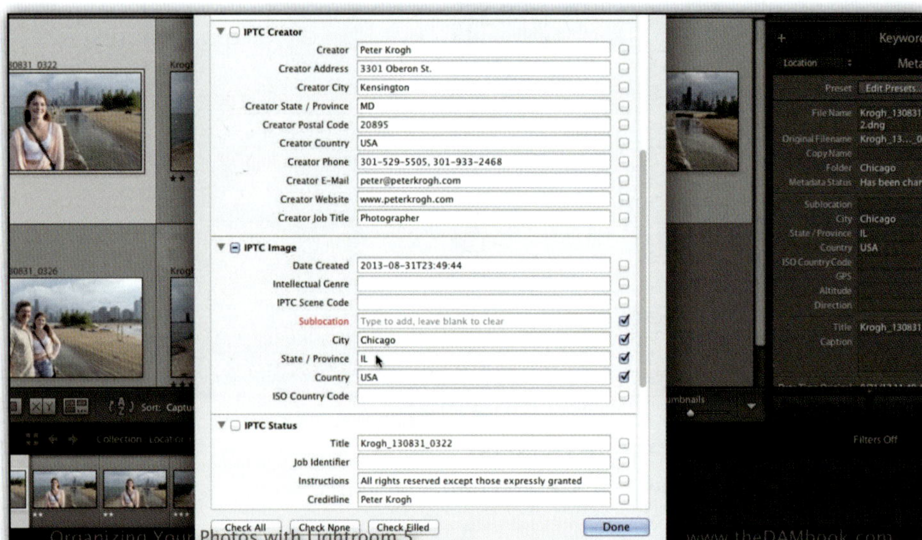

VIDEO 6-4 LOCATION PRESETS (5:51)
In this video, we see how to make and use location presets.

MAKING A PRESET TO REMOVE ALL TAGS

You may want to create a preset that removes all tags from an image. This can be useful if you have files with a lot of junk tags in them, and you just want to start over. It also might be useful if you want to get rid of some information for reasons of privacy.

To make a preset to remove all tags, you'll want to create a new preset and make sure that each box in the preset is empty, and that the checkbox on the right-hand side of each line is checked. This preset, when applied, will set every field to be empty. The video below shows it in action.

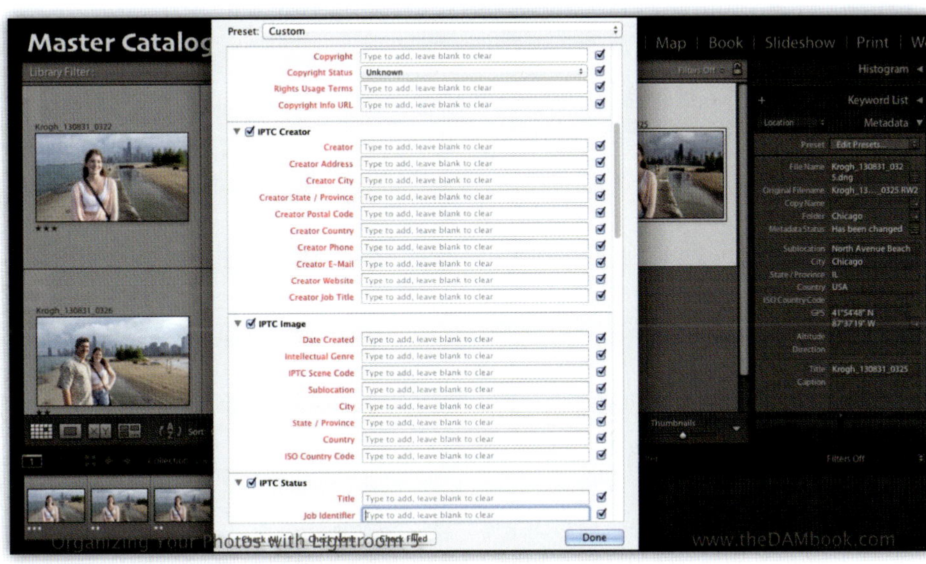

VIDEO 6-5 REMOVE ALL TAGS (2:12)
You can make a preset to remove all tags from a photo.

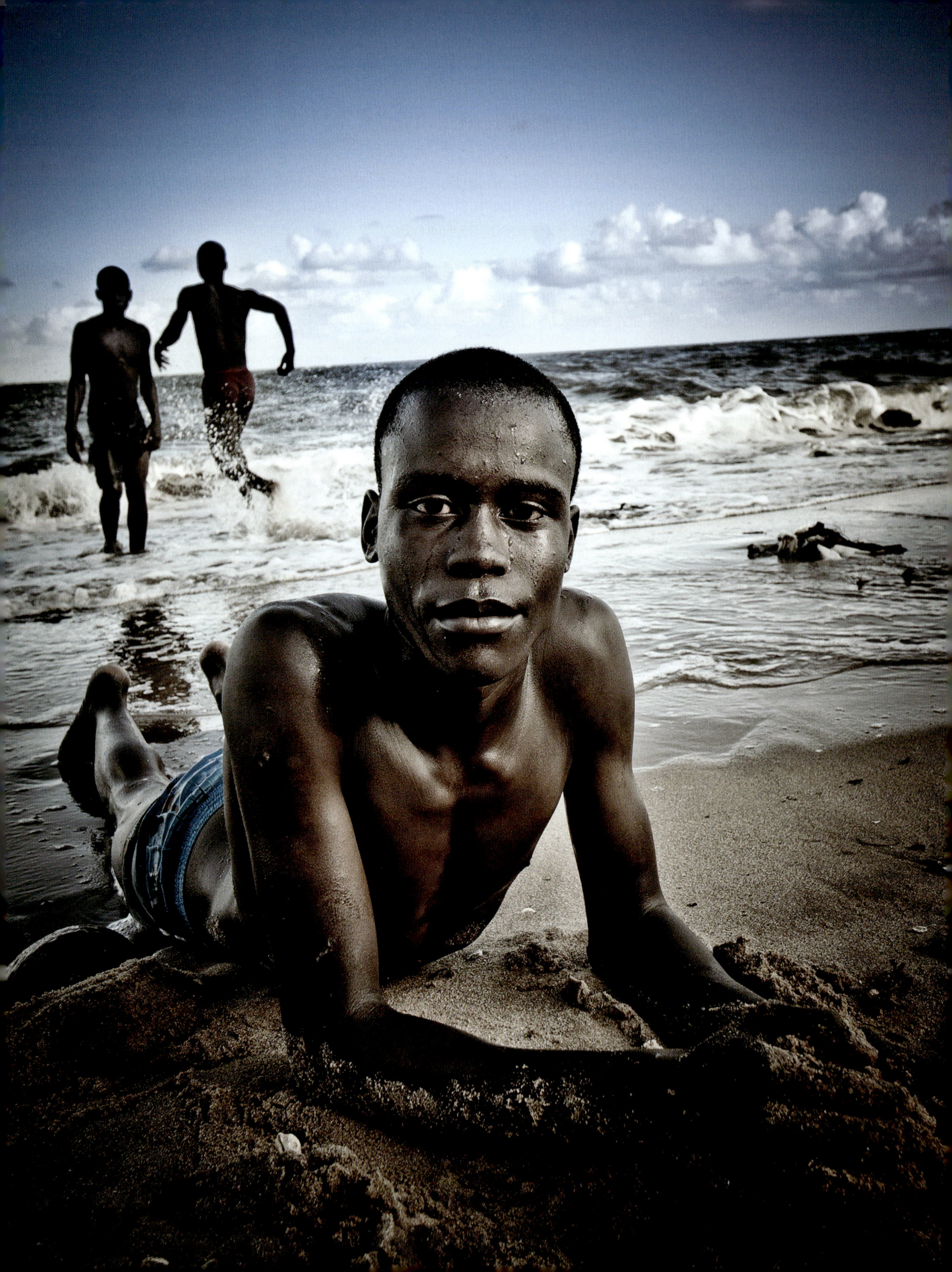

CHAPTER 7

LOCATION TAGS

Most photographers I know have a strong memory link between photos and the location they were taken. If I remember anything about an image, it probably includes the place where it was shot. I have many 40 year-old images in which I've forgotten some of the people's names, but I remember the location.

This strong link between photo and place creates a high value for location tags. A good set of location tags allows most photographers to find pictures quickly and comprehensively.

Location tags are some of the easiest tags to understand. They come in a natural hierarchy that is pretty clear: Country, State/Province, City and Location. They are generally easy to determine, at least for your own use. And, in most cases, you can add the same set of location tags to many images at once.

When your Photo Library is properly tagged, location tags are really easy to navigate. Are you looking for photos from Africa, from San Francisco, or from Mom and Dad's house in Bethesda, Maryland? Filter for the right tag, and the photos show up.

The video below shows how useful location tags are when you want to find some particular images.

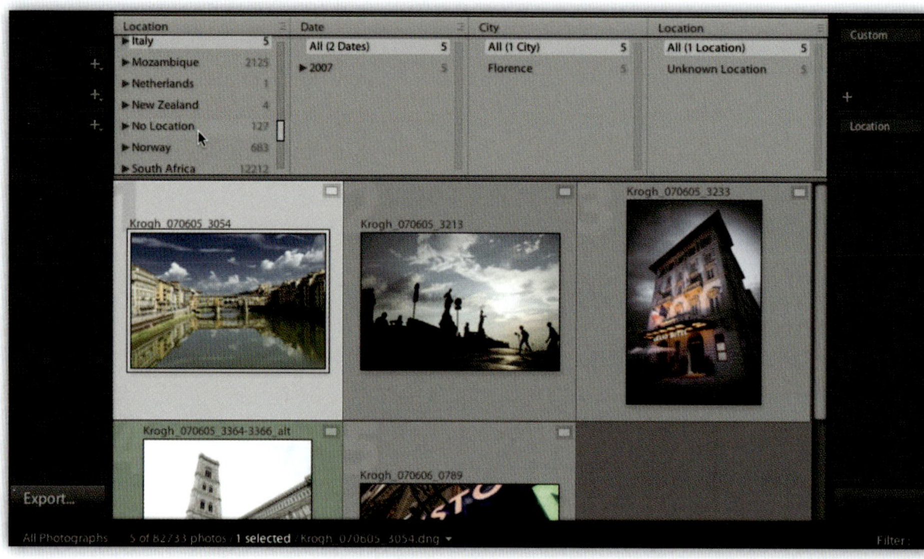

VIDEO 7-1 LOCATION OVERVIEW (3:20)
In this video, we see how location tags make it easy to find photos according to where they were taken.

PRIVACY ISSUES

You may want to be careful about embedding location tags in photos, particularly for files that are exported to the web or somehow transferred to other people. Let's talk about that a little bit.

The location tags may pinpoint exactly where a photo was taken. Tracking your own location for your own use is probably acceptable to most people. However you, or the people you photograph, may not want to announce to the world where a photo was taken.

There are lots of reasons for this. There might be security issues. Additionally, people are sensitive about publishing information concerning minors. And some people just don't want to announce their locations to the world.

If you want to be really secure, you could erase all location information from your Lightroom catalog. (You probably ought to pay some attention to your phone as well, in this case.) A more modest solution may be to keep Lightroom from writing the location tags to any exported files. This will keep the data inside the catalog.

Lightroom is set up to remove the location tags from exported files unless you tell it to include them. You can find this in the Metadata panel of the Export dialog. The video below shows how this works.

Wiping out all location tags

If you really want the location information to be erased, you can remove the tags entirely. There are two way to do this in Lightroom. If you want to do this just once, then it is probably easiest to select the file, open the Metadata panel, and clear each field.

If you will want to do this repeatedly, then it's best to make a Metadata Preset for that purpose. Create a new Metadata Preset as described in the previous chapter and make sure the location tags are blank. Make sure that the checkbox to the right of each field is checked and save the preset as *Location Cleaner* or some other descriptive name. When you apply this to a file, it will replace any existing location tags with the new ones with blank fields.

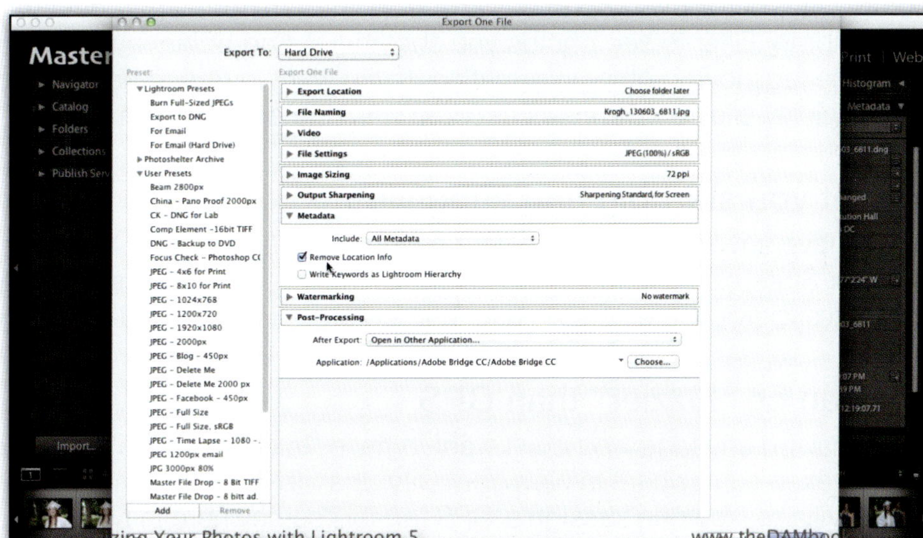

VIDEO 7-2 REMOVING LOCATION TAGS (3:01)

In this video, we see how to include or exclude location information from exported files.

MAP TAG OR LOCATION NAME TAG?

Lightroom offers two main types of location tags: place names and the map coordinates. (Let's call the place names location tags, and call the map coordinates GPS tags.) Each one has its value, but I strongly favor location tags as being the most useful for most people, given current tagging technology. There are several reasons for this.

Location tags can always be seen in the Library

The location tags support a hierarchy that Saved Places do not. In order to use the GPS tags, you'll frequently need to switch over to the Map module. This is a real pain when you are doing some kind of organizational or filtering work.

The location tags can be used in the Library Filter bar.

This gives you easy access to the tags while you are working with your collection. The Library Filter bar also lets you see which location tags are in your collection. When you get as old as I am, you'll probably have a hard time remembering everywhere you've been without a little prompting.

Being in the Library Filter bar allows you to easily see all images from a particular place. Click on *Denmark* in the Library Filter to see photos you shot there. And being in the Library Filter bar lets you use these tags to find other information. If you want to remember when you went to Denmark, you can quickly click on *Denmark* and see what the date column shows.

Location tags let you start big and subdivide

If you don't already have any location tags in your collection, then you'll probably want to start by tagging for City or State. You can make a quick pass through the images dividing them into big groups, and then subdivide later. This is a lot harder to do with the GPS tags.

Location tags can be "fuzzier" than GPS

Whenever you are making any tags, you don't want to have "false precision". It's much better to say "this photo was taken somewhere in New York City" than to specify Central Park when it was actually Greenwich Village. You can't assign a GPS tag for "somewhere in New York City". You must set a GPS tag to "this exact place in New York City".

Lightroom does have a way to find by region. But the GPS tag that is applied to the file is always assigned to a specific point.

This makes GPS harder to get started with, unless your camera tags GPS automatically.

It's easier to create workflows from location tags than GPS

In the end, due to Lightroom's design, I find that it is much easier to make a fast and useful workflow from the location tags than from the GPS tags. It's quicker and easier to make the tags, and it's quicker and easier to use the tags to filter with.

So what are GPS tags good for?

Let's start by saying that GPS tags that are made correctly by smartphones and GPS-equipped cameras are awesome. As long as they are accurate, they can take a lot of work out of tag creation. In a few years, this should be pretty commonplace on most new cameras, but at the moment, it's rare for cameras.

In general, accuracy works out like this.

- Smartphones are usually very accurate. They use GPS chips, WiFi signals and cell towers for positioning.
- Cameras equipped with WIFi and GPS are also usually very accurate.
- GPS-only cameras are good in the natural environment, but they have real problems indoors or around tall buildings. They may be wildly inaccurate or lose the signal entirely.

GPS tags are particularly valuable in situations where place names are too general. This includes undeveloped land like national parks. The place name may be limited to *Tasman National Forest*, but the GPS tag can show you the exact spot you stood to shoot the photo.

Reverse Geocoding

GPS tags can be used by Lightroom to find place names. This is called Reverse Geocoding in Lightroom. I have found these place names to be very accurate for Country, State and City. The location name is **sometimes** correct. If I'm at a landmark like the US Capitol, it will be correct. But there's no way for the GPS database to know that I want to tag a particular map location as "Rod Glover's Apartment".

BY THE WAY

Reverse Geocoding is not fully implemented

I hate it when I have to outline stuff like this, but here goes. When you first see Reverse Geocoding, it's wonderful. Your phone images, for instance, may come in and all show up on the map and have location tags that you can see in the Library Filter bar. Hooray! It would be wonderful to use these phone photos to help tag the rest of your big camera photos. Alas, Lightroom does not let you close the circle. You'll notice that these tags are greyed out in the Metadata panel. And you'll also see that if you try to make a Metadata Preset from them, they will be omitted. Bummer.

You can make them permanent one line at a time. But you'll soon find that this is a nearly-impossible workflow. I expect that Adobe will fix this before too long. So, for now, it's best to just leave them alone.

The video below shows the problem.

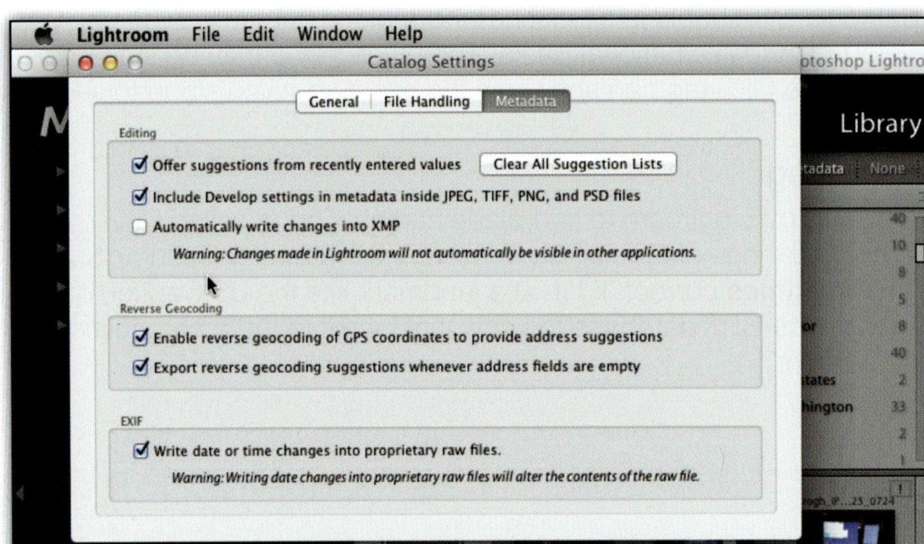

VIDEO 7-3 REVERSE GEOCODING (6:44)

In this video, we see how Reverse Geocoding can add place names to your images automatically, but we also see here that the implementation in Lightroom is not ideal yet.

ADDING PLACE NAMES

There are two basic ways to create place names. You can select files and type directly into the Metadata panel, and you can apply Metadata Presets. Direct entry is okay when you only need to add the place information once. The preset method is good for repeated entry of the same information. The preset method also allows you to apply GPS tags at the same time you make location tags.

We'll look at these a bit more closely in a moment.

How precise do you need to get?

As you think about your tagging strategy, it's good to give a bit of thought to the amount of precision you need. In general, you'll want to be more precise for locations where you shoot a lot of photographs.

If you only visit a particular university campus once in your life, then the name of the university is probably a fine location tag. But if you are a student at the university, you might want to tag each building. Of course, using the Start Big and Subdivide technique, you can alway start with a tag for the university, and then add building tags as time allows.

Your desire for precision will also depend on personal preference. Some people really like their tags to be as precise as is humanly possible. Know thyself, and act accordingly.

Adding place names with direct entry in the Metadata panel

In order to add location tags with the Metadata panel, you need to select the files to tag and then open the panel. It may be easier if you set the Metadata pulldown menu to Location, since this will hide the other fields we're not worried about at the moment.

Make sure that you uncheck *Show Metadata for Target Photo Only* in the *Library>Metadata* menu, otherwise you'll only be tagging one photo at a time.

You can start typing into one of the fields. If you start at the top with Sublocation, you can simply tab to the next field. You'll want to wait for Lightroom to finish updating the metadata for the field you just finished before you start typing again. Once you have filled out any fields you want to, you can select more images and keep moving.

***Warning:**

Be careful to wait until Lightroom has updated your typing before beginning to type in the next field. If Lightroom has not finished updating, then you might start executing keyboard commands. Yikes! This is especially true if you have a lot of files selected.

Adding place names with Metadata Presets

We saw how to make Metadata Presets in the last chapter. You choose *Edit* in the Presets pulldown and fill in the tags you want to apply. Make sure that you only check the fields you want to include. Save the preset with a descriptive name. I like to put the term ***Location*** at the start of all my location Metadata Presets.

To apply, select some files and choose the preset from the pulldown.

The video below shows how to tag in each of these ways.

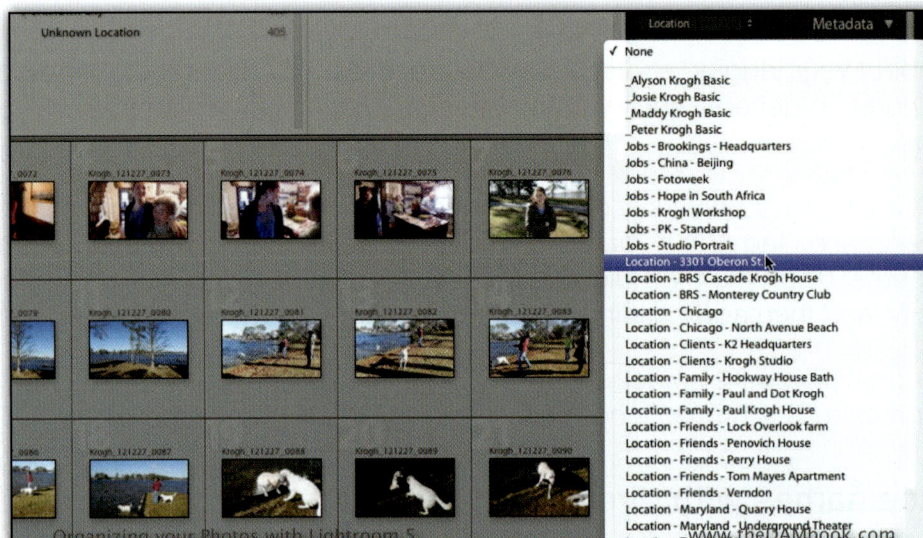

FIGURE 7-4 TAGGING IMAGES (5:50)

In this video, we see how to apply location tags with a preset in the Metadata panel.

ADDING LOCATION TAG NAMES TO A LARGE COLLECTION

If you have a large Photo Library that is not tagged with locations, it can be difficult to get started. Tagging a handful of images at a time can be a really tedious chore. Let's use some of the tools we learned about in the Keywords chapter to get things started.

It's easier to assign keywords than any other kind of tags. So we'll begin by making a keywords hierarchy to assign location information. Once we've made a good pass through the Photo Library, we can make the location tags match the keywords. This may be a little time-consuming at first, but it's definitely worthwhile to use location tags instead of keywords. It will pay off in the long term.

Make a keyword hierarchy for Places in your Photo Library

We start this process by building a keyword hierarchy for the places that our photographs were taken. Build this out as Country/State/City/Location inside a keyword called *Places*. Most people will only need to build down to the City level for most locations. For important locations, you will want to build out the full hierarchy.

You can then start adding your photos to the location keywords you've created. Set your Library to Grid View and make sure to sort by Capture Time. Drag the images to each *Place* keyword. You need to strike a balance between being really precise and getting things done quickly.

Keep in mind that you can always subdivide the photos further at any point. For most people, that will probably be easiest to do with the location tags than with keywords because the Library Filter bar shows you exactly which tags are still blank.

I suggest you start by spending a half hour or so on the process, and see how many you can get done. If you feel good about your progress and it seems reasonable to continue at this rate, keep moving. If it feels like you're never going to be finished, then you might want to start by assigning to a higher level: City instead of Location, State instead of City. Remember, we can always subdivide later.

TRICK

Keeping track of what files have the place keywords

We can use a Smart Collection to keep track of the images that have been added to the place keywords. Make a new Smart Collection and set the Criteria to *Keywords > doesn't contain > Places*. All images will disappear from this Smart Collection as you assign them to one of the places that lives inside the hierarchy. This allow you to spend time on the biggest groups of photos first, which provides the maximum value. Only untagged images will remain in the Smart Collection.

Transferring the place keywords to location tags

Once you have gotten the bulk of your collection tagged with the place keywords, you can transfer that information to location tags. It's probably easiest to use the Direct Entry method. Just make sure that you let the metadata update after you hit tab or enter. Unless you have more than a few hundred place names, this process should not take too long.

Finish the tagging with the location tags and Metadata Presets

Once you have assigned the location tags to the keyworded photos, you should do your future tagging with the location tags. You can do this with direct entry into the Metadata panel, or you could use Metadata Presets.

You can find any photos without a location tag assigned by looking in the Library Filter bar for *Unknown* __________. You can select the images and add the missing tags.

The following video shows the entire process.

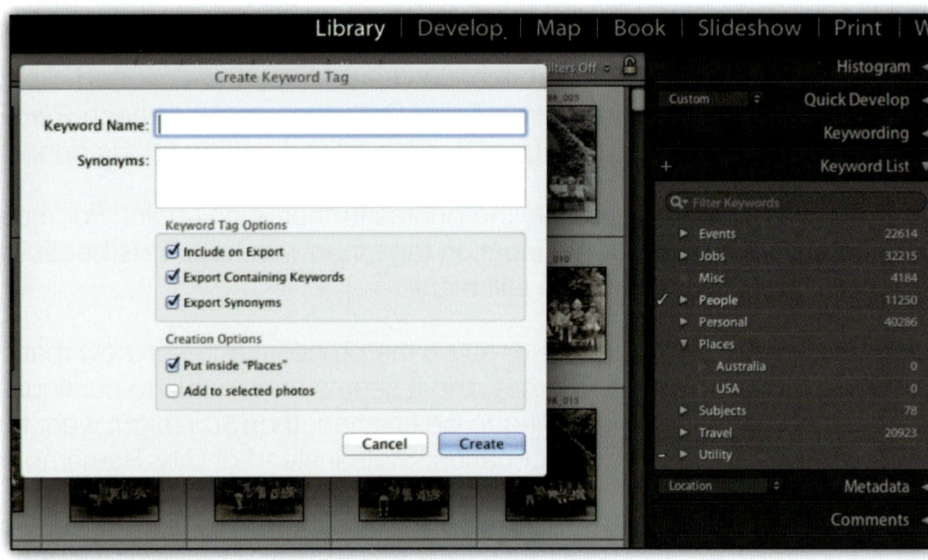

VIDEO 7-5 TAGGING A LARGE COLLECTION (8:03)
In this video, we get some tips for making location tags for a large untagged Photo Library.

DIGGING DEEPER

Import a keyword list of places if you have a large collection

If your catalog has a lot of images and your computer is slow, it can be a tedious process to make your place keywords. In order to speed this up, you may want to import a keyword list that already has your place names. You can make this in an empty Lightroom catalog or you can create a list in a text editor. These are described in the Keywords chapter.

ADDING GPS TAGS WITH THE MAP MODULE

Now let's take a look at the process for adding the GPS tags with the Map module. Because this feature is not fully developed in my opinion, I won't spend a lot of time describing a workflow. If you want a more complete description of what each button does, as always, I suggest you check out Victoria Bampton's *The Missing FAQ* book.

Find the place and drag the file

To assign a place with Map module, you need to have your files showing in the Filmstrip and then find the location on the map. At this point, you can select the images and drop them on the map location. A tag icon will appear on the map where you drop it.

I typically only want to do this for images that are from a specific location I can find on the map, as opposed to images from somewhere in a city. This makes the process pretty time consuming, particularly because, at this time, the Map search in Lightroom does not work all that well. I'm hoping this gets better in future versions.

Using the Map module

Here are some tips on how the Map module works.

- If you have added more than one file to a coordinate, you will see a number on the tag.
- Click on the tag to review images from that coordinate. If there are more than one, you can click through them.
- Tags are yellow for selected images.
- Tags are orange for images that are not currently selected.
- The tags will merge together as you zoom out.
- You can save a location with a name on the left hand panel, but these Saved Locations do not integrate with the location tags.

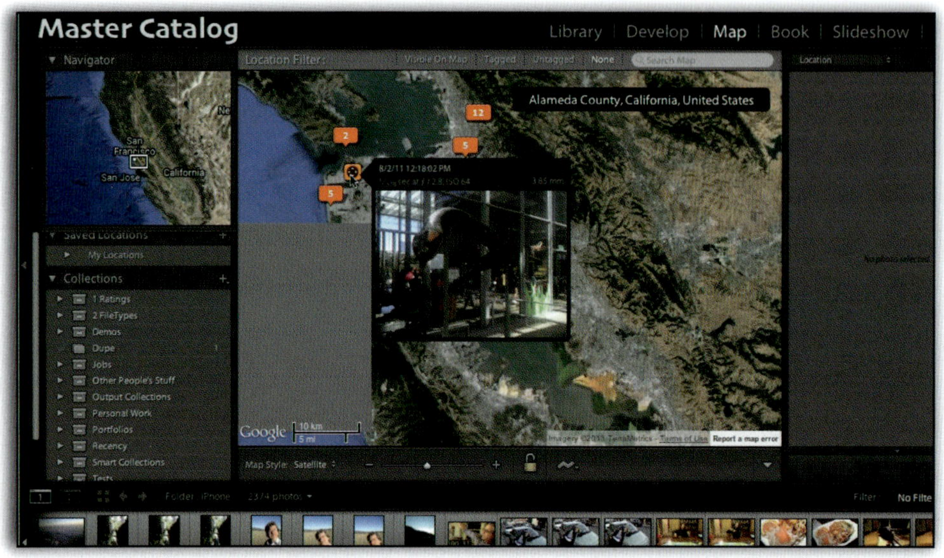

VIDEO 7-6 USING THE MAP MODULE (3:04)

In this video, we see how to add a GPS tag to images in the Map module.

Make and apply presets for your important repeating locations

I think the most valuable first step here is to make presets for the places you visit most often. This is even more valuable if these are places you intend to return to, like your home, your friends' homes and other locations important to you.

Once you have dropped an image on a location, you can use the GPS tags that Lightroom makes to create a location preset.

Add images to Regions

You can also use the Regions tool in the Map module to drop images onto larger areas, such as an entire city. But remember, you will still be tagging them with the point at the center of the circle, which may be right for one and wrong for many more. Fixing this later is a real pain.

So, unless there is some reason you really want to use the maps, I suggest skipping this altogether.

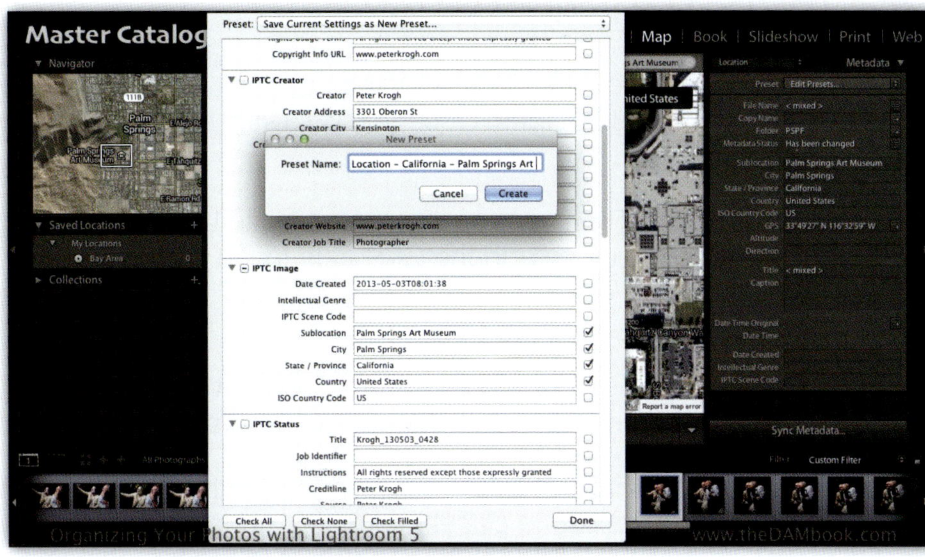

VIDEO 7-7 LOCATION PRESETS (3:44)

In this video, we see how to create a location preset in the Map module.

Here are the steps

1. Select an image that has a location tag you want for the preset.
2. Open up the Metadata panel on the right side of the Map module.
3. Make sure that you are happy with the location tags for Country, State, City and Location. Change them if you need to.
4. If the tags are greyed out, you need to click on the tag name (e.g. City) and it will let you confirm the tag, turning it white.
5. Select *Edit Presets* in the Metadata Preset pulldown menu.
6. Confirm the information you want to include and save the preset with a good name, like *Location — [State] [Location Name]*.

ADDING GPS TAGS WITH A TRACKLOG

There is one way that the Map module can add a lot of tags quickly. If you have kept a tracklog, you can use it to add GPS tags to your images. Once you do a little setup, you can use the tracklog to tag many images at once.

The first step is to create a tracklog. Then you need to import it into Lightroom and match it up with the photos. Once you do that, you can add the GPS data to the pictures.

Creating the tracklog

Unless you are working in the wilderness, it will be probably be best to make your tracklog with your phone. You'll need an application that makes the tracklog and exports it as a GPX file.

After you have imported the photos into Lightroom, you can import the tracklog into Lightroom's Map module. You'll need to set the *Timezone Offset* to correspond to your camera's clock at the time of shooting. Once you've done that, you can tell Lightroom to tag the photos.

If the photos still seem to be off by a bit, you can drag one along the tracklog until it is properly located. All the other images on the tracklog will also be adjusted. If you have enabled reverse geocoding, then these images will also receive their place names, but they will be greyed out until you select them one-at-a-time.

The video below shows this process in action.

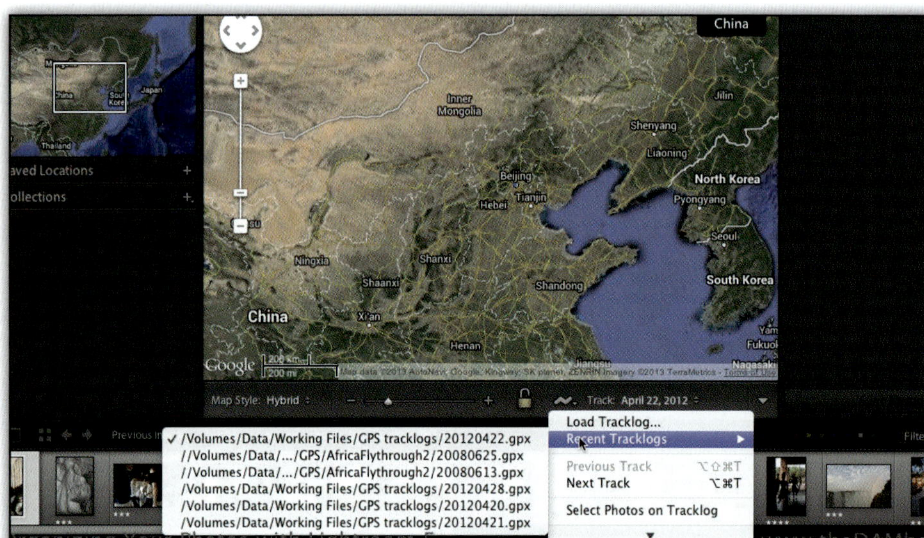

VIDEO 7-8 TRACKLOG MERGE (3:39)
In this video, we see how to use a tracklog to tag a shoot.

DIGGING DEEPER

Using other tools for geotagging

As you can tell, I'm not a huge fan of the Lightroom GPS tagging workflow. If you are serious about geotagging your photos, I suggest you take a look at some third-party tools. Jeffrey Friedl has created a Lightroom plug-in that works better than the built-in tools. And there are a number of tools for Mac and PC that can do the GPS tagging independent of Lightroom.

For more information, check out www.theDAMbook.com/oyp_resources.

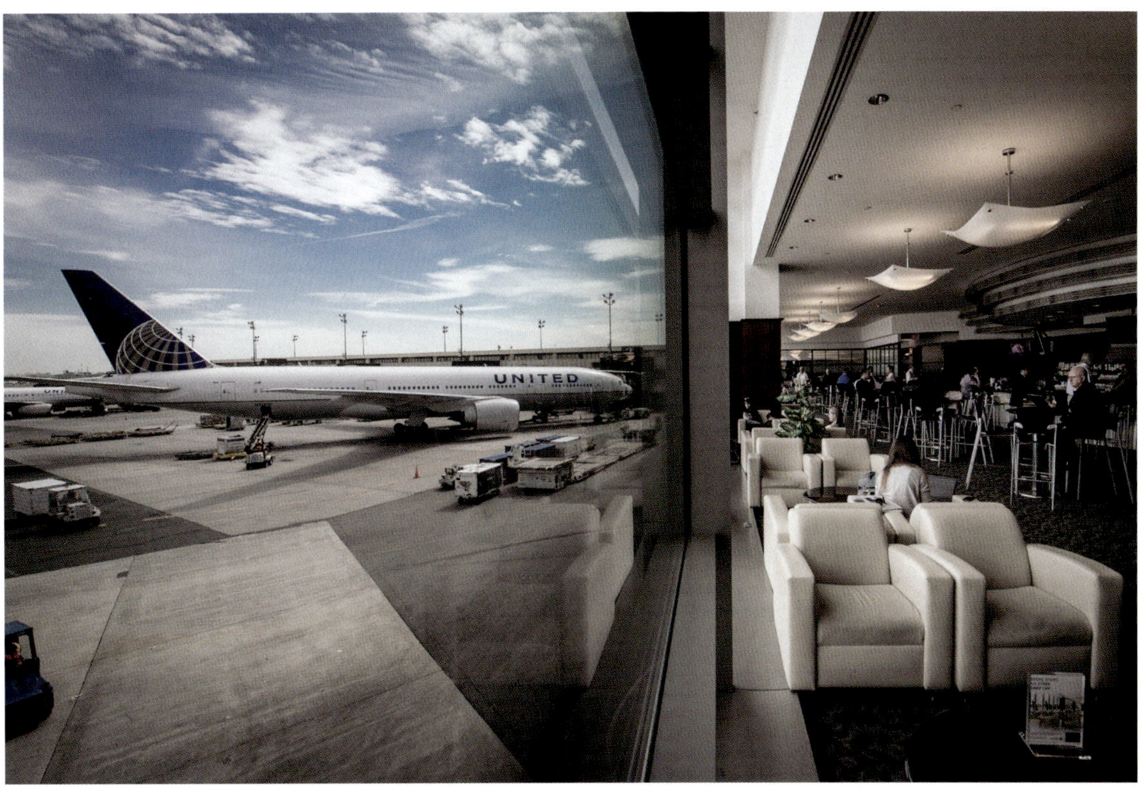

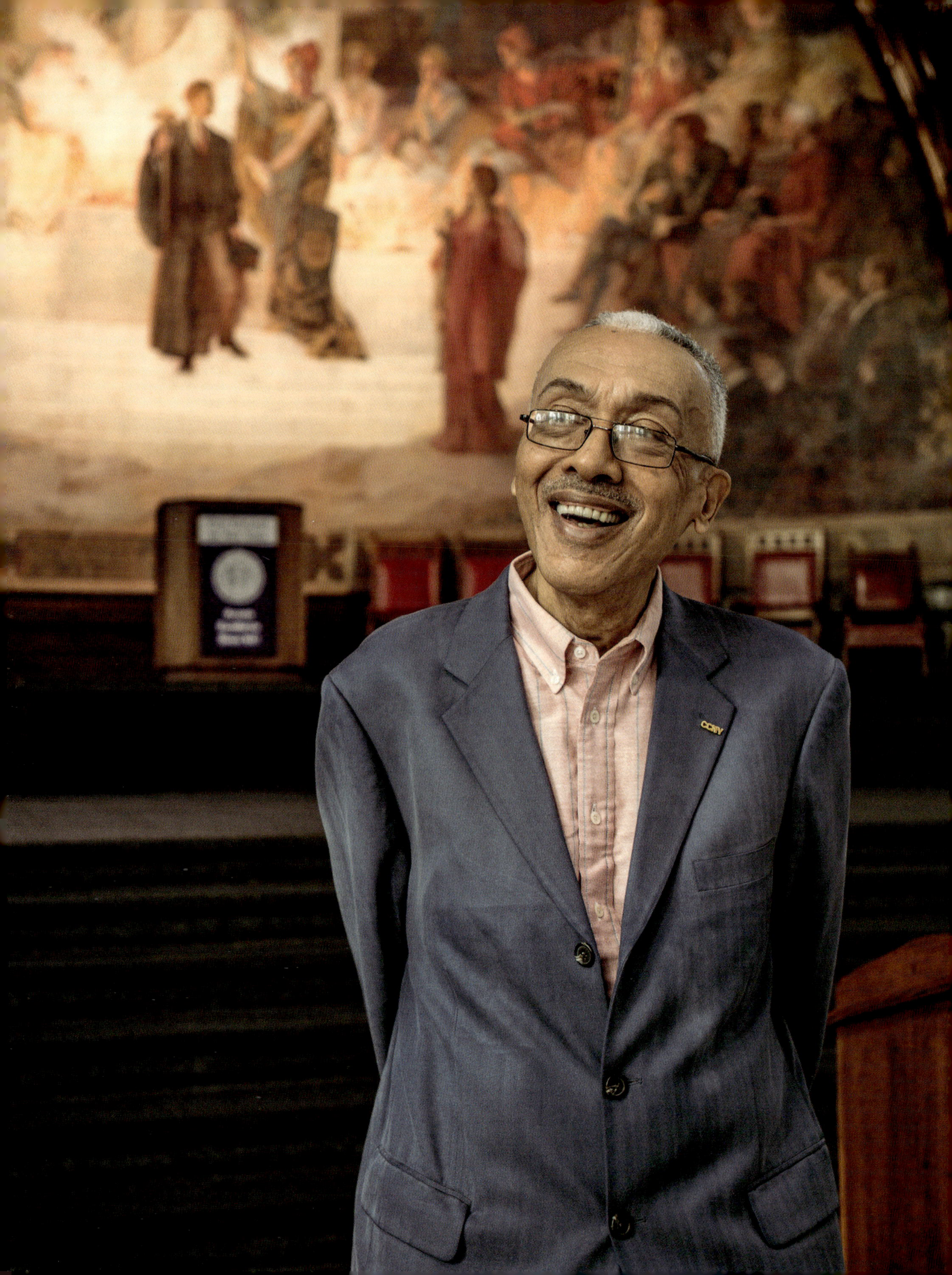
CCNY

CHAPTER 8

COLLECTIONS AND PROJECTS

In the previous four chapters, we explored the use of tags to classify your images and make them easy to find and filter. In the next two chapters, we'll examine how we can build on top of the Storage Layer and the Tagging Layer. In the Project Layer, we will select, prepare and create stuff with our photos.

The Project Layer is where you can actually make something. This could range from a single image you print, to some files for export that tell an event's story, to a book that illustrates a vacation, or a slideshow of your portfolio. In each of these cases, you're making a selection, doing some preparation and then you create something. In many cases, the most important part of this process is the choosing you do. The way you see and tell a story gives it your voice.

The Project Layer will be very straightforward for some tasks, and it may be messy and experimental for others. It may be a simple choice to "export this one photo and email it". Or it may be a complex set of choices, such as "these 100 photos, laid out in this order, with this text and these Develop settings, tell the story of this non-profit organization". These larger projects often require experimentation as you look for the exact selection and sequencing of your photos.

The pinnacle of organization

Projects are the highest value organization you do to a Photo Library. It's where you identify and make use of the best photos in the Library. And it's where you can bring photos together to explore subject matter and create a body of work.

For a fine art or professional photographer, these ongoing efforts might be an assignment or a body of work that spans many years. And the family photographer has the same range of project scope — today's school play or the photographs that document a lifetime. For many, the individual shoot is only a chapter in a larger work of ongoing themes and subjects.

Putting your photos together in projects, whether simple or complex, is one of the greatest joys of photography. And making these projects attainable is one of the greatest advantages of digital photography. Our work here is to build something we like on top of and yet inside of our digital Photo Library.

Lightroom has provided a wonderful set of tools to bring these projects to life, and to always have them at our fingertips. Collections, coupled with the Output modules — Book, Slideshow, Print and Web — allow us to seamlessly create stuff with our photos, and to save, reuse, revise, republish and remix these projects in an unlimited number of ways.

We'll want to put a little order on top of the chaos. I'll show you how to think about Collections as the home of this important project work, and how to keep them organized in a way that helps to lubricate the creative process and also helps you to preserve the work.

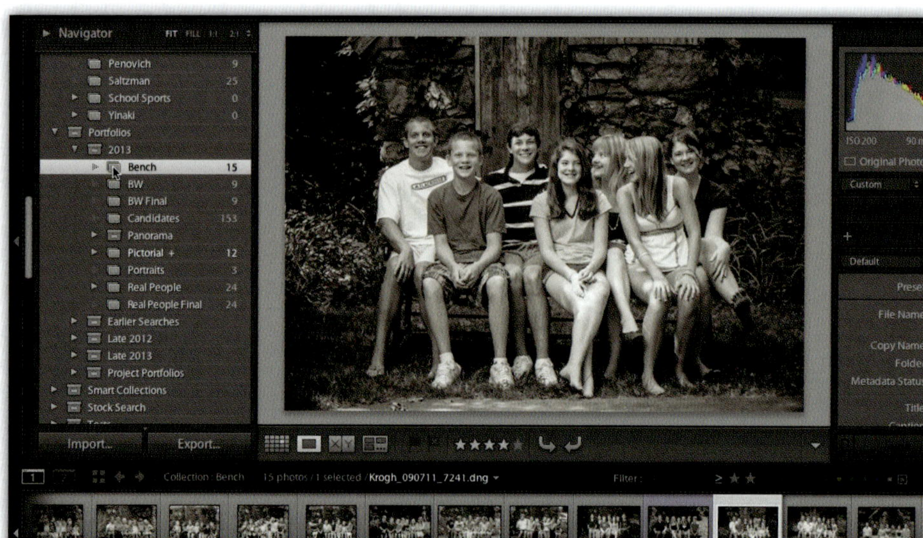

VIDEO 8-1 COLLECTIONS AS PINNACLE (1:30)
In this video, we see how Collections can build on top of the work you do to store and tag your photos.

History repeats itself

For most people, it's worth saving **all** your output choices as Collections. Whether this is a group of files to export, or a slideshow, print, web gallery or book. The images that you have used in the past are more likely to be used in the future.

Every photographer knows the frustration of searching for an image that was used in the past, and yet remains elusive. Was that from three years ago or four? Was it part of this shoot or that one?

Do yourself a favor and put your images into logical, well-named Collections as you work on them, and you'll be able to find them again next time without a lot of wasted effort.

SHOOTS AND PORTFOLIOS

As we talk about the creative work you do with projects, it can be helpful to distinguish between shoots and portfolios.

Let's use the term "shoot" to mean a set of photos from a particular event over a limited time frame. This could be a portrait sitting, a soccer game, or a trip to New York. In many cases, we want to work with shoots as an independent group of photos. You select, optimize and output them.

A portfolio, by contrast, is a group of photos that is brought together from multiple shoots to tell a larger story. It expresses an idea or tells a story or showcases a technique. This might be a commercial portfolio like *My Architectural Photography* or it might be a personal one like *Swim Team 2013*.

The way we use Collections for shoots and portfolios will usually be different from each other. This is because portfolios tend to draw from more sources, and require some kind of storytelling sequencing. They also may need more levels of refinement along the way.

COLLECTIONS ARE THE HUB OF YOUR PROJECTS

The design of Collections in Lightroom makes this the ideal place to create and manage projects. Here are the main reasons the Collections panel is the right tool for this:

- Collections are the only Library sources that are visible in all the different modules.
- Collections allow you to gather photos from any source to create a single new source.
- Collections allow for custom sequencing, which is essential for many projects.
- And finally, the Collection panel is the the only place where you can make output settings "sticky" to a group of photos.

Together, these capabilities make Collections the tool of choice for your important project work.

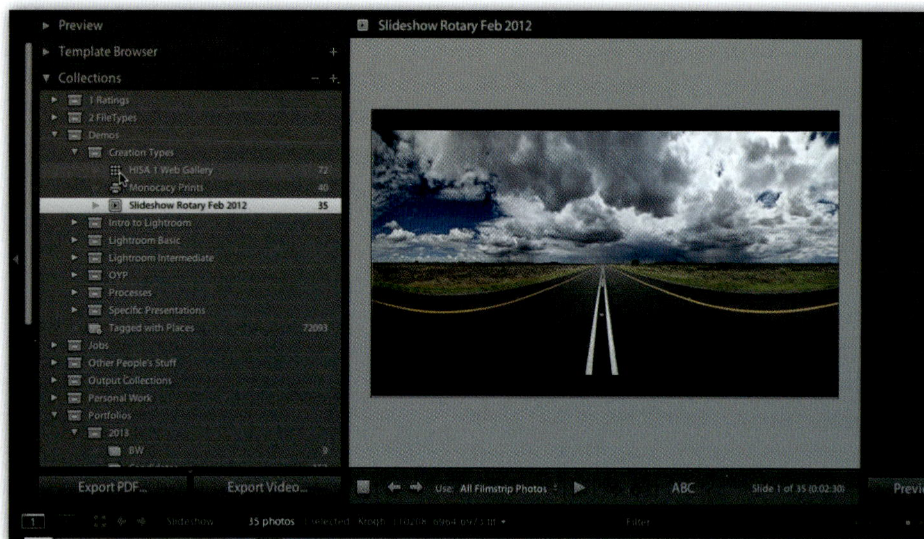

VIDEO 8-2 COLLECTIONS ARE THE HUB (2:12)

In this video, we outline the benefits of using Collections to manage your projects.

WORKING WITH COLLECTIONS

Okay, let's outline the functions we find in Collections. We'll start with the three kinds of Collections.

Collections can hold Photos. (They can also hold Creations.) Creations refer to saved Books, Slideshows, Prints and Web Galleries that you can make from each of these modules.

Collection Sets hold other Collections. You can't put photos directly into Collection Sets.

Smart Collections are really saved filters. We looked at those in Chapter 4. While Smart Collections may help us find images to put into Collections, most of this chapter deals with the images that you choose for some purpose and deliberately set aside in a Collection, rather than the ones that you find by filtering.

Creating Collections

Here are the tips on creating your Collections.

- You can make any of the three types of Collection by hitting the + button at the top of the Collections panel.
- When you first make a Collection, you can have it add all selected images. You can also choose whether to put the Collection inside a Collection Set.
- You can create Virtual Copies when you first make a Collection. This is useful if you want to make sure that the Develop settings stay as-is for this particular project.
- You can create a duplicate Collection with the same sequence order. Select all images in the first Collection, and right-click. Choose *Create Collection* and check *Include Selected Photos*. The photos will inherit the current sequencing.
- You can rename and reorganize your Collections whenever you want.
- You can sort your Collections by type, or alphabetically. You can put a number in front of your Collection names to make them line up in order.

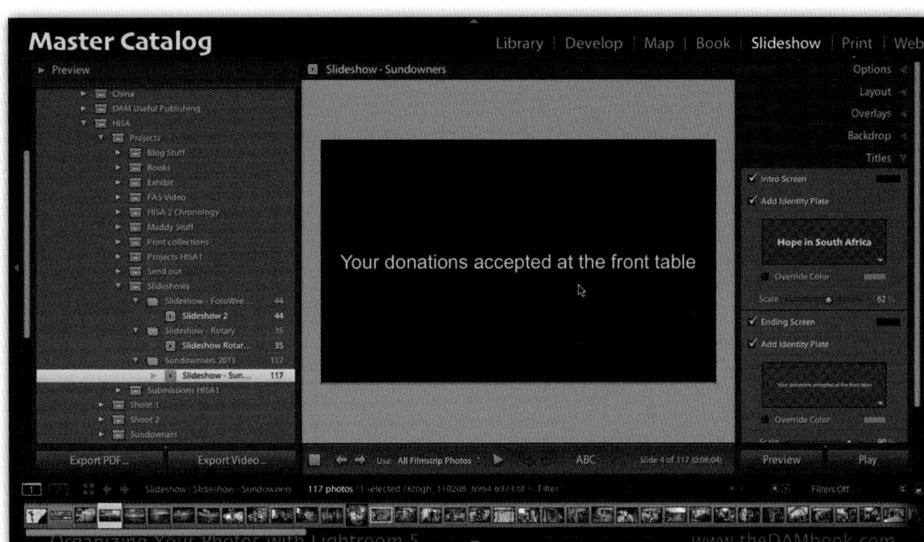

VIDEO 8-3 MAKING COLLECTIONS (5:19)

In this video, we outline the various ways Collections work.

Working with Collections

You can drag images into a Collection to add to that Collection. If you want to remove an image from a Collection, start by selecting the Collection as a source. Then, select all images you want to remove, right-click on the image and choose *Remove from Collection*.

You can set a Collection as a Target Collection by right-clicking on the Collection name and choosing *Set as Target Collection*. Selecting a photo and tapping the B key will add that photo straight to the Target Collection.

You can see what Collections an image belongs to by right-clicking on it and hovering over *Go to Collection*. You can also click on the Collection Badge on a photo's thumbnail.

You can make a custom sequence in Collections called a Sort Order. You can switch between your User Order and one of the sorting methods that is based on metadata.

When you select a Collection, all included images will be shown. If you "close" the Collection Set that contains the Collection, all images in the Collection Set will be shown.

Each Output module has its own dedicated Collection type which saves the sequence and all the module-specific settings.

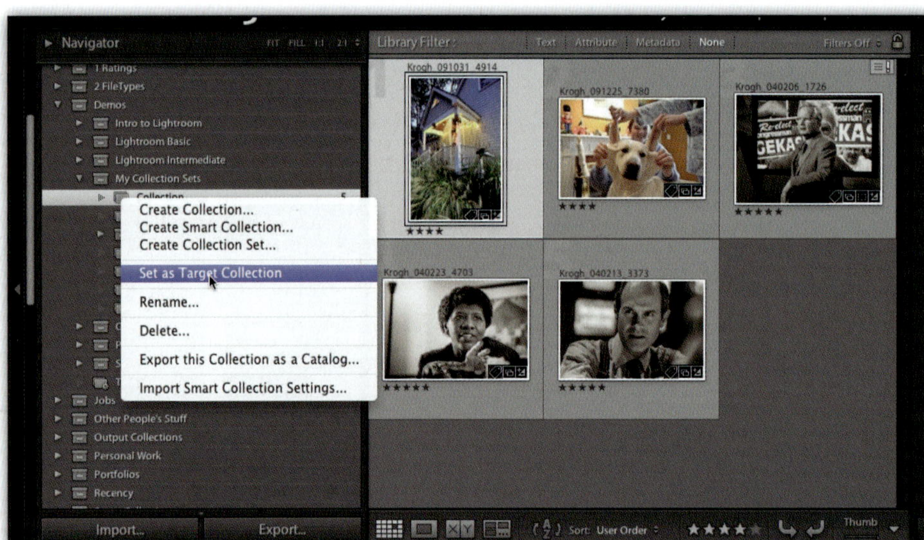

VIDEO 8-4 WORKING WITH COLLECTIONS (5:06)
In this video, we see some more techniques for working with Collections.

ORGANIZING YOUR COLLECTIONS

As with your keywords, the organization of your Collections will depend on the subject matter in your Photo Library, and the ways you are interested in making use of those photos. One photographer may need to organize assignments and another will want to manage family vacation projects.

In each case, we'll want to create some kind of hierarchy that fits the Photo Library and your goals. We can use Collection Sets to manage an individual project, and then use other Collection Sets to keep related projects grouped together. As with the keywords, you can easily rename and reorganize these over time. And, as with keywords, we can start big and subdivide.

Note that we are not trying to duplicate the keywords structure here. We don't need to make a Collection for *Beach 2013* just because there was a *Beach 2013* shoot. We want to make a Collection only when we are trying to do something with the photos.

Build a Collection hierarchy

You'll want to have a handful of top-level Collection Sets to contain your projects. As your number of projects grow, you will want to add intermediate Collection Sets as necessary. So *Assignments* may contain *Client 1* which may contain *Project 1.* For the family photographer, *Family Projects* may contain each *Vacation* that you have turned into a slideshow or book.

You may also want to create a Collection Set to store *Completed Projects* alongside a Collection Set for *Current Projects*.

Standardize your use of Collections

While the creative process may be messy at times, we should try to keep the mess under control in our workspace. You should try to use Collections in a similar way across all your projects. This helps you to understand your workflow better, and it helps you standardize the way you do things.

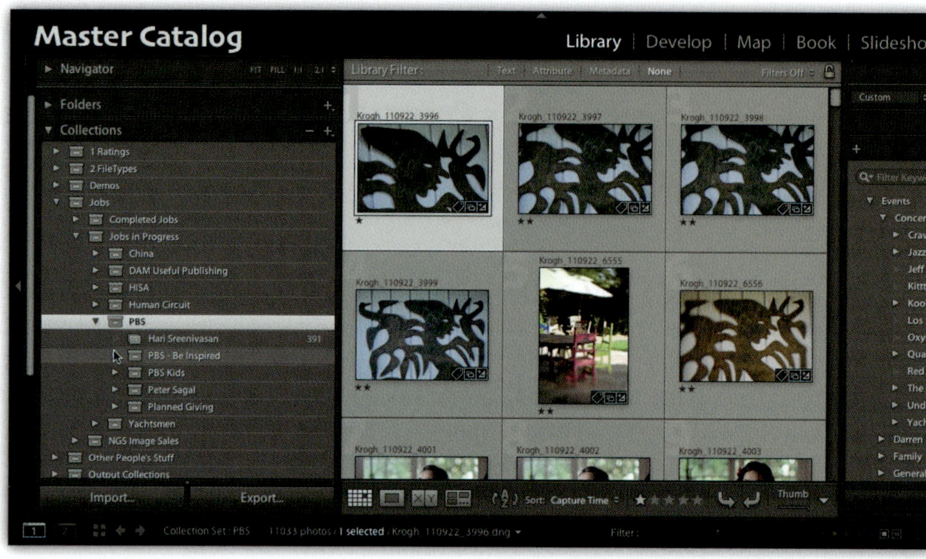

VIDEO 8-5 BUILDING A COLLECTION HIERARCHY (3:52)

This video shows how to build a Collection hierarchy.

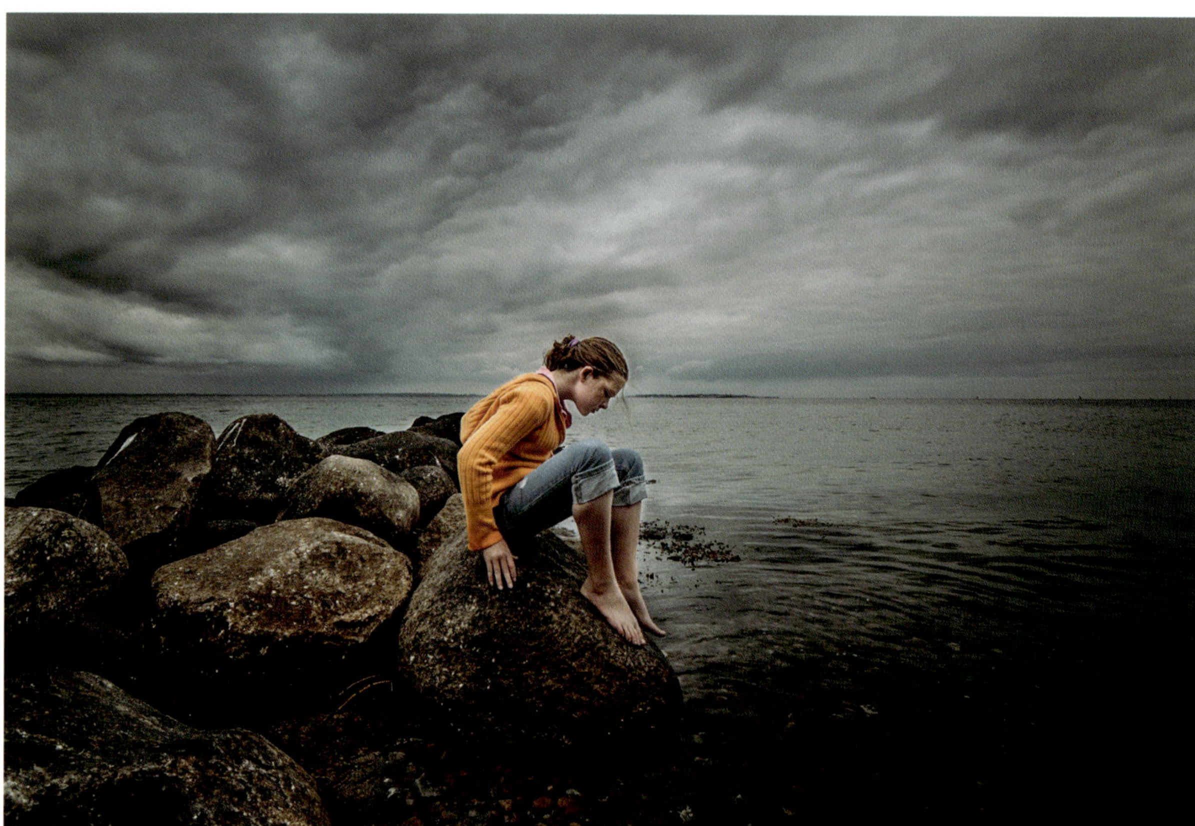

MANAGING A SHOOT WITH COLLECTIONS

When I'm working with a shoot in Collections, I'm typically using them to help with three steps. I'm gathering the images together to do the rating and selection process. Then I use the ratings and selections to focus my attention in the Develop module. And finally, I'm creating the output from the shoot as a Collection.

In a case like this, my Collections will include these elements:

All Images: This Collection brings all the images from a shoot together. I'll use this as a source when I do my ratings and selections. This gives me a one-click place to find all images from the shoot, even if they are stored in different download folders.

Send to Client: After I have reviewed the images, I will send off a selection of images for client review. In many cases, this is done by selecting all two-star and better images and putting them in a Collection. For some clients, I will send only the 3-star images to begin with, and send the 2-star photos if requested. I can make my output from this *Send to Client* Collection, whether it's a file export, web gallery or Publish Service.

It makes sense to name this Collection for the kind of output you're creating. If the output from Lightroom is the final delivery, I'll call it *Send to Client*. If it's a Web Gallery for proofing only, name it *Web Gallery Proof* or something similar so you'll know exactly what this Collection was used for.

If you use a service like PhotoShelter to deliver your shoots, you will probably want to make a Published Collection to send the photos out. We'll look at that in the next chapter.

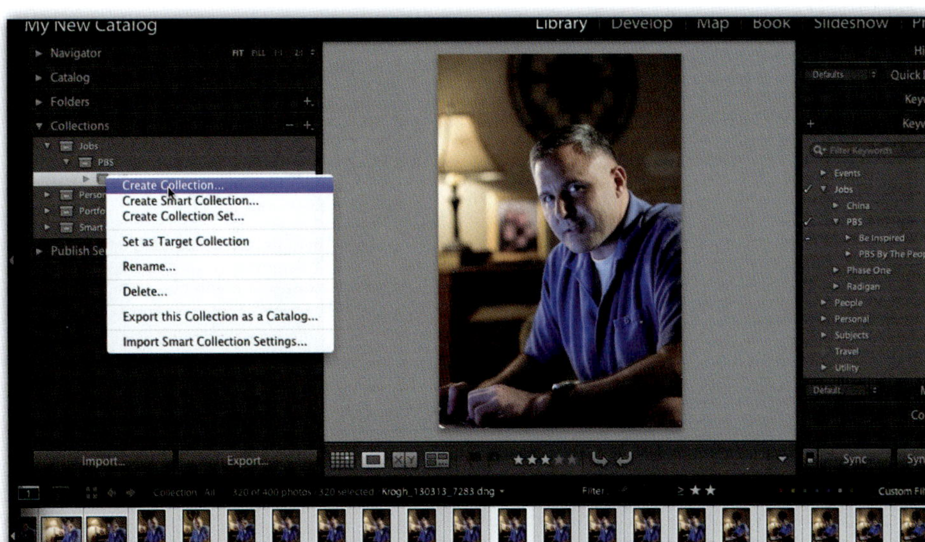

VIDEO 8-6 SHOOT COLLECTIONS (4:57)

In this video, we see how to structure Collections for a simple shoot with a batch output.

Managing a multi-level shoot

Sometimes the work on a shoot goes beyond this simple batch output. A client may return to me with a selection of images to optimize in Photoshop. Or I may need to create a more finished project from the photos. In these cases, I'll continue to use Collections to manage as much of that work as possible.

These Collections might include:

Client Select: I'll make a Collection for the images that the client wants me to further optimize. This Collection helps me manage the output workflow and keeps a record of which files the client used for the project.

Additional Output Collection: For some shoots, the client may require several different outputs. One may be for their website, one for their printed communication, and one for social media. Again, it's helpful to make a Collection for each of these to help with workflow and keep a record.

Module-Specific Collections: Any work you do in one of the Lightroom Modules should be saved in a module-specific Collection. These will retain your sequencing and the module-specific settings.

In the video below, let's look at a project that makes use of these additional types of Collections.

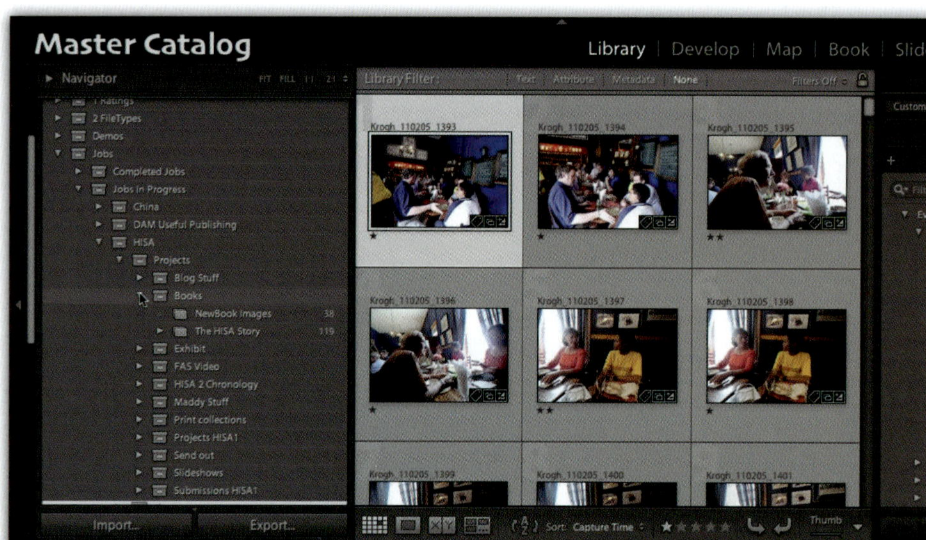

VIDEO 8-7 MANAGING A COMPLEX SHOOT (2:14)

In this video, we see how Collections can help you track large and complex projects.

MANAGING A PORTFOLIO PROJECT WITH COLLECTIONS

We're using the term "portfolio" to include any project that pulls photos from different shoots together into a single entity. This might be a portfolio to sell your photography services, or it might be a personal portfolio. The workflow for these will look a lot like the multi-level shoot outlined above.

Portfolios typically require more levels of refinement than shoots do. The gathering process is usually more broad, the selection process is usually more difficult and the sequencing may take several attempts before you've got it right. And a good portfolio, once it's been finalized, may be exported to different kinds of output. Collections can help you with all of these.

Portfolio Collections

Here's a typical set of Collection types I will use in a portfolio project.

Portfolio Collection Set: I'll start with a Collection Set that identifies the portfolio subject. I may date these Collection sets if it's a type of portfolio search I've done before.

All Candidates: I'll do a search for all images that might be useful in the portfolio. I may search by ratings, since I've already identified some images as my best. And, as I round out the storyline of the portfolio, I may do deeper searches into particular shoots or into particular keywords.

Trial Groupings: Getting a portfolio just right may take several attempts. You can gather images together and see how well they tell a story. It can be helpful to save multiple versions so you can come back later and compare.

Trial Sequences: Choosing the order of the photos can be as important as choosing which photos to include. This is another place where you may want to experiment.

Module-Specific Collections: Once you have your selection and sequencing done, it's time to make Collections for any Module Creations you want to make.

Internal Collection Sets: If you've done a bit of experimentation, you may want to create a Collections Set for the experiments. This allows you to save them, but keeps them from cluttering things up.

The video below outlines how all these types of Collections may be useful.

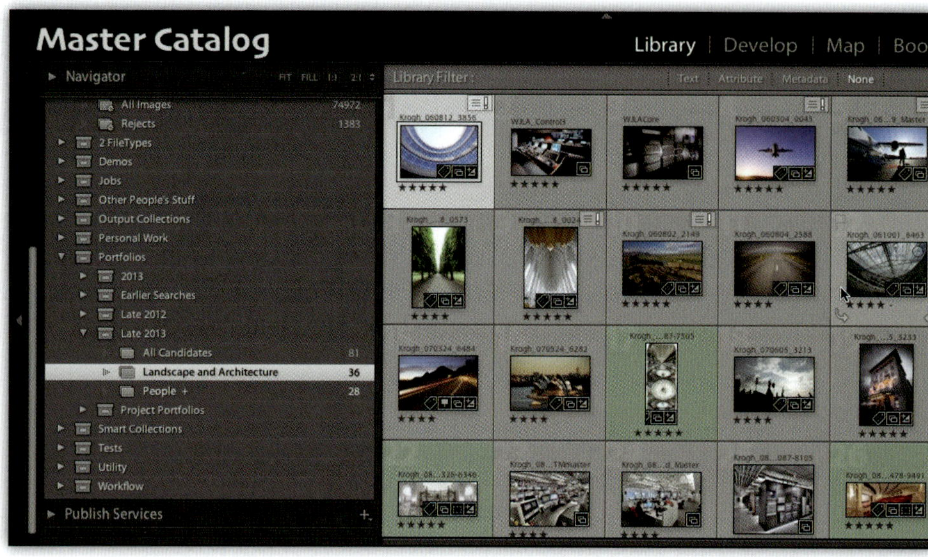

VIDEO 8-8 CREATING PORTFOLIOS (7:54)
In this video, we see how Collections can help you create portfolios.

MODULE CREATIONS

Lightroom 4 introduced a new type of Collection — one that is designed to be used in the individual output modules: Print, Slideshow, Web and Book. Each of these creation types has its own icon. These individual creations will remember the sequence of the images, and they will remember the settings that you have chosen.

We'll be looking at these from the organizational perspective.

In many cases, you'll want to use a regular Collection for your selections and sequencing before creating the Module Creation. Once you've got things set, you can select all the photos and create the Module Collection. Check the option to Include Selected Photos and they will come in with the sequence you have made in the source Collection.

The video below shows how this works.

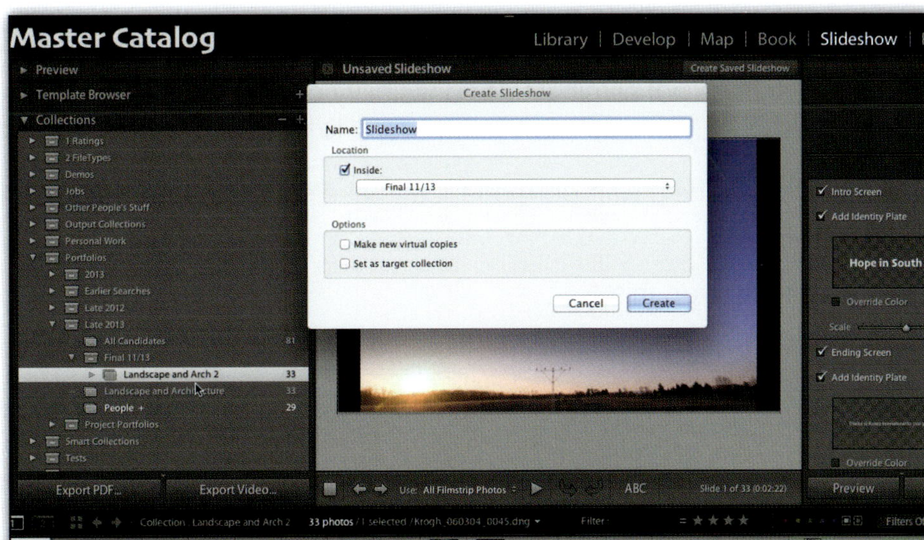

VIDEO 8-9 CREATIONS (3:05)
In this video, we see how to make Module Creations.

MAKING A COLLECTION "PERMANENT"

Over time, you'll have lots of important organizational work stored in your Collections. Unfortunately, there is no way to lock a Collection in Lightroom. And there is no way to lock Develop settings with Lightroom either. This means that images you use for a Creation or other Collection may be changed unwittingly. You may be looking at the image in a totally different collection and change the crop or color balance.

If you want to make sure you can return to the project in the future and have it look exactly the same, you can do a couple of things.

Use Virtual Copies for your Creations

If you use Virtual Copies when you make some kind of Portfolio Collection, then you can reduce the possibility of making a change to the images. The easiest way to do this is to make the Virtual Copies at the time you first create the Module Creation, because that can be done for all images with a single keystroke.

However, the Virtual Copy does not eliminate the possibility of changing an image, because the Virtual Copy is not locked. And you also have a new copy to deal with, which may be confusing.

If you do use a Virtual Copy to help with permanence, make sure to name it appropriately, so you'll know why you made it.

The video below shows how to do this.

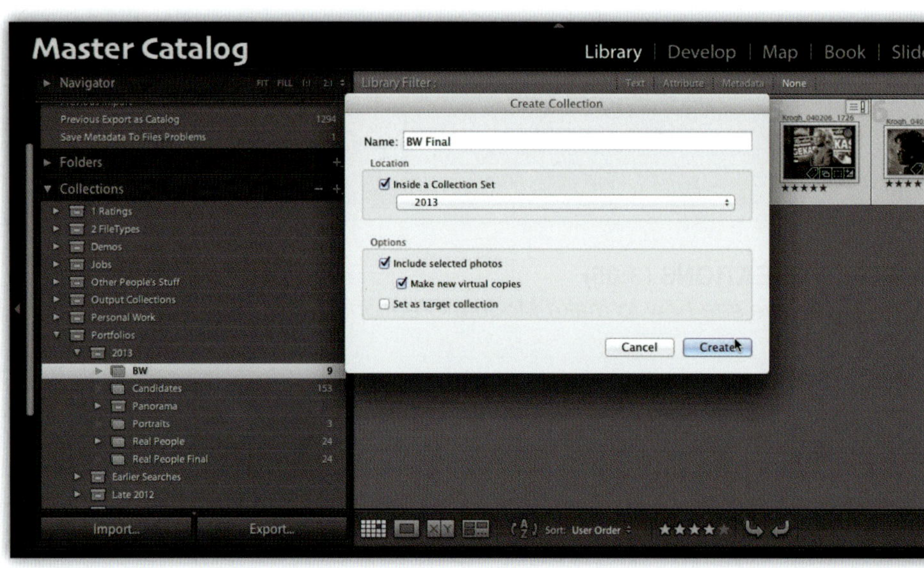

VIDEO 8-10 USING VIRTUAL COPIES (3:04)

In this video, we see how to use Virtual Copies to reduce the possibility you might inadvertently change an image that is part of a project.

Transferring Collection information to keywords

The Collections information lives inside the Lightroom catalog. Unlike other metadata, like keywords, it can't be exported back to the file by Saving Metadata. If you want to tag an image as being part of some project more permanently, you may want to add a keyword for that designation.

Once you've created a *Portraits* portfolio, for instance, you could add the word *Portraits Portfolio* to the keywords. This makes the information easier to find, and allows you to see the tag in exported files. The video below shows how this works.

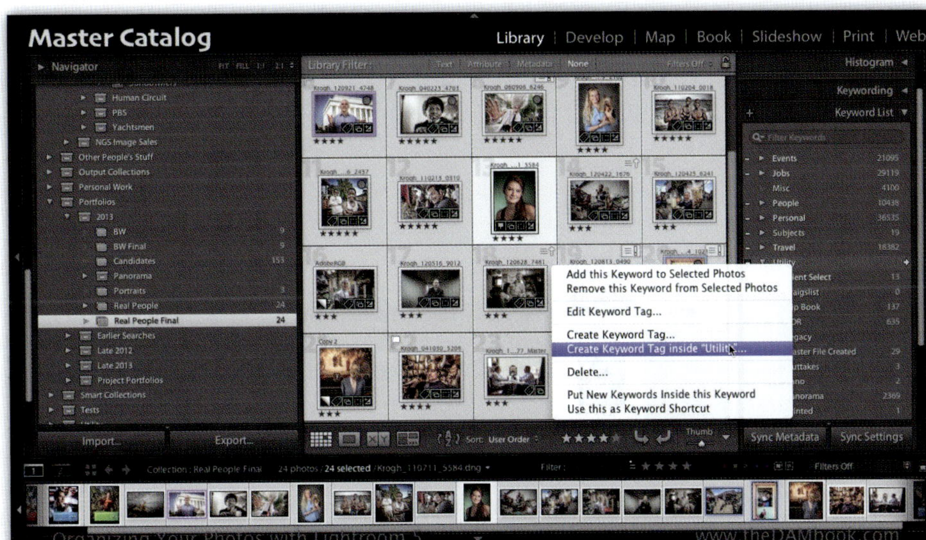

VIDEO 8-11 SAVING COLLECTIONS INFO TO KEYWORDS (1:34)
In this video, we see how to transfer Collection tags to Keyword tags.

TRICK

Creating an Exported Catalog

There is one way to make sure that none of the settings for a project get changed. You can export that Collection as a catalog, and the settings will be part of the exported catalog. If the settings for an image do get changed in your Master Catalog, you can still find the earlier version in the Exported Catalog. When you open the catalog, you'll see that all the old settings are still there.

If you want to make the exported catalog totally self-contained, you can also export the "negative files" as part of the process. This provides the catalog with full export and adjustment capabilities, whether it's connected to the Photo Library or transferred elsewhere.

The video below shows how this works.

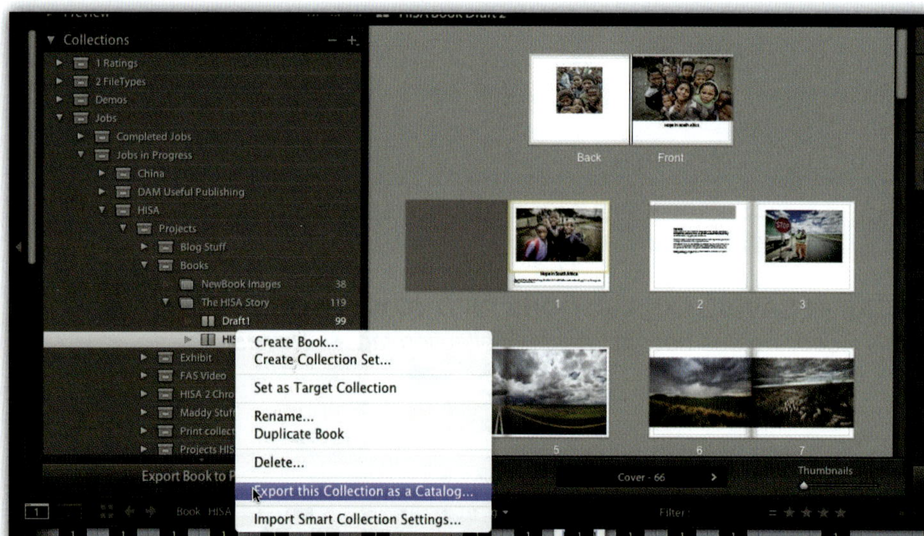

VIDEO 8-12 EXPORTING COLLECTIONS AS CATALOGS (2:50)
This video shows how to export a catalog to preserve project settings.

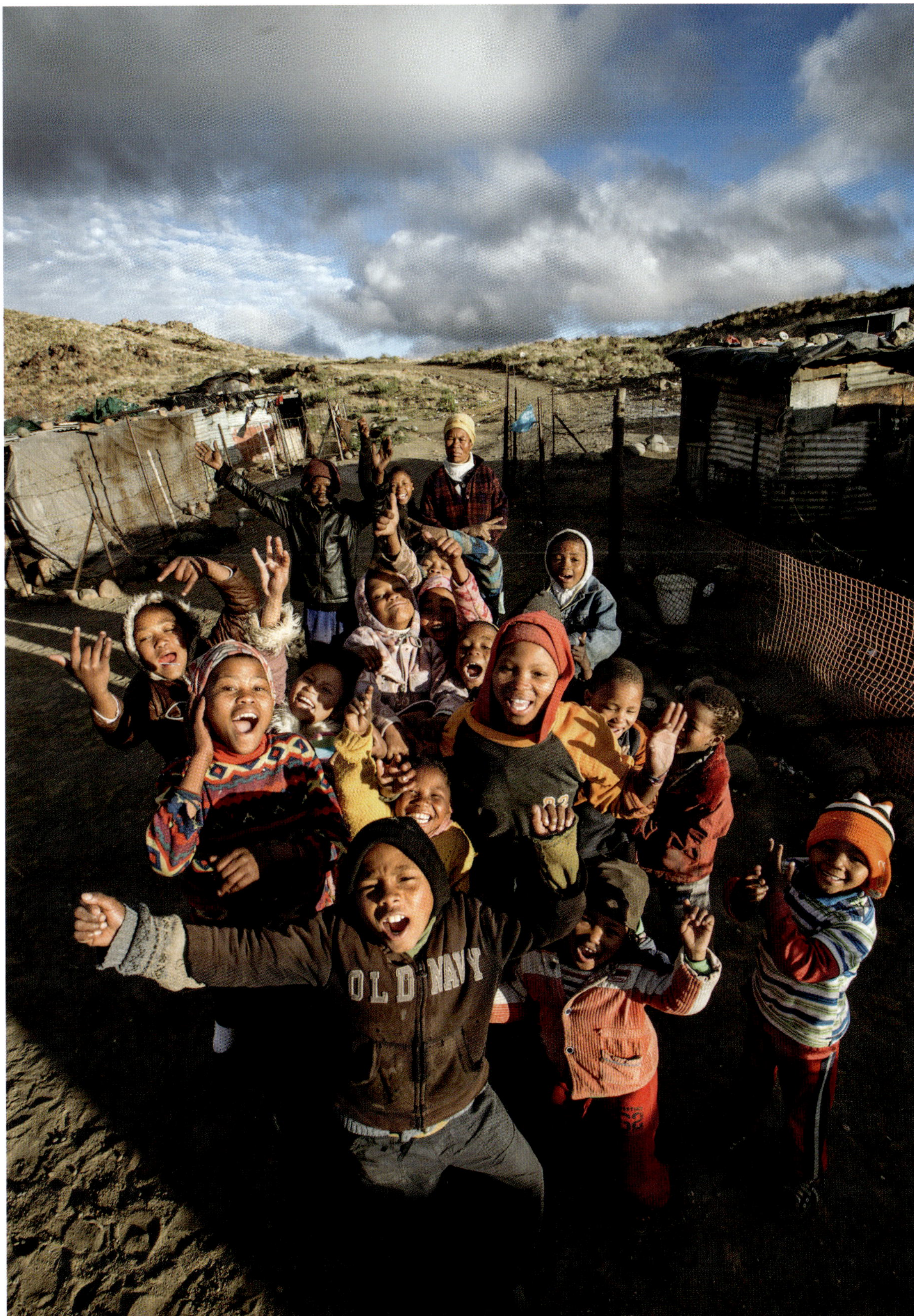
OLD NAVY

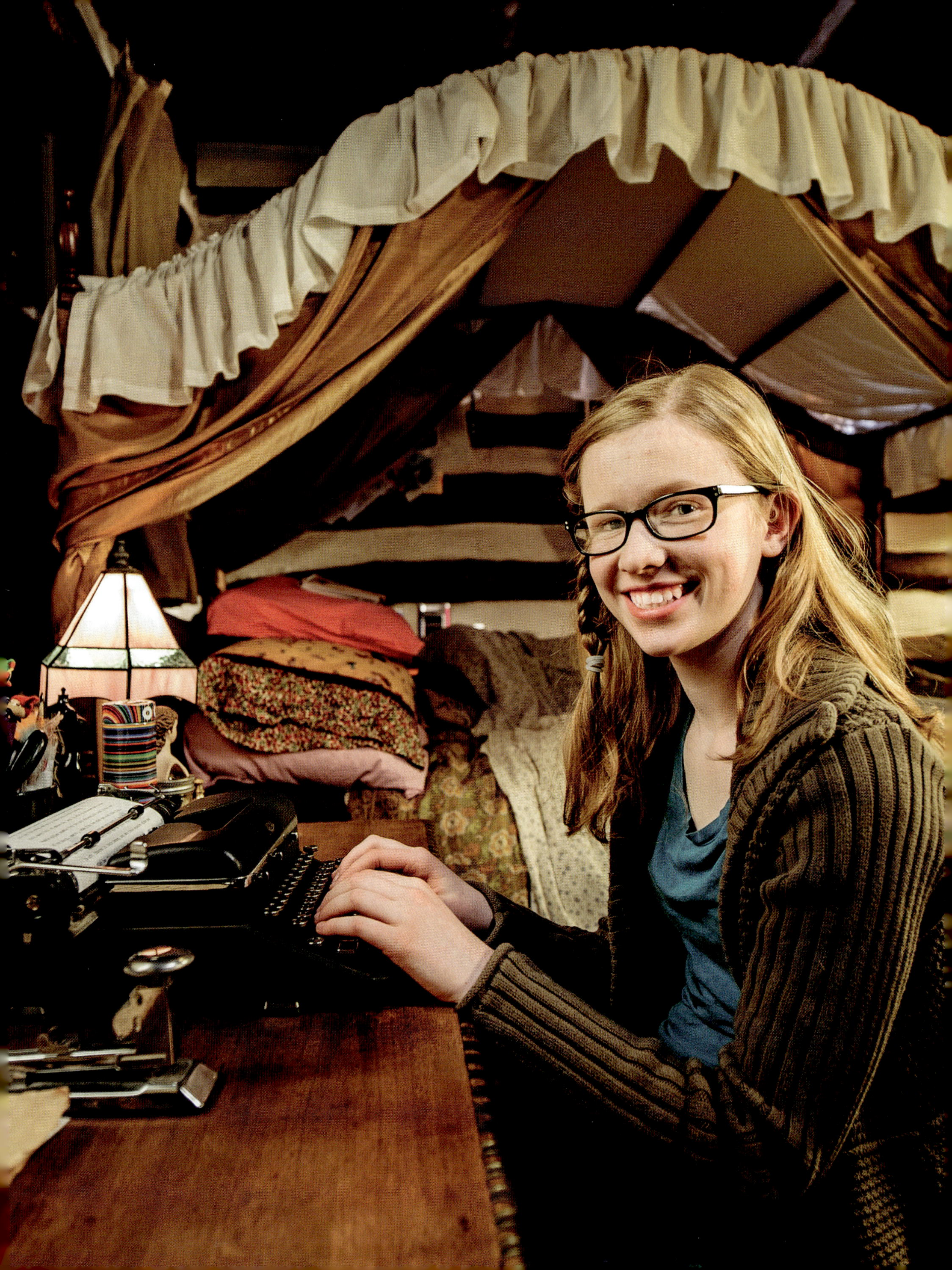

CHAPTER 9

USING PUBLISH SERVICES

Lightroom's Publish Services create special Collections that export a set of files and keep a connection to those files. If you change the Develop settings for an image, or remove a photo from the Published Collection, Lightroom can update the published files.

Publish Services also allow a two-way communication between the Lightroom Catalog and some web services. When you publish an image to Facebook, for instance, it's possible for Lightroom to import all the likes and comments that the photo has received on Facebook.

Publish Services allow Lightroom to act as an extension of online services and vice versa.

Do your sorting in Collections and use Publish Services for output

In most cases, I suggest that you do your project preparation in Collections before you make a Publish Collection. It is best to consider the Publish Collections as a tool for smart export of files, rather than a Collection to do your organization.

WHAT DOES PUBLISH DO?

Let's break up Publish Services into three categories.

Publish to Hard Drive

You can publish directly to your hard drive. In this case, Lightroom exports a copy of the selected files to a chosen location. Once published, you can tell Lightroom to update these exported files whenever the photo is changed.

Lightroom can update the metadata in the file and the Develop settings that are applied to the file (in other words, the appearance of the photo). It can also add new files to the Published export and delete files. All of these capabilities are possible on both Mac and Windows.

This capability is useful for creating a constantly-updated set of images. You might want to use these published files in another application, or you might want to send them to another device, like your phone or tablet. You could also send them to a folder that is shared by Dropbox or another sharing service.

There's no two-way communication when you publish to a hard drive. Publish Services simply allows you to keep a set of exported files updated.

Publish to a sharing service

If you use a sharing service like Dropbox, you can add some extra functionality to Publish to Hard Drive. You can publish to a shared folder, and those images will be available to any person or device you share with. This is useful for friends, family and co-workers. It's also great for sharing to your own smartphone or tablet.

Publish to web service

When you publish to a web service like Facebook, SmugMug or Flickr, Lightroom adds the ability to establish a two-way communication with the web service. This allows comments, likes and other metadata to be brought back into the Lightroom catalog.

Lightroom can update the file name, metadata and look of the published image as outlined above. It can also add and delete images from the Published Collection. It can also bring in likes, comments and metadata changes if the web service is set up to do so.

Some web services, like PhotoShelter, Flickr and SmugMug, offer a lot of cool features for photo sharing. This includes permission-control over who can see or download photos, e-commerce applications and other sharing tools. Using Publish Services can provide an excellent integration between Lightroom and these flexible photo services.

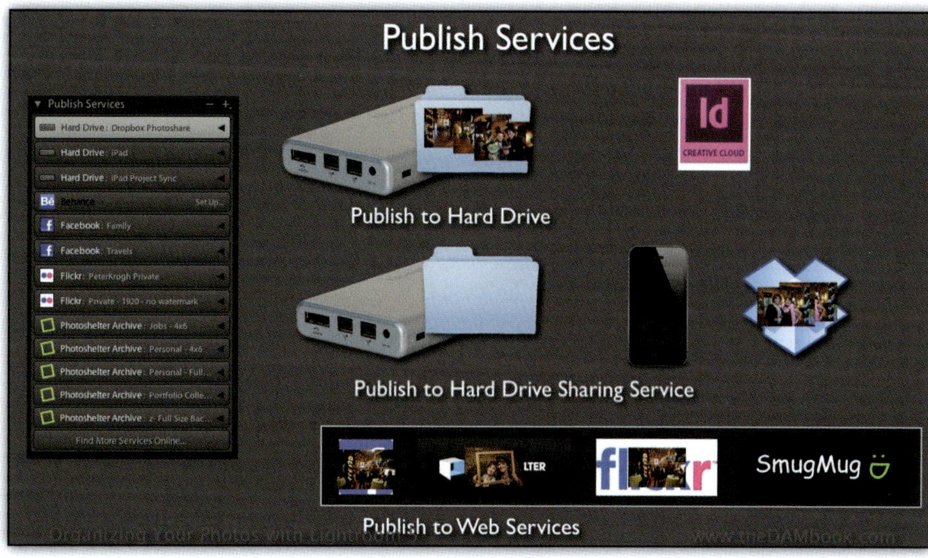

VIDEO 9-1 WHAT ARE PUBLISH SERVICES? (4:28)

This animated flowchart explains what Publish Services do.

Just because it's possible, doesn't mean it works

It's important to make a distinction between the capabilities that Publish Services can provide, and the implementation in an individual service. While Publish is capable of updating a filename, for instance, many of the web services may not be able to handle this kind of update. Facebook, for instance, may simply see the updated file as a new file, and lose the previous connection. Facebook does not allow Lightroom to delete a file from the service, but some other services do.

To make matters more confusing, not only does each web service implement things differently, but they are constantly changing their own services. So something that works today may not work very well tomorrow.

It's safest to assume that most web services will lose the connection to a file if it gets renamed. Professional level services like SmugMug and PhotoShelter are more likely to accept updated metadata, but will probably lose track of renamed files. And social media services like Facebook will, at best, allow likes and comments to move back to the Lightroom catalog.

This is a place for some testing, especially if any of these connections is critical for your plans.

BASIC HARD DRIVE PUBLISHING

Let's start by looking at the process to publish images out to your hard drive. You click the setup button and open the Publishing Manager. Give the service a name that helps you remember the settings, or your intended use of the service. You then need to choose a place to publish the photos to, which can't be changed after you've saved it.

You then work down through the settings, choosing the ones that are appropriate for the need you have. You'll want to make a new Publish Service for each different group of output settings you need. So publishing full-sized images should be a different service than those published at low resolution.

Finish by saving that Publish Service. Once you've done that, you can create Published Folders. This is almost exactly like creating the various types of Collections, including Published Folder Sets, Published Folders and Published Smart Folders. Each of these folders creates a new folder in the Publish Services panel.

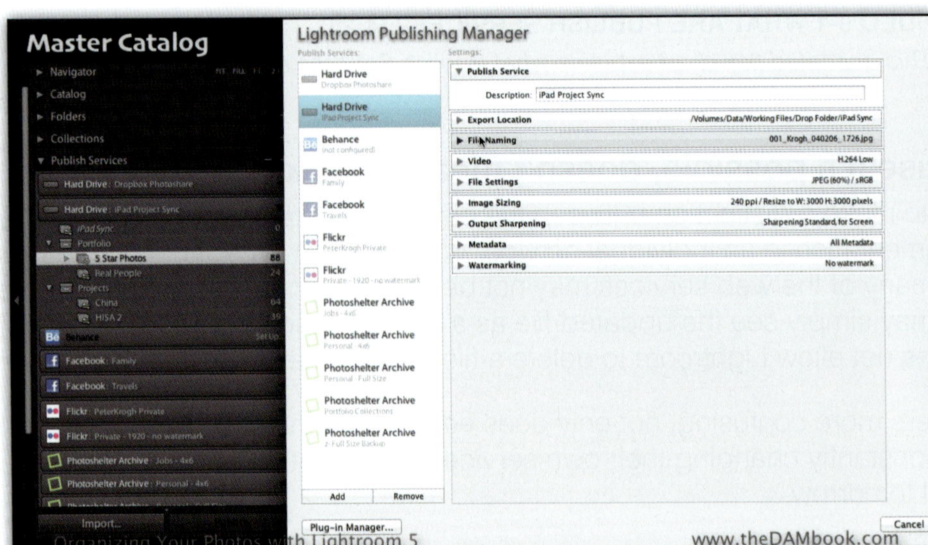

VIDEO 9-2 PUBLISH TO HARD DRIVE (4:12)
In this video, we see how to set up Publish to Hard Drive.

Here are the steps

The steps outlined here are for publishing a collection of images to an iPad or iPhone. You can use similar methods on different devices and different platforms.

1. Set up to Publish to Hard Drive.
2. Choose a name for the service, a location for the folders, size, format, etc.
3. Rename the files with a sequence number in front of the file name if you want them to line up in order.

Creating Published Folders

In part two of Publishing to a Hard Drive, we see how to create Published Folder Sets, Published Folders and Published Smart Folders. We also see how to add images and start the Publish process.

Refining and Republishing

Lightroom assumes that you will want to keep your published images updated.

Whenever you add photos to the Publish Folder, they will show up at the top in a group called New Photos to Publish and the Publish button will become live. Hitting the Publish button will add these to the existing group.

Whenever you make a change to an image that has been published, Lightroom marks that image for republication. If you would like to update the photo, simply hit the Publish button. If you don't want to republish, then you can right-click and choose Mark as Up-To-Date.

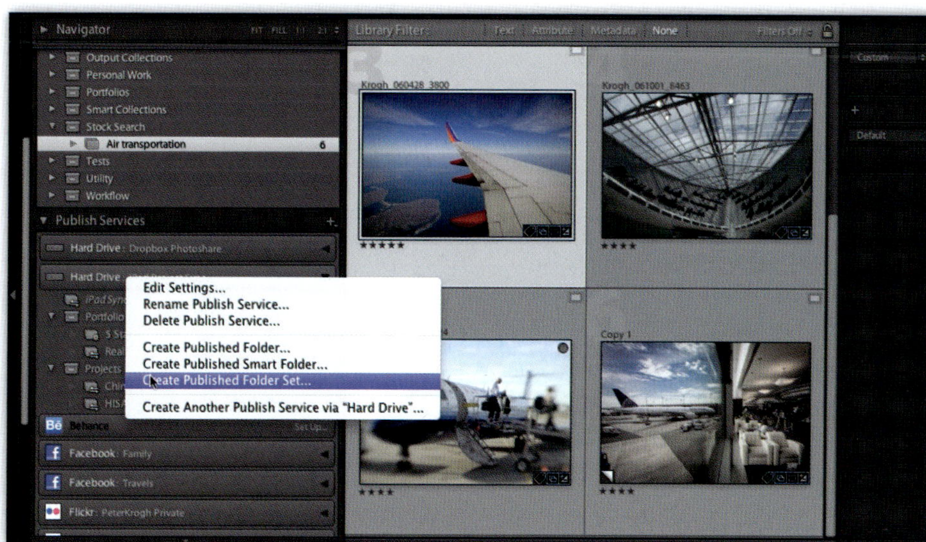

VIDEO 9-3 CREATING AND UPDATING PUBLISHED FOLDERS (6:12)
You can add images to Published Folders in the same way that you add to Collections.

Here are the steps

1. Make a Folder Set inside the new Publish Service.
2. Make a Published Folder for each group of images you want to publish.
3. Add the images to the Published Folder.
4. When you're ready, hit the Publish button.
5. Make new Published Folders as desired, and update files as desired.

PUBLISH TO SHARING SERVICES

When the folder you publish to is part of a Sharing Service, you can distribute photos directly from your Lightroom catalog. Dropbox folders can be shared to other computers, devices or users seamlessly. Lightroom takes care of the creation and updates of the images, and Dropbox takes care of the distribution.

Sharing Services give you control over the people who have access to the shared folders. This could be limited to you, to people you invite, or it could be shared openly to the world.

These services do not offer the sophisticated access controls that some professional photo services do, but they do make sharing really easy. The following video outlines the process.

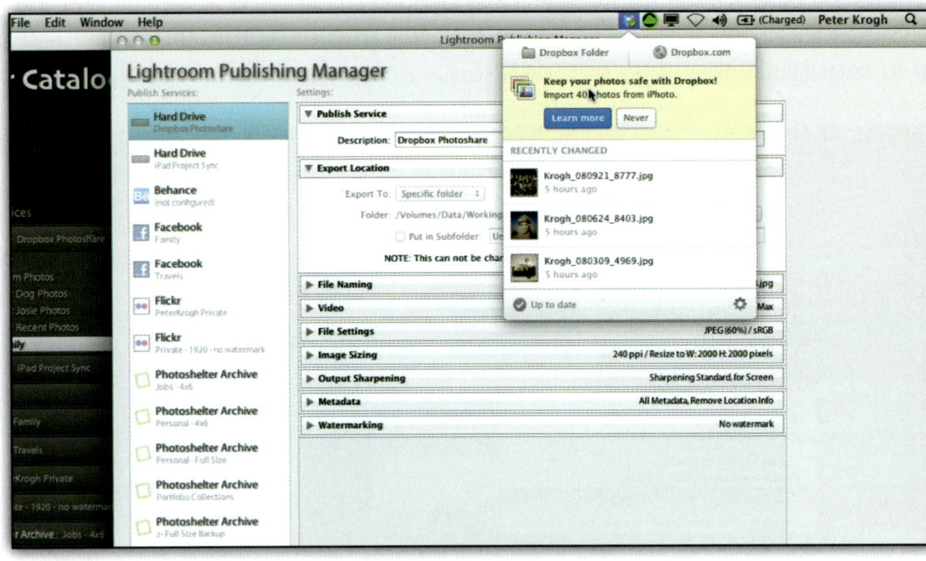

VIDEO 9-4 PUBLISH TO SHARED SERVICES (4:54)

In this video, we publish to a folder that is shared by Dropbox.

Sharing with Smart Publish Folders

You can also use Smart Publish Folders to backup or share your favorite photos about a particular thing, or your favorite recent photos. If you can create a Smart Collection to find images, you can make a Published Collection to share them.

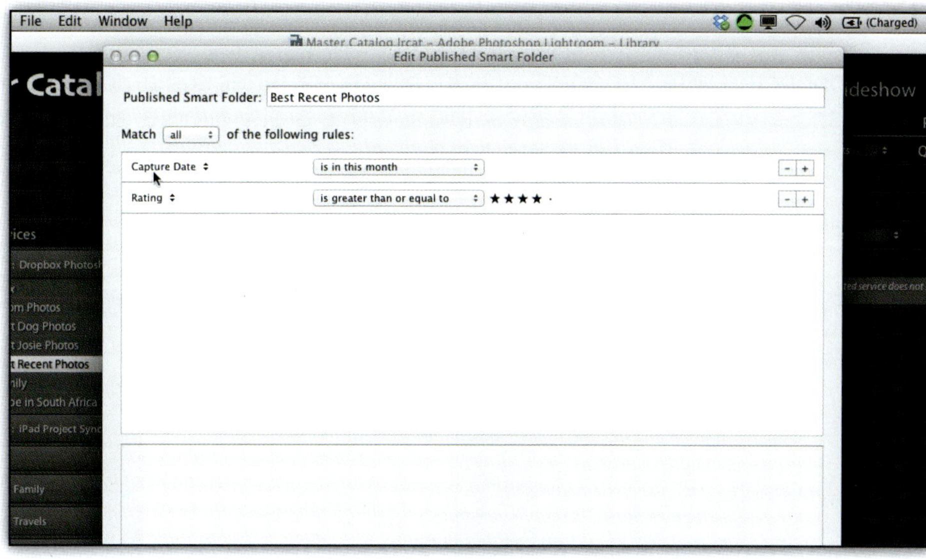

VIDEO 9-5 PUBLISH SMART COLLECTIONS (2:13)

Smart Publish Folders allow you to keep your shared folders updated as you create new work.

PUSH IMAGES OUT TO SOCIAL MEDIA

If you want to stay connected with Facebook, Flickr, 500px, or other social media services, you can do so with Publish Services. In most cases, the setup is pretty simple, and the service works well. Many of these services will also send the comments and likes back to Lightroom.

The video below outlines how this works.

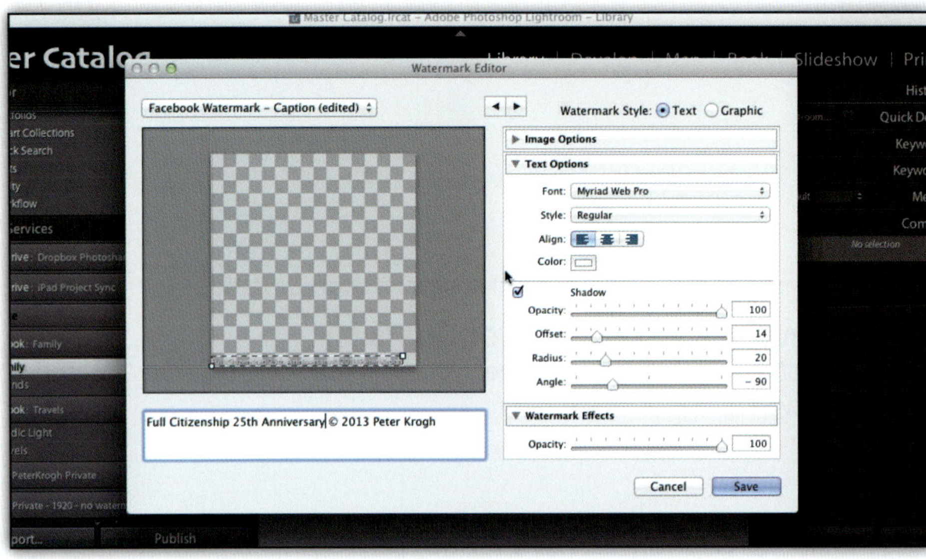

VIDEO 9-6 PUBLISH TO FACEBOOK (4:45)
In this video, we see how to publish to Facebook.

Here are the steps:

The steps outline here are for publishing a few images to a Facebook album. Other services work in a similar way.

1. Set up to Publish to Facebook. You'll need to authorize your account and give the service a name.
2. Choose the Album you want to publish to.
3. Select images to publish.
4. Drag to the Publish Collection.
5. Change the watermark, if you use one.
6. Publish.
7. Make comments through the Comments panel.
8. Check for Comments by clicking the refresh button in the Comments panel.

BY THE WAY

Publishing to multiple accounts

Note that you can create multiple Publish Services for different accounts, even for the same service. So if you use one Facebook account for personal work, and one for business, you can make a Publish Service for each.

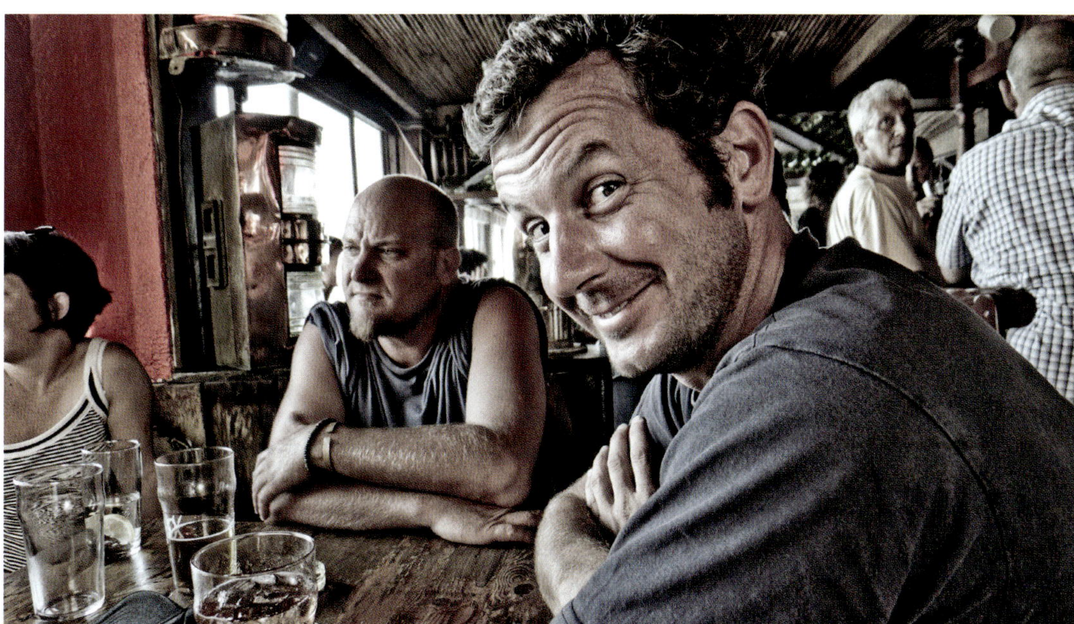

DELIVER SHOOTS

You can use Publish Services to deliver shoots to your clients by uploading the files to a web service like PhotoSheter, Flickr or SmugMug. This allows the web service to handle security, image resizing, lightboxes, and e-commerce. Once you have finalized the selection and optimization of the photos, you can create a Published Collection and upload. The video below outlines how this can work.

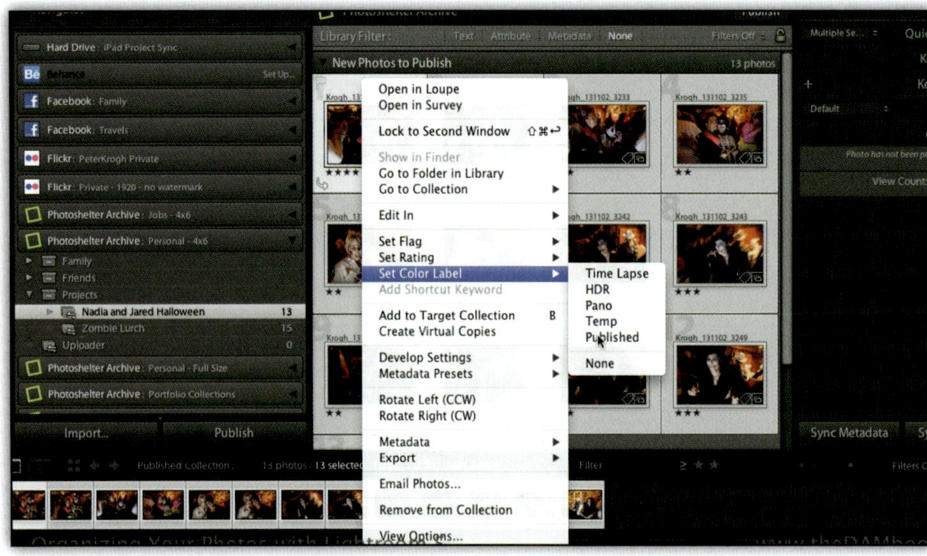

VIDEO 9-7 PUBLISHING PROOFS (4:42)

In this video, we see how to deliver a shoot for proofing or final delivery with Published Collections.

Here are the steps:

This video shows how to deliver a shoot with PhotoShelter. In this demonstration, the account has already been set up, and I'm just uploading a shoot.

1. Finalize images to publish in Collections.
2. Make a new Collection in the proper Publish Service. My considerations here include what size images I'll be publishing, and the collection area that the shoot will appear in.
3. Create Publish Folder and add the selected photos.
4. When satisfied, click Publish.
5. After the images are done uploading, go to the Publish Collection set permissions and notify the client.

UPLOAD ONLINE PORTFOLIOS

I have started using Publish Services to upload my commercial photography portfolios to PhotoShelter. This provides a quick and easy bridge between the work I do in Lightroom to refine my vision, and the web services that can showcase this vision.

This workflow is almost identical to uploading a shoot, except that I will use a custom filename to make sure everything shows up in the desired sequence in the web service.

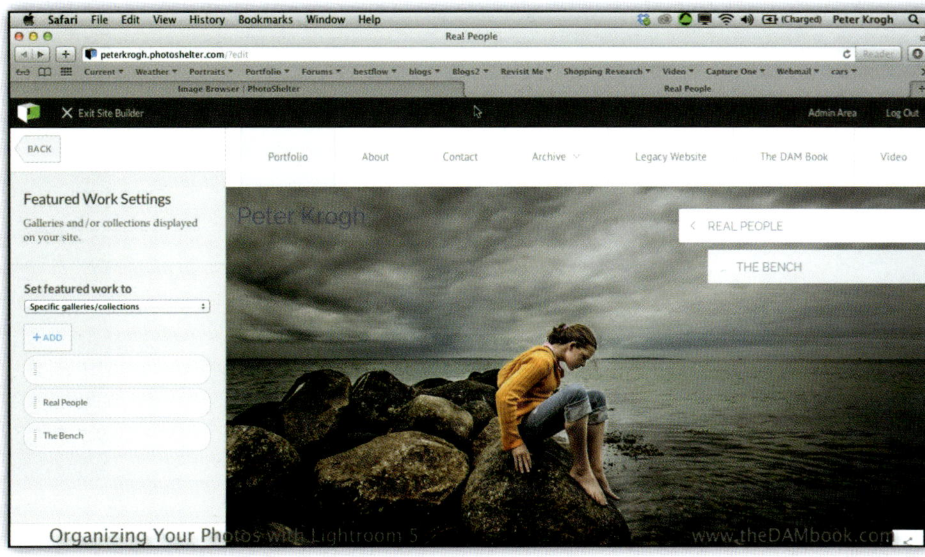

VIDEO 9-8 PUBLISHING A PORTFOLIO (2:31)
In this video, we see how upload a portfolio to PhotoShelter.

Here are the steps

1. Finalize images to publish in Collections.
2. Make a new Collection in the proper Publish Service. My considerations here include what size images I'll be publishing to, and the collection area that the shoot will appear in.
3. I'll also make a new File Renaming Template that adds digits to the front of the filename in order to preserve the sequencing.
4. Create Publish Folder and add the selected photos.
5. When satisfied, click Publish.
6. After they are done uploading, go to the Publish Collection and set permissions.

BACKUP YOUR MOST VALUABLE PHOTOS

You can use Smart Publish Collections to backup your most valuable photos to the cloud. You can, for instance, tell Lightroom to publish any 4-star-and-better photos to a web service like PhotoShelter or Flickr or to a shared folder on Google Drive or Dropbox. Whenever a photo gets this rating, it will be added to the Smart Published Collection.

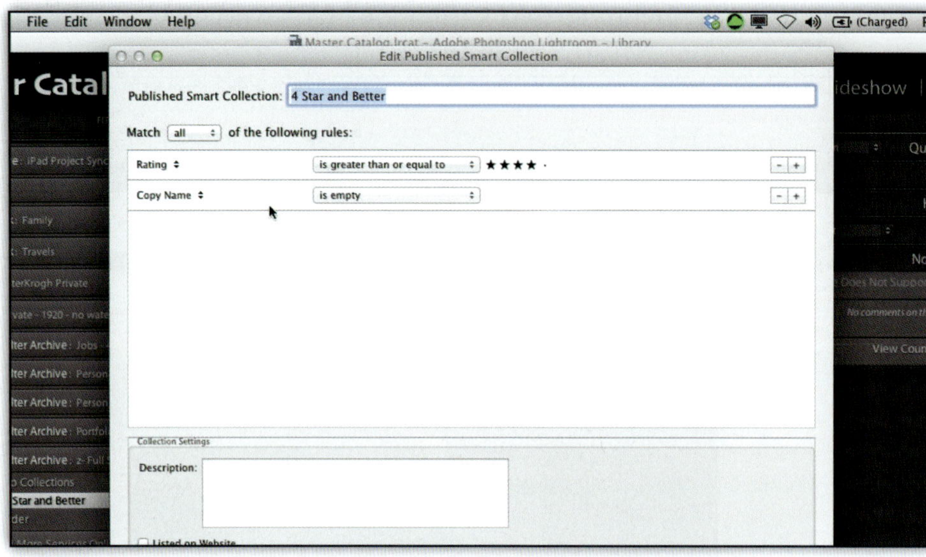

VIDEO 9-9 BACKING UP YOUR BEST PHOTOS (4:26)
In this video, we see how to backup your best photos to an online service by using a Smart Publish Folder.

Here are the steps

1. Create a Publish Service with the appropriate settings, such as full-size JPEG and maximum quality.
2. Set up a Smart Publish Folder with the proper criteria, such as all 4 star images.
3. Once the images have come in to the Publish Folder, you can start the Publish process.
4. Check periodically to see if new images have been added, or if any other images have been changed since first published. Update as desired.

YOU MIGHT BE WONDERING....

When should I make a new Publish Service?

There are several settings in the Publish Services that cannot be changed once the Publish Service has been created. And even the ones that can change should generally be left alone, unless you have made an error of some kind and will want the changed settings for all images published by the service. Any modification of the settings will trigger a request for republishing, and generally causes confusion.

If you want to have the option to choose different settings for the same web service or hard drive export, it's best to make a new Publish Service for those specific settings. So if you want to export some images at full size and some at small proofing size, it's best to make a Publish Service for each size of export, and name the service accordingly.

So, for instance, I will make one Publish Service for full-size photos, and another one for downsized images. When I publish a new collection of photos, I'll choose the appropriate one.

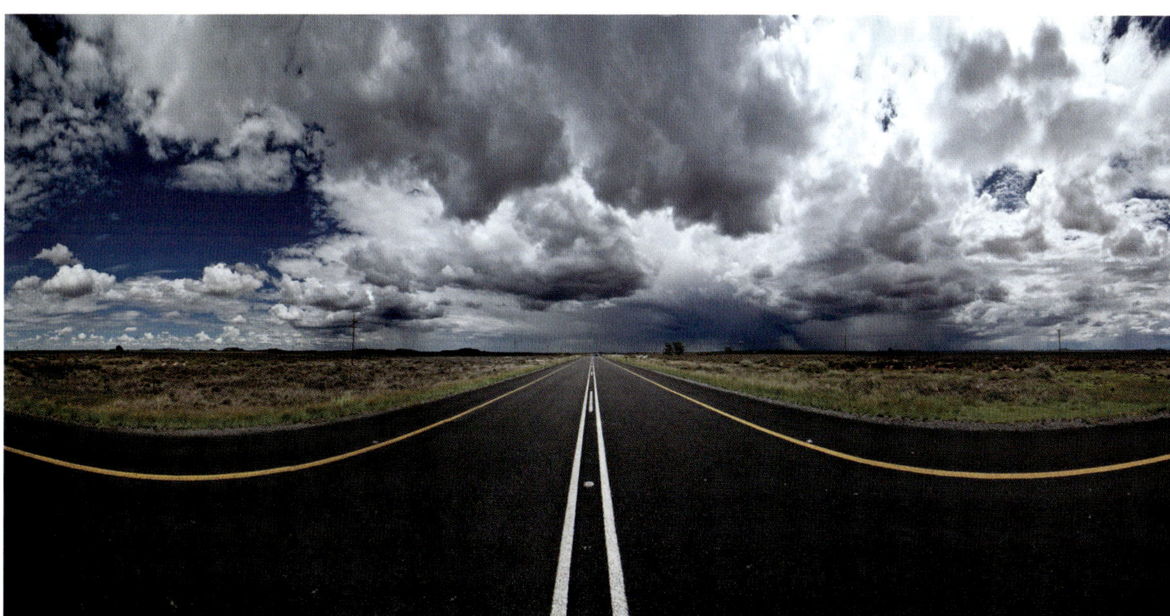

PUBLISH SERVICES DETAILS

Now that we've seen what Publish Services can do, let's take a look at the setup details. Keep in mind that this will be a basic overview, since each service works differently.

What does a Publish Service contain?

Each Publish Service you create will have a saved group of output settings. These include the export location, file naming, file type, file size, metadata, watermark settings and more. All the web services will also require you to sign in and authorize Lightroom to access your account.

The elements of Publish Services

Let's start by defining the elements of Publish Services.

Publish Service: This is the top level line. You specify the name, output location, size, file naming, watermarks, etc. when you make a Publish Service. If you need to export files with a different file size, destination or naming convention, you should make a new Publish Service, even if it is still publishing to the same hard drive or web service.

Publish Folder: This is like a Collection. You can add images to the Published Folder and put them in a custom sequence. In most cases, each Published Folder shows up as a folder or album on the hard drive or in the web service.

Published Folder Set: This is like a Collection Set. It is used to organize the Published Folders, but you can't put any photos directly inside it.

Published Smart Folder: This is like a Smart Collection. You can set up some filter rules, and images will be added and removed automatically according to the filter criteria.

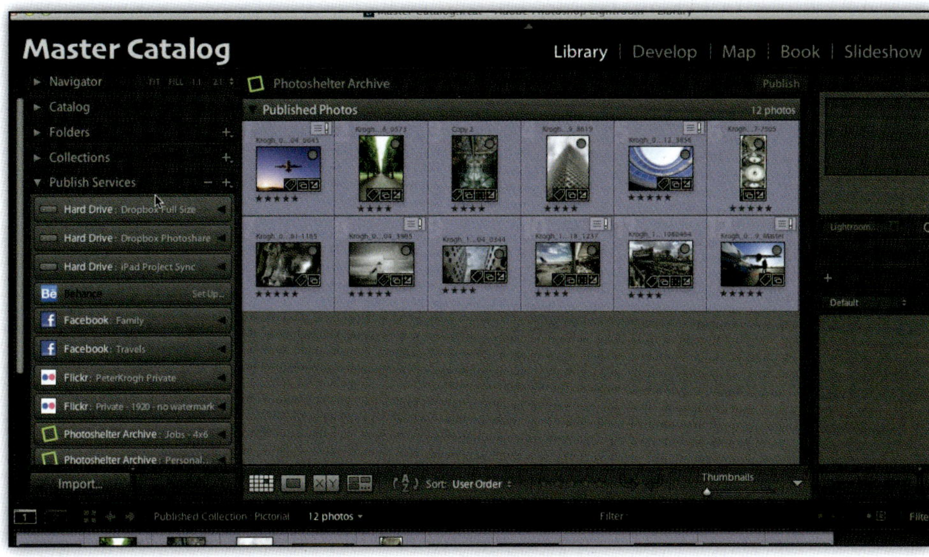

VIDEO 9-10 WHEN TO CREATE A NEW SERVICE (1:25)
I suggest that you make as few Publish Services as you can, and use the Publish Collections and Publish Folders to subdivide your published photos.

DIGGING DEEPER

Third-party Plug-ins

Publish Services is a part of Lightroom that is built for integration into other web services. This means it's a place that is going to be changing pretty rapidly. You'll see lots of third-party plug-ins, and new capabilities becoming available. These third-party services will use the same basic structure and setup that we have shown here, but the details will be different.

Check out www.theDAMbook.com/plugins for more current information.

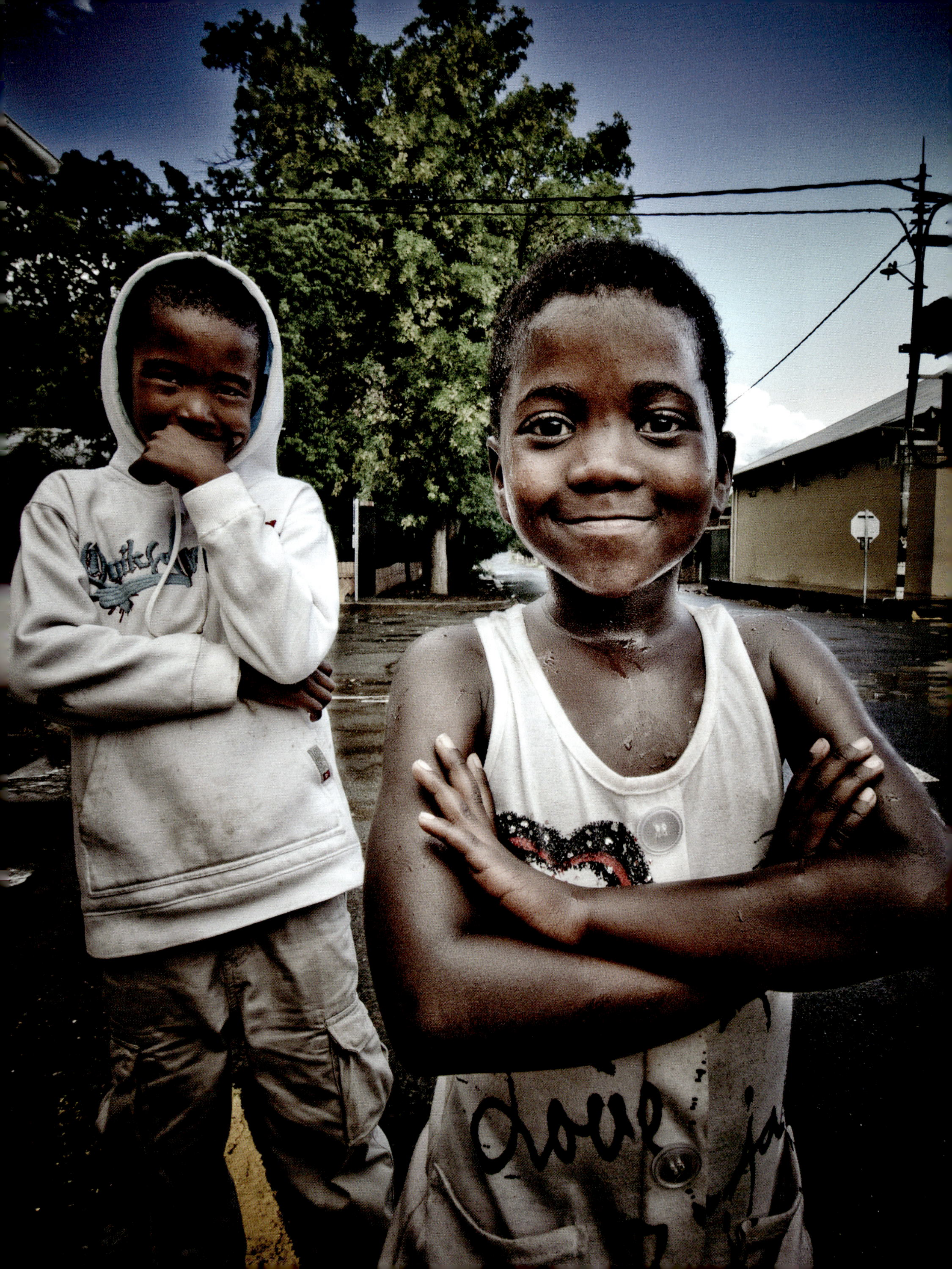

CHAPTER 10

MANAGING DERIVATIVE FILES

Lightroom allows you to do a lot with your photos without ever making additional copies of them. This simplifies the organization and management of your Photo Library. But there are some times when you'll need to make additional copies of your photo files. In this chapter, we'll look at some strategies for organizing and managing these derivative files.

YOU MIGHT BE WONDERING....

What's a derivative file?

A derivative file is a version of a file that is different in some way from the original. (If it's exactly the same, then it's a copy, not a derivative.) A derivative might be a small version of a photo used for email. Or it might be a large version of a photo sent over to Photoshop for retouching. Or it might be a panorama that is made from several different images stitched together. Any time you export from Lightroom, or Edit in Photoshop, or create Published photos, you are creating derivative files.

KEEP IT SIMPLE

The management of derivative files makes things harder, no question about it. Even the simplest methods for managing derivatives add complexity. Think about your real needs to make, keep and catalog derivative files, and try to keep things as simple as possible. Listed below are some rules to follow whenever you are considering the creation of derivative files.

Only make derivative files because you have to

The first thing to say may be obvious, but let's put it on the table. You should only make additional copies of your files because there is a reason to do so. You should try and do as much as possible inside Lightroom without making new copies. Each time you make a new copy, you introduce the possibility of confusion as well as some additional complexity. Now you have (at least) two files instead of a single Camera Original.

Only keep derivative files because you need to

Sometimes you'll need to make a new file, but you won't need to keep it. If you want to email a file to someone, and you want your Lightroom Develop work to show in the new file, you'll need to make a version for emailing. But you don't need to keep that file once it's been sent off.

Lightroom can easily recreate JPEGs like the ones you use for email. There's generally no reason to keep files that can be easily recreated.

Only catalog derivative files because you need to

You may want to keep a derivative file, but that does not mean that you need to add it back to your catalog. A professional photographer may want to create a set of files to send off for copyright registration, and to keep these as a record of that registration. But there is probably no reason to bring these files back into Lightroom.

Use Snapshots and Virtual Copies whenever possible

Sometimes people make derivatives because they need a different look for a version of a photo. If you can use Snapshots or Virtual Copies for this, you may not need to make a new file.

Use Publish Services whenever possible

Publish Services allow you to create derivative files and keep those files updated. This can be quite useful when you need to make finished images available to another person, computer, program or web service.

The Publish Services allow you to treat the published derivative and the original file in a seamless way, as though they were one file. If you can make this fit your need for a derivative file, then it's probably the best way to go.

BUMMER

Lightroom is not made to sort out lots of duplicate derivative files

Lightroom is designed to help you make sense of a Photo Library made of digital camera original files. It can catalog derivatives, but it's really not made to help you sort between multiple versions of the same photo.
If you are hoping that Lightroom is going to help you sort out the 30 different copies of *My Best Photo*, then you'll be disappointed. The Lightroom team made a conscious decision to build software that helps you prevent this kind of mess, rather than to sort the mess out. Because this is not what Lightroom was designed to do, we're only going to touch on this problem briefly.

If you really need to sort out multiple versions of many different files, I suggest that you take a look at Phase One Media Pro.

WHY MAKE DERIVATIVE FILES?

There are three basic reasons you might want to make derivative files. You need to do some work to the photo that can't be done in Lightroom, or you may need to make the photo available to another person or program. It's also possible that you want to make a derivative file because the picture is really important to you, and you want to have a version of the finished image that is not dependent on Lightroom to display properly.

Before you start making lots of derivatives, it's important to understand why you're making them.

You need to edit in Photoshop or another image editor

Sometimes you need to use the tools in Photoshop to finish your photos. You might need significant retouching that Lightroom can't do. You might also need to make a derivative in order to create a panorama or HDR composite image. Or perhaps you need to send photos outside of Lightroom for image compositing, or conversion to CMYK.

When you edit photos in Photoshop, the new derivative file will probably become the most important version of the file. You'll want to keep it, and keep track of it. You'll need to make some choices about where you store the derivative, what you name it, and whether you add it back to your Lightroom catalog.

This workflow is generally going to fall under the umbrella of Master File workflow.

You need to make the files available to another person, computer or application

Sometimes you may need to make derivative files so that they can be used by someone else, or so that they can be used in another program.

If you only need these on a temporary basis, it may be best to erase them after use. If you need them on an ongoing basis, then I suggest using Publish Services to create the derivatives and keep them updated. You can also use Publish Services to delete them when you're done (probably).

When these exported derivative files become part of a project in other software, then you'll probably want to think of them as part of that project, and not a part of your Photo Library that is managed by Lightroom.

You want a rendered version

When you export a derivative file using Lightroom, all the Develop settings get applied and "baked in" to the new file. This "rendered" version will allow any program to see the photo in its finished form, rather than the way it originally showed in Lightroom. (Remember, Lightroom's non-destructive image editing never changes the original pixels. If you want to see the changes when you open the photo in another program, you'll need to make a derivative file.)

You might want to make rendered versions of your most important photos so that the final versions are independent of Lightroom. In general, I think this is only advisable when you are preparing to stop using Lightroom.

If you do want to have rendered versions of your best files, just to have them, you can use any of the methods for making derivatives that are outlined below.

STORING DERIVATIVE FILES

In Chapter 3, we outlined the options for organized storage of your Camera Original files. This is pretty straightforward for many people. The files stack up neatly in a chronological order. And all the work done in Lightroom is non-destructive, so the photos can be put away safely without constantly needing updates.

Derivative files are more complicated. You may need to make multiple versions of a file. And you may only want to keep some of those versions. Some images will be composited from multiple originals, which may produce a folder full of images you need to manage. How do we get a grip on this?

Let's divide the storage of derivative files into four storage groups.

Drop folder

When you need to export files for temporary use, such as email or other transfer, you can use a dedicated drop folder to hold the files. I only put files in this folder which don't need to be cataloged. Inside that drop folder, I'll make a new folder for each exported group of images, according to the subject matter or purpose of the export. Once I've filled my needs for the photos, they can be deleted from the drop folder.

Application project folder

You may need to export your photos or videos so that they can be used in some other program, like video editing software or a page layout program. In this case, the files are probably not temporary, but you probably don't need to manage them with Lightroom.

These should be sent to a project folder for the other application, which will take over custody of the files.

Store with original

When you're making files you want to keep, such as Master files edited with Photoshop, you can store them inside the same folder as the Camera Original image. This is a good arrangement for many people, especially those with modest sized collections. Lightroom makes it easy accomplish this export and round-trip back to the Lightroom catalog.

Dedicated derivatives storage

Busy professionals who do a lot of work with Photoshop and other imaging applications may want to create some kind of storage that is dedicated entirely to derivative files. This allows you to keep the Camera Original files in a nice orderly storage, and confine the messier derivative files to their own sandbox.

In my own case, I have several terabytes of derivative files, and many were made before Lightroom even existed. So this is the method I use personally.

The video below outlines each of the arrangements outlined above.

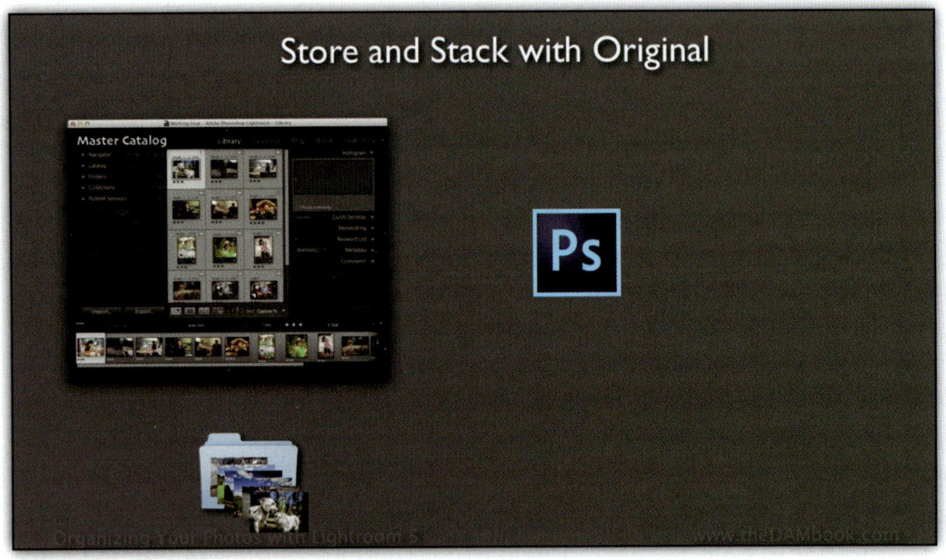

VIDEO 10-1 DERIVATIVES STORAGE (4:35)
In this video, I outline the four basic methods for storing derivative files.

NAMING DERIVATIVE FILES

You'll do yourself a favor if you standardize the way you name your derivative files. This can help avoid confusion and keep you from erasing one file by replacing it with another. Here's what I suggest.

Root name: When you make a derivative file, it should keep the main part of the source image's name, the root name. As I outlined in Chapter 3, I suggest that this looks something like *Krogh_131115_1234* or *PHK_131115_1234*.

Master files: When you send a file to Photoshop for optimization, I suggest that you add the word Master to the filename. For me that looks like *Krogh_131115_1234_Master* for a single image.

Delivery files: When I deliver a file straight from Lightroom, I typically keep the original root name. Since I only shoot raw, it's easy to tell the original from the delivery file since the original will be saved as DNG and the delivery file will be a JPEG or a TIFF.

When I convert a Master file for delivery, I like to replace the word *Master* with *Delivery* to help distinguish these from simple proofs made from Lightroom.

Panorama stitch: When I make a stitched file out of multiple source files, I like to add the number range to the file name. So a panorama made from the files *Krogh_131115_1234* to *Krogh_131115_1238* would be called *Krogh_131115_1234-1238.*

Prepend with sequence: If you want to send a set of derivative files to someone and you want to specify a certain sequence for them to retain, you can prepend the name with a sequence number, such as 001_, 002_, 003_. This will make the files show up in order on the other computer or other program.

Total rename: Sometimes you want to rename a derivative file entirely. If you are posting to a website, perhaps you want to choose a name for search engine optimization. This could include the subject of the photos, or some other search term you think is relevant to the photo. In these cases, it's helpful to put the original file name in the *IPTC Title field* (found in the Metadata panel), so that you can trace the original file from the derivative.

VIRTUAL COPIES AND SNAPSHOTS

Virtual Copies (VCs) and Snapshots provide some useful ways to minimize the need for derivative files. For instance, you can use VCs or Snapshots to save an image as both black-and-white and color. You can make different Develop settings, crops, captions and other metadata for each of the VCs, without having to make new files.

VCs and Snapshots allow you to make multiple interpretations without having to make and manage multiple versions of the image files. This saves space on your hard drive, and makes your workflow more straightforward.

Snapshots

The Snapshots tool allows you to save Develop settings for an individual image, and to restore those settings at any later date. You can create a name for the Snapshot to help you remember why you saved the Snapshot. And you can recall the Snapshot with a single click. When you hover your mouse over the Snapshot name, the Navigator will show what the Snapshot looks like.

I suggest you create a simple naming system for your Snapshots. Call black-and-white snapshots *BW*, for instance. If you are saving a Snapshot because it was used in output, save that output in the name. And if you create specific "looks" for your photos, you should create a name that is specific to that look.

The video below shows how to use Snapshots.

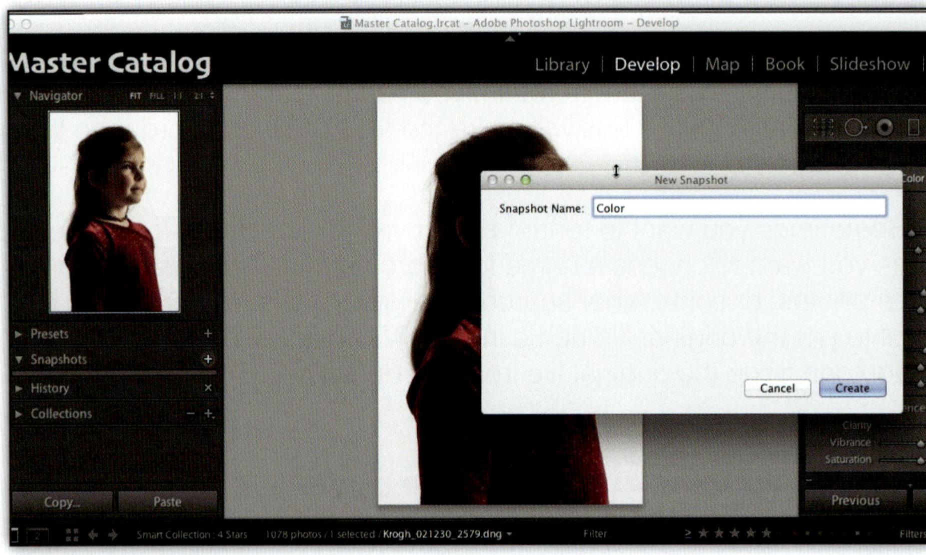

VIDEO 10-2 SNAPSHOTS (1:25)
In this video, I outline the use of Snapshots to save and recall a set of Develop settings.

Virtual Copies

Lightroom allows you to create Virtual Copies of an image. When you make a VC, you create an additional item in the Library for a single image. You can have different Develop settings for each VC, and even different Metadata settings. Each VC can be added to Collections independent of the Master copy of the file.

Using VCs allows you to create a second interpretation of an image, and to use that second version as though it were a derivative file. You can use a black-and-white version for a printed book, and a color version for a slideshow.

VCs are really helpful when you want to pin a group of settings to a file. The VC can help you from inadvertently changing Develop settings for an image that has been used in a book or other collection. While you can't actually lock a VC to prevent it from changing, it does allow a group of settings to stay put even as you make changes to the Master.

VCs can also cause confusion if you get too many of them, or if they aren't named properly. Here are some tips on using VCs. Let's outline why you might want to make VCs, and how they work.

Making VCs

Only make a VC because you need one for a specific reason. If you just want to save a version of your Develop settings, then make a Snapshot.

The VCs I make are nearly aways tied to a use in a particular Collection.

You can create a VC when you make a new Collection. Select the files you want VCs for, and open the *Create Collection* dialog in the Collections panel. Choose the *Make new virtual copies* checkbox in the dialog.

You can also make a VC by selecting an image in the Library, right-clicking on the file, and choosing *Create Virtual Copy*.

Name your VCs appropriately. If you've made the VC for use in a particular Collection, that Collection should be part of the name. You can change the name of the VC in the Metadata panel.

To find the Master Copy from a VC, select the VC and open the Metadata panel. Click the arrow to the right of the Copy Name. The folder that holds the Master Copy will be selected as a source, and you'll see the Master and all VCs.

The video below shows all this in action.

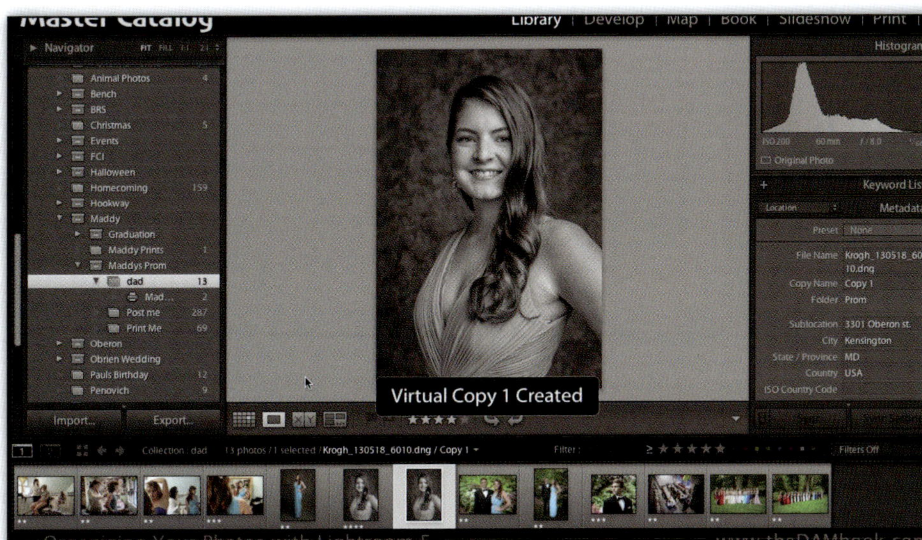

VIDEO 10-3 VIRTUAL COPIES (4:27)
In this video, we see how to use Virtual Copies.

STORE AND STACK WITH ORIGINAL

The easiest way to manage derivative files is to tuck them away with the original version of the photo. You can even tell Lightroom to display them as a single image in a stack. If you are sending an image to Photoshop for enhancement, then this is the simplest way to deal with the derivative file.

You must tell Lightroom to save the new file to the same folder as the original for this to work. And the stacking that is created in the process will be available in the Folder view and Catalog view, but it won't replace the original image in any Collections it belongs to.

Although it's possible to accomplish this using the Edit command, I suggest using the Export tool to make the derivative files. This allows you to have a lot of control over the way the derivative is created and to name each variation descriptively.

The video below shows how this works.

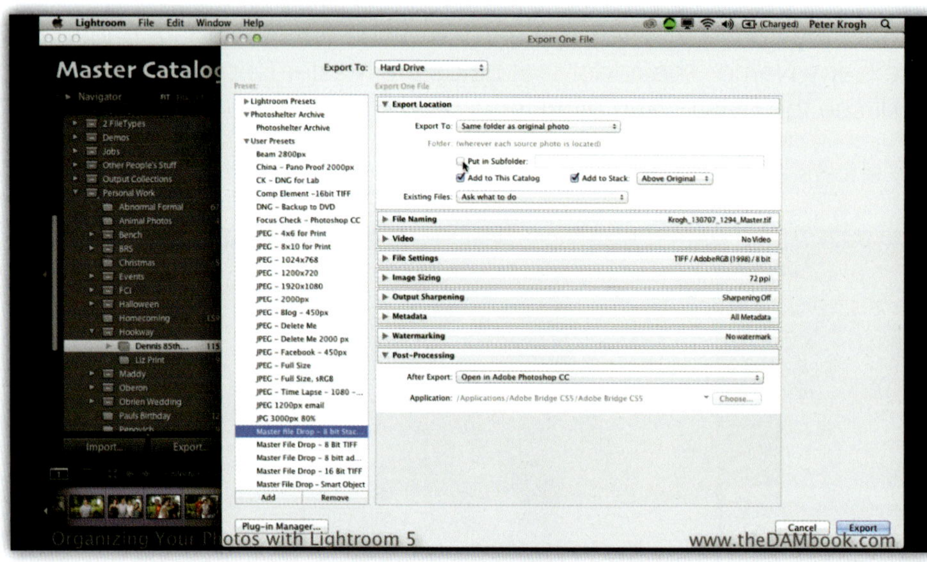

VIDEO 10-4 STORE AND STACK WITH ORIGINAL (4:41)

In this video, we see how to use Export to make a derivative file, store it in the same folder as the source image, add it back to the catalog and stack it with the original.

Here are the steps

1. Identify the image(s) you want to make derivative files for.
2. Choose *File > Export.*
3. In the *Export to* line, choose *Same Folder as Original.*
4. Do not put in a subfolder.
5. Check *Add to This Catalog.*
6. Choose *Add to Stack, Above Original.*
7. You can save this as a preset for future use.
8. Once you've created the derivative, make sure to run your backup program.

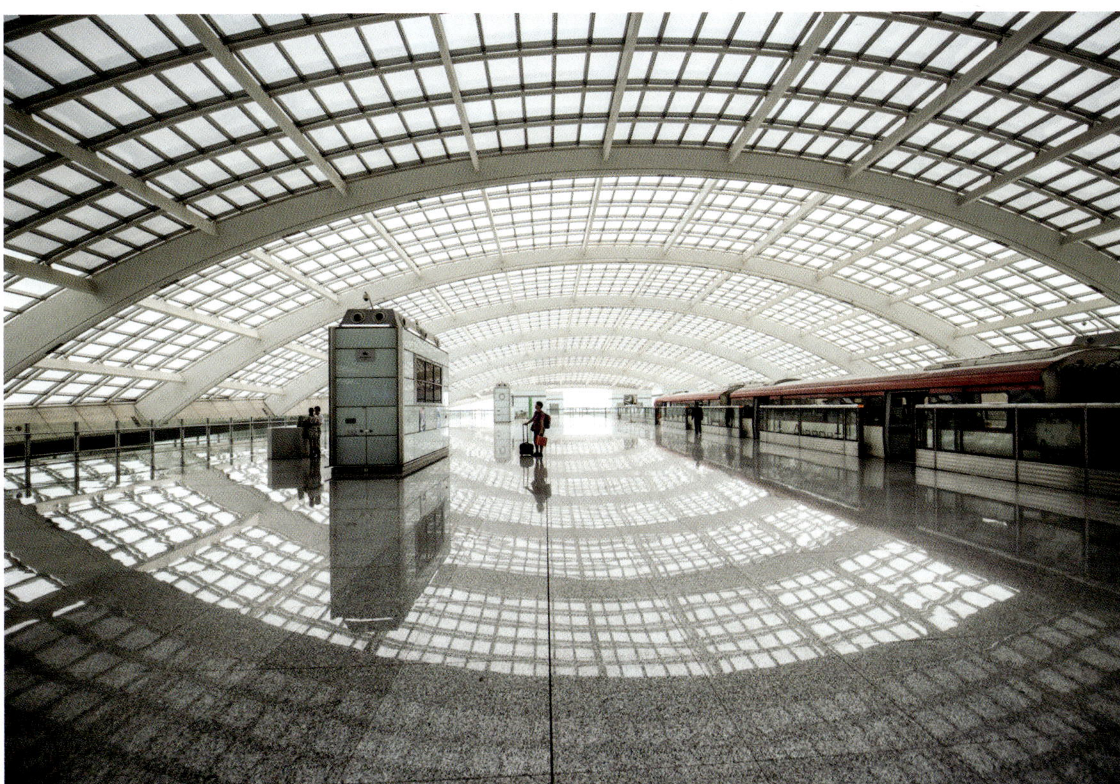

EXPORT AND FORGET

In this section, we'll look at the process for creating derivative files that we don't want to keep. This is appropriate for situations where you need to send an image to another person by email or Dropbox. It might also be appropriate for sending images to another program, such as a word processor.

In this case, we make the derivative with the Export function, and tell Lightroom to ignore the exported files. We can use Collections to keep a record of the exported files, but we don't need to keep (or to catalog) the actual files in many cases. We'll send the files to the drop folder, in a folder specific for this export.

The video below shows this in action.

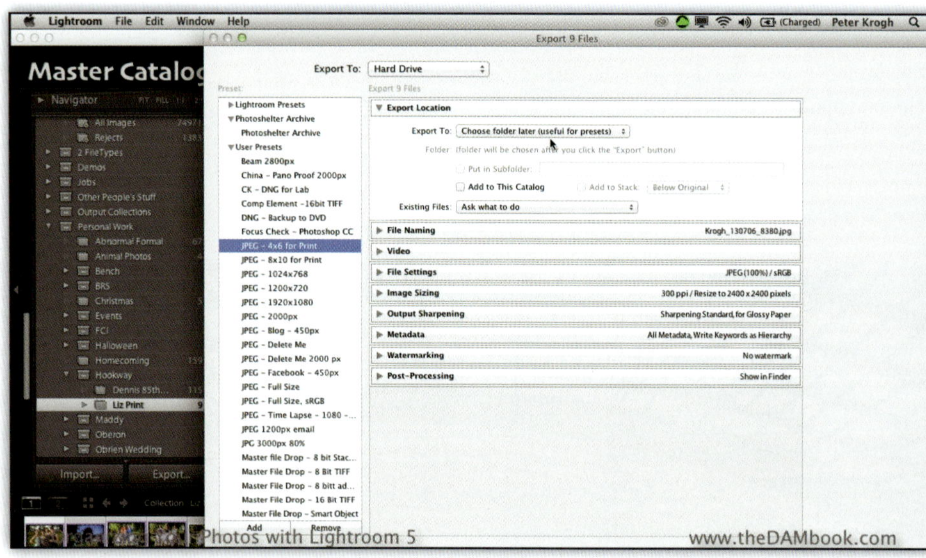

VIDEO 10-5 EXPORT AND FORGET (2:40)
In this video, we create the derivative files in a drop folder, and tell Lightroom to ignore the new files.

Here are the steps

1. Select the files for export.
2. Choose *File > Export* and select the proper settings for file size, etc.
3. Set the *Export to:* pulldown to *Choose folder later (useful for presets).*
4. Save these settings as a preset, if you like.
5. After you hit Export, make a folder for the export in the drop folder.

DEDICATED DERIVATIVE STORAGE

Note: This next section is written for those of you who have a lot of derivative files to manage. It's also appropriate for people who have a set of existing derivatives that are not already stored in the same directories as the camera originals. If you've already started down this road, it's a good one to stay on. If, however, your need for derivative files is minimal, it's probably best to stay with Store and Stack as outlined above.

If you have a lot of derivative files, it may make sense to create dedicated storage just for these files. Unlike the Camera Originals, they tend to be more disorganized. You'll probably have multiple copies of your most important images. You may have a bunch of project folders here. And these files may be created long after the Camera Originals have been put away in the Photo Library and backed up.

You have several choices of organization for your dedicated derivative storage. As with your Camera Originals, you'll want to make an organized folder structure that scales easily. This can live on the same drive as the Camera Originals if it all fits, or it could live on a dedicated storage device if you need the extra capacity.

You can make a parent folder to hold all your derivative files. This can be split up into date-based subfolders, subject-named subfolders or numbered subfolders.

If you need to open images or video in video editing software or a page layout program, you will probably want to use project folders.

If your derivative workflow generates a lot of files you don't want to catalog, you may want to bring the final Master files into their own directory in the OS and add only these back to your Lightroom catalog.

EXPORT FOR ANOTHER APPLICATION

In this workflow, we're sending the files out for use with another program. This might be a video editing or page-layout program. In this case, I suggest that your project live in a *Projects* folder, like the one I am using as I write this book. The images files should be placed inside subfolders to help to keep them organized.

In most cases, you probably don't need to add these new files to your Lightroom catalog, so we will not be doing that in this demonstration.

Use Publish Services when appropriate

Don't forget about Publish Services when you're working on a project in another application. If you have an ongoing need to add new files and to update the ones you've exported, it may be better to Publish, rather than Export the files. Of course, this is most useful if the application that will be using the Published photos can see the updates you make and refresh the files to show those updates.

The video below shows how all this work.

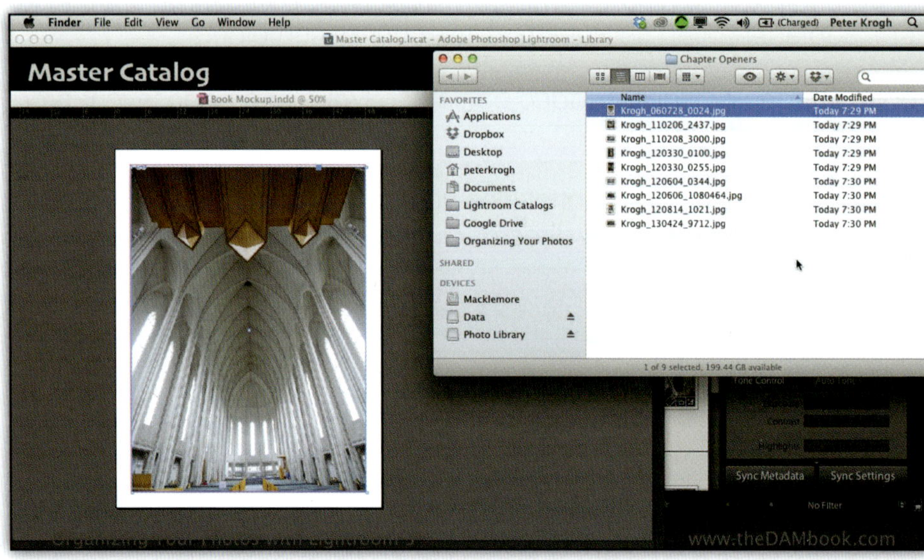

VIDEO 10-6 SENDING TO A PROJECT (5:22)
In this video, we create the files for another application. Lightroom can forget about them immediately, or wait until the project is complete.

EXPORT TO DERIVATIVES FOLDER AND CATALOG

In this variation, we're going to export the files to a dedicated *Derivative Files* folder tree, and then we're going to catalog the images with Lightroom when we're done. This is an appropriate workflow for those who want to create Master files with Photoshop or another image editing program.

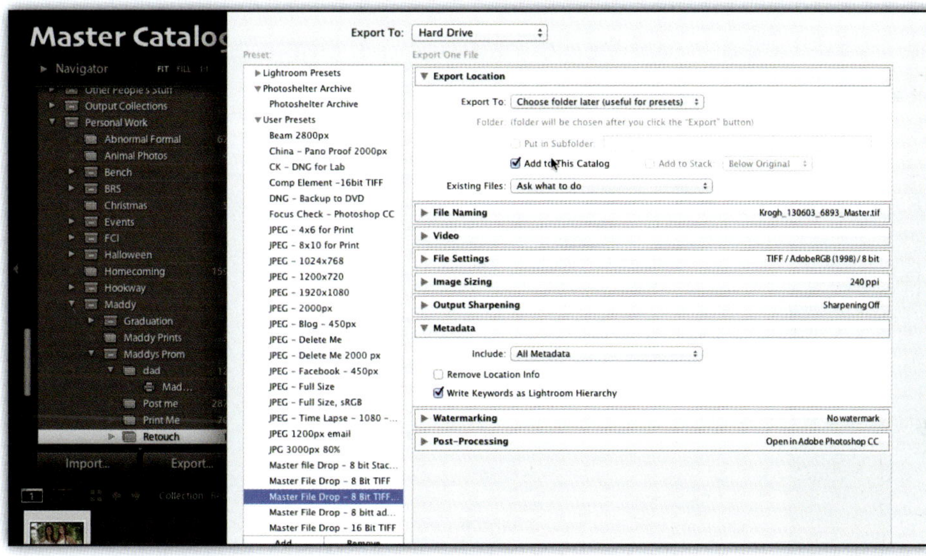

VIDEO 10-7 SAVE TO DERIVATIVES FOLDER (4:04)

In this video, we create the derivative files in a drop folder, and tell Lightroom to ignore the new files.

RE-CATALOG MASTER FILES ONLY

In this demonstration, we're sending several files out to Photoshop for compositing, but we only need to bring the final finished image back into Lightroom. In this case, the folder of images used in the compositing is much like a project folder outlined above. We export to the folder, but Lightroom ignores it afterwards.

We'll gather the finished images together for cataloging in Lightroom, and archive the project folder separately.

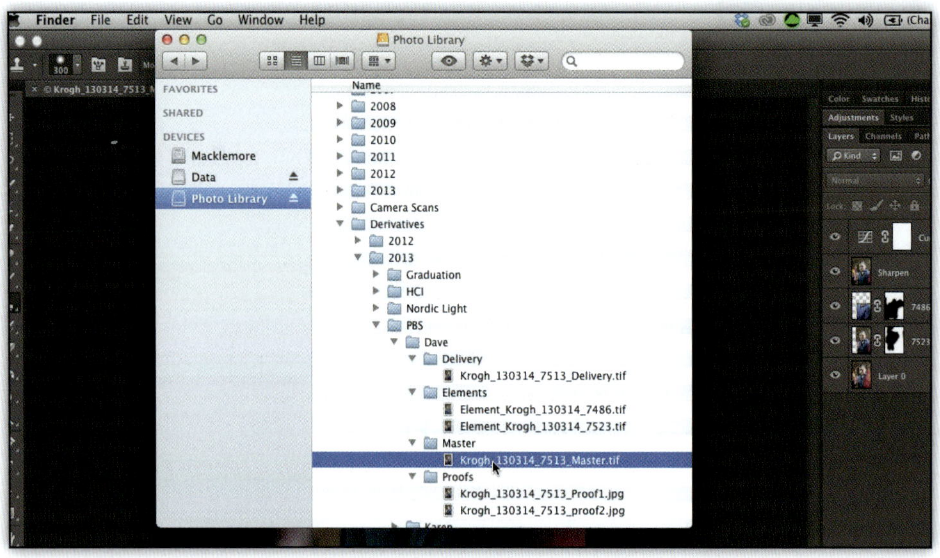

VIDEO 10-8 COMPOSITE WORKFLOW (4:22)
In this video, we create a number of derivatives for compositing, but only the final image gets cataloged in Lightroom.

DIGGING DEEPER

WHAT ABOUT THE DERIVATIVES I ALREADY HAVE?

If you've been working with digital photography for a while, it's possible that you have a lot of derivate files hanging around your hard drive. This can make a confusing mess. Programs like iPhoto have a bad track record of making lots of duplicates that can be nearly impossible to sort out.

I can give you a bit of advice for sorting this out, but Lightroom's tools are limited for this task. Here are some tips.

- It may be easier to create a separate catalog to sort out a lot of duplicate derivative files. This can be a messy task.
- When you import a big collection of derivatives into your catalog, turn off the Don't Import Suspected Duplicates checkbox in the Import module.
- You can sort files by Capture Time or File Name to make versions of the same image show up next to each other.
- Set up your View Options for the Grid to include File Name and Cropped Dimensions to help you see file type and pixel size. Unfortunately, you can not display other useful information like Modified Date or File Size in the grid.
- Set up some Label Sets to help you tag the types of files you find in your Collection. This could include Master files, Delivery files and Obsolete files.
- Review the techniques I showed in Chapter 3 for collecting and sorting your existing photos.

Phase One Media Pro

The Lightroom team at Adobe has concentrated more on preventing the mess than sorting it out.

If you really need to straighten out a giant disorganized and duplicated library of derivative files, I suggest using Phase One Media Pro. It has many more tools for sorting out duplication and variations of the same root file. Although I have switched over to Lightroom for my own Camera Original photo management, I'm still using Media Pro for the management of my derivative files.

DIGGING DEEPER

CONSULT THE DAM BOOK

Derivative file workflow can get complex for a busy photographer or production house, and the needs of these workflows may go beyond what Lightroom has to offer. While I've outlined some of the basic approaches here, there are plenty of additional options. If your derivative file workflow requires more complexity than I've outlined here, you may be a candidate for *The DAM Book*.

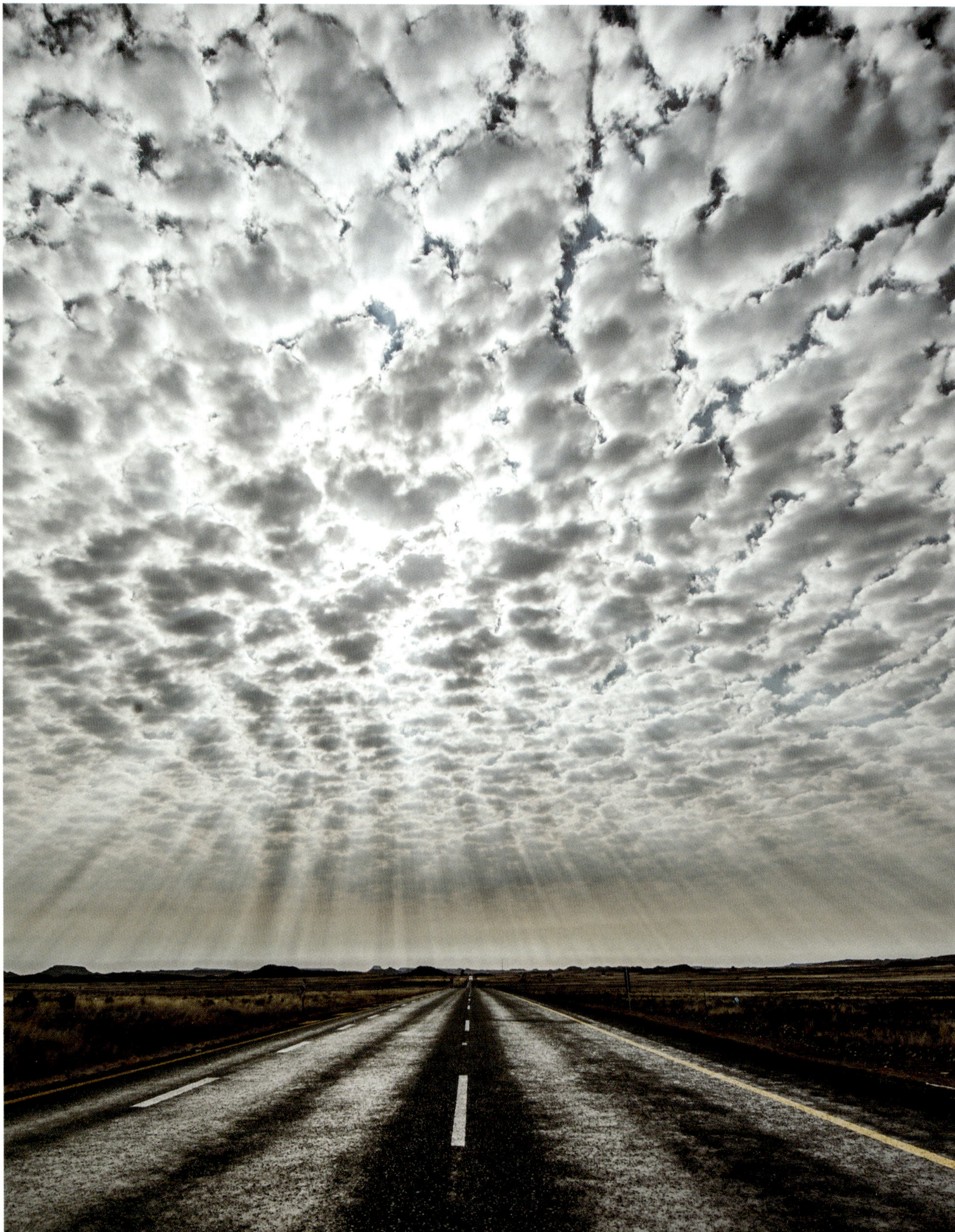

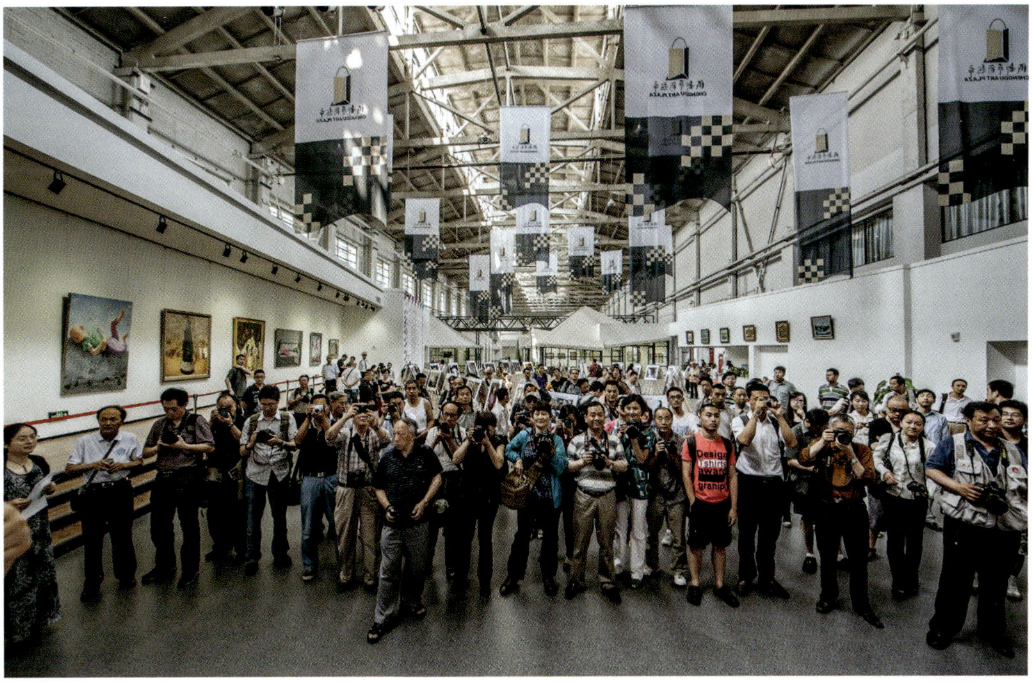

AFTERWORD

My relationship with my Photo Library has been an ongoing affair, and has only deepened with age. The photos serve as memory and self-expression, profession, and my self-appointed role is as personal documentarian. What you've read in this book represents a holistic approach to Photo Libraries.

Digital photography has added new richness to the photo experience, and promises to continue to add even more. We're seeing a constant stream of new ways to capture, store, create and share media. A new language of visual communication is being developed right now.

I'm excited by these changes, and I feel privileged to have a front-row seat in the arena (and also, frequently, a back-stage pass). It's been challenging and fun and deeply rewarding to help shape the tools of the digital media era, and to help my fellow photographers put them into practice.

I'll continue to work in service of photographers and the photographic image. I intend to continue this long into the future, until a time when the remarkable tools we have today seem quaint and outdated.

When new developments arise, as surely they will, I'll do my best to put these into a context that serves the photographer. I'll bring you research and analysis, but be always mindful of the higher purpose of the creative process and self expression.

It's going to be an interesting ride.

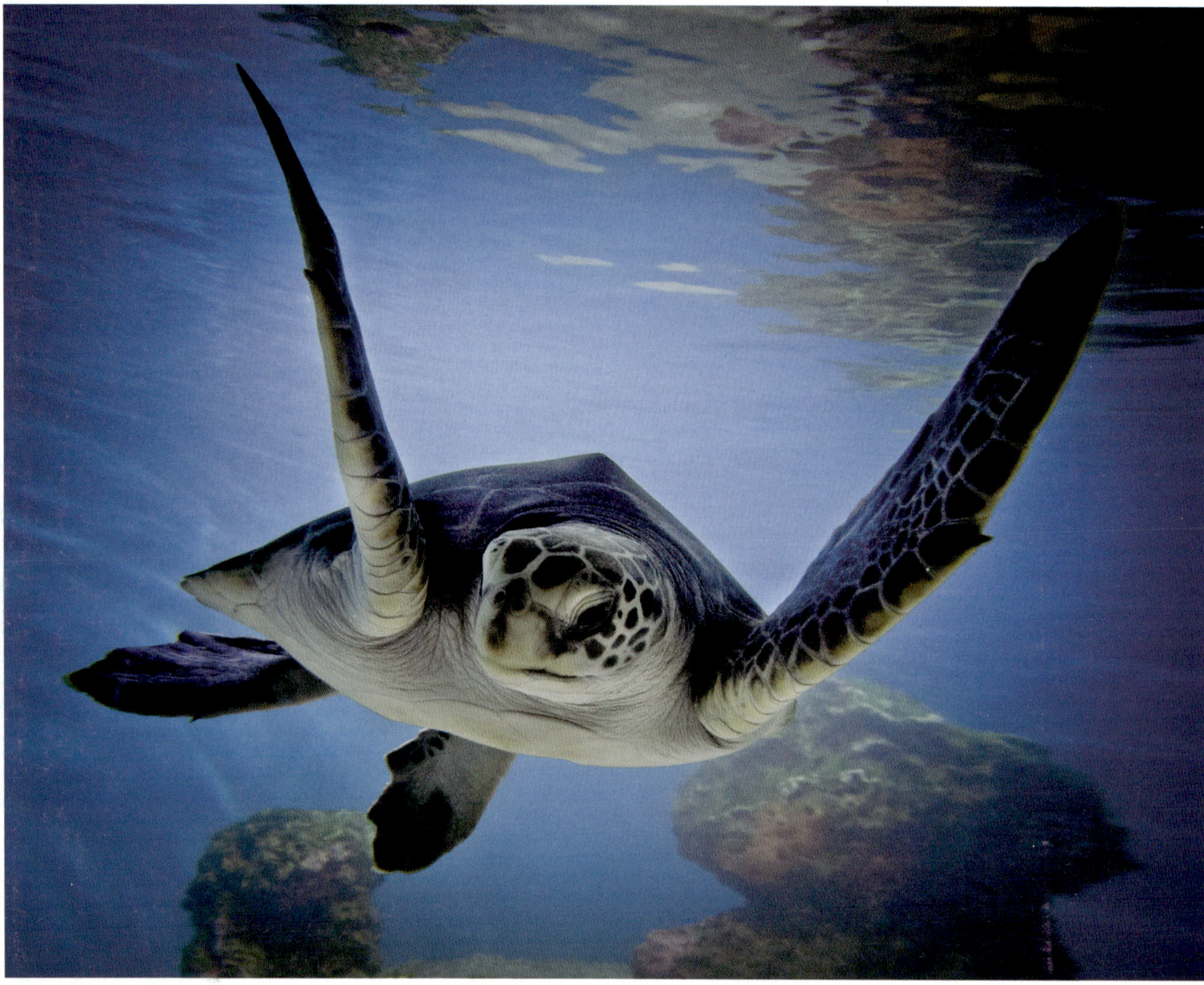